Many thanks for your contributions to the Funsiders. Continue the great work in your AF career.

*Kev McGwin
490 MS/CC*

Unlike Any Land You Know

The 490th Bomb Squadron in China-Burma-India

James M. Vesely

Writers Club Press
San Jose New York Lincoln Shanghai

Unlike Any Land You Know
The 490th Bomb Squadron in China-Burma-India

All Rights Reserved © 2000 by James M. Vesely

No part of this book may be reproduced or transmitted in any form or by any means, graphic, electronic, or mechanical, including photocopying, recording, taping, or by any information storage or retrieval system, without the permission in writing from the publisher.

Published by Writers Club Press
an imprint of iUniverse.com, Inc.

For information address:
iUniverse.com, Inc.
620 North 48th Street
Suite 201
Lincoln, NE 68504-3467
www.iuniverse.com

ISBN: 0-595-09699-9

Printed in the United States of America

This book is dedicated to my uncle, Sgt. Adolph Malovich, and to his comrades aboard the B-25 Mitchell Medium Bomber # 43-4977—1st Lt.William B. Plunkett, 2nd Lt. Donald E. Thorn, Sgt. Stephen Mercer Collins, and Sgt. J.D. Cobb.

As well as to all the veterans of the 490th Bomb Squadron who served so gallantly in China-Burma-India.

The author wishes to thank the following people for their invaluable assistance in researching this book: Don Harkins, Clyde Dyar, Fran Posey, Ivo Greenwell, Tom Quinlan, Howard Bell, L.P. Bloodworth, Doug Knokey, Ed Tengler, Dick Goodwin, and Robert P. Hyde, who was my uncle's tentmate, for reviving memories of almost sixty years ago, and for all their information on the men, operations, and history of the 490th Bomb Squadron.

In addition, throughout a great portion of this book, the author has borrowed liberally from Howard Bell's "The Burma Bridge Busters," from Ivo Greenwell's "My War Years in CBI," and finally from John J. Poister's "New Hope for Occupied Peoples—The Story of "The Burma Mail" as well as from the same author's contemporary account "The Saga of the 490th Bombardment Squadron," a narrative history completed July 31st, 1945, at the squadron's tactical airbase in Hanchung, China.

Also to Erma Peknik, Floy Plunkett Luppen, Pat Moyle, and Michael Moyle, for sharing their remembrances of Otsie Malovich, Bill Plunkett, and Mercer Collins.

And finally, to my long-lost aunt, Zoe Novak, who shared her loss with me. She'll know who she is.

"Then a golden mystery upheaved itself on the horizon—a beautiful, winking wonder that blazed in the sun, of a shape that was neither Muslim dome nor Hindu temple spire…the golden dome said: *This is Burma, and it will be quite unlike any land you know about.*"

Rudyard Kipling, *Letters From the East* (1898)

Contents

Prologue—Grand Rapids 1
Part One—Growing Up 15
Part Two—The Squadron 39
Part Three—Assam Province 123
Part Four—Warazup 139
Part Five—Kehsi Man Sam 181
Epilogue—Grand Rapids 217
Appendix 225

Prologue—Grand Rapids

I

As you drive southeast from Chicago, through the grit and steel town grime of Gary, and then around the bottom of Lake Michigan and north along its eastern shore, you see the crudely lettered road signs one after another, advertising fresh fruit and vegetables for sale.

All along the way are tiny clapboard stands offering the highway traveler apples and peaches, sweet cherries, cucumbers, beans, squash, and asparagus, plums, grapes and strawberries. These are the sweet, ripe days of harvest in central Michigan.

But out the car's windshield, September skies are already turned dull and dirty gray, with the promise of long, cold winter days and a veiled threat of heavy snows in the clouds that drift east over Chicago and scud out across the big lake toward the Wolverine State.

Grand Rapids was once a fur trapper's town. Now it's a cabinet-making center—the thriving furniture industry took hold here and thrived in the 1840s, fed by the area's thick, abundant hardwood forests of oak, maple and hickory.

In 1990, seventy-five percent of the city's population was Caucasian, eighteen and a half percent Black. The Asian and Hispanic portion of the mix is almost too small to count, and although the Ottawa tribe occupied the area until the early nineteenth century, Native Americans are represented here by only eight tenths of a percent.

Gerald R. Ford, 38th President of the United States, came to live in Grand Rapids in 1913, after his mother left her husband and returned there to live with her parents. The former president's museum is located here, and a tour of it is on the schedule for the four-day event taking place at the Holiday Inn East, this second week in September, 1999.

I'd come here—to a reunion of the 490th Bomb Squadron—searching for scraps of information about my uncle, Sgt. Adolph "Otsie" Malovich, from Chicago—a radioman and waist gunner aboard an ill-fated B-25 Mitchell bomber during the waning months of World War II.

I'd searched for him once before—or at least for a memory of him—almost twenty-seven years earlier.

It had been a similarly gray day in January 1972. A chilly south Texas wind swept through the neat, geometric rows of markers of the Military Cemetery at Fort Sam Houston, in San Antonio.

On either bank of the San Antonio River, and northeast of the city along small Salado Creek, the cottonwoods still stubbornly held a few brown leaves and stood in gnarled silhouette against the sky.

I looked down and studied the cemetery map, trying to hold it taught and flat against the wind. So many graves were here, so many names.

There is something about a military cemetery that demands from a visitor a hushed and gentle reverence, a much greater than usual degree of respect. Most of those buried in this place had died young—the collective result of chance, political decisions, large and small events out of another time.

Chance is a part of every life, and the men beneath these markers had no part in making those political decisions. In the last brief moments of their young lives, they were most probably very surprised at the occurrence of events that had conspired to kill them far from home.

I'd stopped here on a long, cross-country trip back to Chicago after leaving an advertising job in the Pacific Northwest. More than a week earlier, I'd packed the car and drove south from Spokane, Washington, crossing the great Columbia River and following it west to the coast. I'd been in no particular hurry to get back home, opting instead to see a big chunk of country at my own easy pace.

Taking a roundabout, leisurely route through the morning mists of Oregon's Willamette Valley, I followed the ragged, breathtaking California coast through Big Sur, passed through San Francisco and Los Angeles, and finally drove into sunwashed San Diego. From there it was due east across the Mojave, through Arizona and New Mexico and on across the endless miles of flat, southwestern Texas.

By the time I reached San Antonio, I was halfway home. At the time, I knew only two things about the city—the story of the Alamo, and the fact that my uncle was buried there.

After stopping for directions at a Chevron station, I found my way out of town and drove to Fort Sam, stopped at the gate for clearance, and went on to the National Cemetery.

Looking back on it, I think curiosity brought me here. As well as some deeply buried sense of family connection—some need to reach back across time and touch the memory of a young airman who I knew only through faded photos, and dim, childhood memories of overheard conversations about him, usually tinged with tears and sadness.

I had kin here among the rows, beneath the grass.

Adolph Malovich had been a flyer in those distant days when military flying was still a part of the army. He'd been my mother's younger brother, and was resting beneath this unfamiliar Texas earth for the better part of a quarter century, far from home and seldom thought of anymore by those who'd buried him here twenty-three years earlier.

I parked the car and walked into a drab brick building, not too much larger than the guard station at the entrance gate. It was serving as an information center and graves registration office.

Standing behind a polished wooden counter was a young corporal whose name badge read *Chavez*.

Corporal Chavez was polite and professional, with the look and bearing of a career soldier, yet he seemed barely out of his teens.

"May I help you, sir?"

"I'm looking for the location of a grave."

"Yes sir, what's the name?"

The corporal moved from the counter and across the room to a row of metal file cabinets strung along one wall. The room itself was drab and spartan—a desk and two telephones, a furled flag in one corner, and above the desk an official portrait of that favorite son of the Texas hill country, Lyndon B. Johnson. From another small storeroom off to the right I could hear a radio playing Janis Joplin's "Me And Bobby McGee."

"It would be Malovich," I said. "Sgt. Adolph Malovich."

Corporal Chavez dug through an open drawer and brought out a file in a matter of seconds. It occurred to me that this particular manila folder had probably been untouched since being put away so many years ago. I thanked him for the cemetery map and his help, and stepped back outside. On the map, Corporal Chavez had circled Section J in red pencil and written the number 135 on the line marked *Grave*. I briefly wondered if I was to be the grave's first visitor since that last, long note of taps sounded over it on a hot August afternoon in 1949.

My mother and grandmother were there that day.

They'd traveled to San Antonio for the service together, and I doubt that up to that time my grandmother had even known where San Antonio was. Aside from her great, youthful adventure crossing the ocean in steerage, Josephine Malovich's travels had been limited to the south shore homes in which she worked as a domestic servant, and perhaps twenty square blocks of her own neighborhood. San Antonio would have been as alien to her as the moon. But she'd worn her best dress and came to this strange place to watch them lower her son's remains into the Texas earth, and then gone back home with a neatly folded flag to replace her loss.

I found the grave quite easily—a well cared-for, ground level slab of stone, not very large, with five names cut into its face. The engraving was simple and in alphabetical order—with no regard for rank.

I was only four years old when Otsie went away for the last time. There still exists somewhere a photo of me dressed in a miniature army officer's dress uniform, complete with its own Sam Browne belt, looking at the camera and squinting into the sun. My back had been turned to the field as his C-47 taxied out onto one of the runways at Chicago's Midway Airport.

As a small boy, I'd been bounced on his knee and he gave me the nickname of *Jimmer*, but I was too young to remember that, or much of anything else about those times.

In years to come, as I grew older, he was little more than a name to me. Like skinned knees and schoolyard fights, the fact that my Uncle Otsie had been killed in the war was just a thing I accepted as a part of life. I had no physical memory of him at all. He was an occasional topic of conversation at holidays and family get-togethers, always talked about quietly, in hushed tones that I eventually came to recognize but never fully understood.

Maybe my visit to the gravesite that winter was motivated by some degree of that sense of mortality that seems to develop with age. Perhaps it was also an attempt at continuity, a way to recognize the family heritage and to reinforce the fact that he was once part of the same small group of people that I cared so much about.

Fate—unexplainable, impartial, and uncaring—had put him under this small piece of Texas earth, so far from everyone and everything he knew, and if he was allowed to be forgotten in this place, he might always be a question mark to grandnephews or grandnieces still unborn.

Looking back on it, these thoughts were somewhat cosmic stuff. Maybe my reasons for coming there were much simpler—just realizing that I would have been the first of his family to visit might have been motive in itself.

I've never been overly religious, but at that time and in that place, I very much wanted to believe that he knew I was there, that he was aware someone had come.

I spent about twenty minutes at the grave, sitting on the close-cropped winter-brown grass and talking to a ghost. I finally grew cold and knew it was time to get on with the trip home. Running my fingers lightly over the smooth stone marker, I touched his name with my thumb—then mumbled some sort of lame goodbye and made my way back to the car.

Ten years later, my mother passed away. Among her papers was a short stack of letters from my uncle, covering a two-year period from his induction to shortly before his death.

She'd saved them all these years and as I read each page, I grew fascinated with him as a fully fleshed-out personality, and with the fact that the letters reflected a time that I'd lived through, too, but had been much too young to recall.

I remember making a brief, ineffectual effort to find out more about him and his death. But in the early 1980s, The War Department and its vast bureaucracy were difficult to wade through and my search eventually petered out to nothing.

It wasn't until the miracle of the Internet and the advent of E-mail that I began searching for Adolph Malovich again.

In 1998, while doing on-line research for another book, I stumbled upon the aviation history web site of Martin Winter. I wrote Mr. Winter and asked for any information he might have on the China-Burma-India Theater. In response, Martin pointed me in another direction—to Tony Strothman's web site, dedicated to the 341st Bombardment Group in the CBI.

It was here that I discovered the name and e-mail address of Don Harkins, who'd been a 1st Lieutenant and navigator with the 490th during the same period my uncle was there. I immediately e-mailed Don and received the following reply:

"Appreciate you contacting me about your uncle. I left the 490th just a week after your uncle became MIA. I did not know him personally, although I did know the pilot, Bill Plunkett, and navigator, Don Thorn. In fact, I spent a couple of hours talking to Plunkett the night before they went down."

Reading these words made the hairs on my neck crawl. After more than half a century, I'd found someone, almost by accident, who actually was there—who could still remember the incident and two of the crewmembers aboard that doomed aircraft.

"We do continue as a squadron," Don went on. *"With a reunion every year (next September in Grand Rapids, Michigan) and you would be welcome to attend."*

II

They've come from all parts of the country, some by air, but most by automobile—they're retired now, and have the time to drive and see the sights along the way. As I walked through the Holiday Inn parking lot, looking at the license plates, I noticed no Hondas or Toyotas.

The memories are long.

The lucky ones still have their wives with them, while a few are widowers with new wives—building fresh relationships late in their lives. They're all old warriors now, most of them plagued by the stiffness of joints and the various infirmities of age, ever mindful of pensions, social security, and lives regulated by fixed incomes.

But once these were young men, healthy and strong—often brash and foolhardy, and always very brave.

As they come together in the lobby, or in a large suite dubbed the "Orderly Room," shaking hands and slapping each other on the backs, I have little trouble seeing them again as they were more than half a century ago. A montage of young faces—faces that would seem more suited to a high school yearbook than grinning out of crew pictures in the midst of war; pilots and copilots, navigators and radiomen, engineers, armorers, waistgunners, tailgunners, line chiefs, mechanics, and administrative staff.

These few gathered in Grand Rapids harbor many memories. The good ones they won't trade for anything. The bad ones they can't give away.

They were, and will ever be, the men of the Skull and Wings. The 490th Bomb Squadron—the *Burma Bridge Busters*—and their camaraderie and pride has been strong enough to last them all their lives.

In the first squadron newsletter of January 1972, former T/Sgt. and ordnance crew chief Ivo Greenwell wrote: *"Who among us can forget our youthful adventure in the strange lands of CBI? We toiled in steaming jungle, infested with cobra and mongoose, while the drenching monsoon put a thick coat of mildew and mold on our clothes and equipment...names like Ondol, Asansol, Dacca, Tezgon, Kermitola and Tezpur sound strange now, but back in the '40's they were as familiar to us as St. Louis, Houston, New York or Chicago."*

Describing the 490th in November 1944, my uncle wrote that he'd been *"assigned to the hottest bomb squadron in the CBI."*

Word Payne, of Albuquerque, was a 1st Lieutenant and a pilot during the same time Otsie served. Word told me that the 490th was sort of a "bastard outfit" with official ties to the 341st Bomb Group and the 10th Air Force, but unofficially far out on a limb and almost forgotten, fighting its own little low-level war in the skies over Burma.

On one memorable visit to the squadron in Warazup, Burma, Lord Louis Mountbatten told them: "I know you men think that this is a forgotten Theater of War. Let me assure you that it is *not* forgotten—most people don't even know you are over here."

Field Marshall the Viscount Slim added to that by stating: "When you go home don't worry about what to tell your loved ones and friends about service in Asia. No one will know where you were, or where it is if you do. You are, and will remain, the Forgotten Army."

And when asked what memories he had of his time in India and Burma, 490th Cpl. Ed Branning, crew chief and engineer gunner just shook his head and said: "It was about the worst place anybody could have ever been."

But in both time and distance, these three days in Grand Rapids are as far from the steaming jungles of Burma as the moon. The Holiday Inn is showing its age, but comfortable and clean. The surrounding restaurants serve up ample portions of solid, Midwestern food.

Above all, the camaraderie is heartfelt and real.

The first day's tour, a trip to the "Kalamazoo Air Zoo" reconnects these aged airmen to many of the war birds flown during their war. On the bus, I sit next to a tall, good-looking gentleman named Dick Johnson. In the 490th, I learn, he was Maj. Richard Johnson. After becoming the 490th's last CO of the war, Dick stayed in the Air Force, retired as a Lt. Colonel, and then spent the next 38 years with Boeing.

"I had my private pilot's license before I got my driver's license," he told me. "We were all young guys during the war. Blowing up bridges was a lot of fun, and I never worried too much about getting killed."

I was to later discover that Dick, a 1st Lieutenant then, had been one of the three flight leaders on my uncle's very first combat mission—a high-altitude raid against *Lashio*, the strategic railhead at the end of the Burma Road—fifty-five years before.

Aboard a tour bus in Michigan, in some strange way that was perhaps only meaningful to myself, the long, dark gap of time and generations was somehow being bridged.

As the men and their wives climb down from the buses and file up the ramp to the museum's entrance, a faint, far-off howl is heard. We all stop suddenly to stare in its direction, squinting to make out a small, dark object hurtling low over a line of hangars. It is the Air Zoo's salute to the 490th—its Bridge Buster guests.

Growing larger by the second, the object—a single, beautifully restored P-51 Mustang, its 1400hp Packard V-1650 screaming like all the banshees of hell—makes a low-level pass over the airfield. The pilot waggles his wings, then pulls a sudden, hard, climbing turn to the right until he's in the low clouds and out of sight. It's a show designed to bring a catch of breath and maybe a tear to the eye—and it succeeds.

Inside, the Air Zoo's display area features a totally rebuilt B-25 Mitchell, and the entire group is drawn toward the plane like moths to a flame. The B-25 gunship has been painted in a scheme representing the "Air Apaches"—the 345th Bombardment Group of the 5th Air Force in the Pacific. The "Air Apaches" specialized in low-level attacks on Japanese shipping and airfields.

"Not much different than us," one of the men tells his wife. "Except that we earned our wings on Jap held bridges." It's a fact she already knows. She's heard it many times over the years.

Depending on the area chosen for these reunions, the group satisfies itself with the local sights and whatever entertainment is available. The next day, it's a long bus ride to the Cornwell family's "Turkeyville, USA" for a slightly corny, but thoroughly American sit down lunch of turkey and dressing, and an earnest, enthusiastic dinner-theater stage production of "Hello Dolly."

The last day of the reunion takes the group to the Gerald R. Ford Museum in Grand Rapids. Here, displays feature the life, times, and presidency of Gerald Ford. The original burglar tools used in the June 1972 Watergate break-in are on display, along with a six-minute multi-screen presentation of the notorious political scandal.

But it seems as if most of the group's attention focuses on a Vietnam-era Huey helicopter that recalls April 29th, 1975, when President Ford finally ordered the evacuation of Saigon.

In the Holiday Inn later that evening, the Saturday night banquet brings everyone together again for one last time this year, and the end of dinner brings the squadron to the silent roll call—the naming of those members who have passed away during the preceding twelve months.

Clyde Dyar, a line chief with the squadron in Burma and China, is at the podium, while Texas rancher, L.P. "Boogie" Bloodworth, a 490th navigator at the same time Clyde was there, calls the roll. The men at the tables are silent. This yearly tradition is never an easy one.

"Arthur Smith," Boogie Bloodworth calls out, repeating the name three times, as was squadron protocol when the man whose name was called would fail to answer "…Smith…Smith."

"Victor Kadanka. Kadanka…Kadanka."

"Jack Manning. Manning…Manning."

I'm sitting at a far corner table with George Townsend and his wife, Edith. They've made the drive north from their home in Lady Lake, Florida. George was an aircraft armorer in CBI, and as the names are read, I see him shake his head and hear him catch his breath. "Oh damn," he whispers—almost imperceptibly. Edith gently pats his knee.

All around the room, it is the same. As Boogie calls out the names, men stare at the floor and self-consciously wipe tears from their eyes while the women knowingly reach out to lightly touch their husband's hands.

"George A. Chapman. Chapman…Chapman."

And like the faded, yellowed leaves of a Michigan autumn, the years just fall away.

Part One—Growing Up

1

"Otsie" Malovich was the son of Slavic immigrants, born on the 6th of September 1919, at 3229 S. Hamlin Avenue, in Chicago, Illinois.

He was delivered without complications by the neighborhood midwife, Elizabeth Pergl, and was the third child of Marco Malovich and Josephine Cepin—young immigrants from Slovenia—until 1918 a part of the Hapsburg-ruled Austro-Hungarian Empire.

Duly christened Adolph Marek Malovich by the priest at Blessed Agnes Catholic Church, the little blond-haired boy arrived into a family already blessed with two older sisters, Mildred and Erma, to spoil and fuss over him.

In 1919, the Chicago newspapers were reporting the first transatlantic flight, by a Vickers Vimy bomber powered by two Rolls-Royce Eagle engines. There was famine in Yugoslavia and much of the rest of Eastern Europe. Postwar prices remained high. Milk was fifteen cents a quart in Chicago, fresh eggs thirty-two cents a dozen, and sirloin steak sixty-one cents a pound. Sirloin was never seen in the small brick bungalow of Marco and Josephine Malovich.

Two months before Otsie was born, a race riot broke out in the city—the result of the sweltering hot summer temperatures and a disturbance at a Lake Michigan beach. By the time the riot ended, twenty-three blacks and fifteen whites were dead, and hundreds more were seriously injured.

In 1919, Jack Dempsey took the heavyweight championship away from Jess Willard with a third round knockout in Toledo. The Cincinnati Reds beat the White Sox five games to three to win the World Series, and along store-lined 26th Street, young people were humming "The World Is Waiting For The Sunrise" and "Let The Rest Of The World Go By."

In Washington, Congress had passed the Eighteenth Amendment prohibiting the future manufacture, sales and distribution of alcoholic beverages—a law that did not sit well with Otsie's father, twenty-seven year old self-employed carpenter, Marco Malovich.

Marco was a talented cabinetmaker. He worked for the Crane Company, but his daughter Erma remembers him as being distant and uninvolved with his family.

Marco was a hard drinker. So much so, that it would finally destroy his marriage. After twenty-two years of an unhappy union, Josephine threw him out, hired a neighborhood attorney named Anton Zeman, and filed for divorce on grounds of "habitual drunkenness." She was a proud woman, and determined to raise her three children alone.

Josephine was awarded the small brick home on Hamlin Avenue, along with all its furniture, but no provisions were requested or made for alimony, support and maintenance, or child support for Otsie, who was still considered a minor.

Otsie was seventeen when his father left the house. There was no father and son relationship between them. Zoe Novak, who married Ots in 1941, recalled that he rarely spoke of his father. Zoe said that she never met her father-in-law, never heard much about him, and until I contacted her, hadn't even known that his name had been Marco.

After the divorce, Josephine fell back on the only thing she knew how to do. She supported her family as a domestic, a housekeeper for the wealthy families who lived along Chicago's south shore. Marco Malovich disappeared from their lives, and years later died a derelict on Chicago's streets.

Josephine Malovich was from the poor Slovenian mountain town of Planina. She'd immigrated as a young woman, sponsored by Josephine and Frank Venk, who lived in the neighborhood.

Josephine worked hard, and after her children were grown and married, she would grow old alone, living in the basement of the same house in which Otsie was born, renting out the upstairs for extra income.

He and his sisters grew up on Chicago's West Side.

The old Czech neighborhood of Lawndale was a solid and stable lower middle-class enclave of brick bungalows and two-flats, mostly mortgaged by the Savings and Loans that were strung out like pearls along Cermak Road.

Lawndale was peopled by blue-collar Czechs, Poles, and other Slavs who worked hard, saved their money—and who, aside from their mortgages, shunned credit like the plague. These were folks who'd found their dream in America, who took pride in their small, modest homes and gave no second thought to washing and scrubbing their concrete sidewalks on Saturday mornings.

When they bought, they paid with cash, and looking back on it, it often seemed they spent all they earned on food. On Sunday afternoons, the streets of Lawndale were filled with the smells of cooking. If the pickings were slim during the week, all the stops were pulled on Sunday, and somehow, these working class Slav immigrants managed to eat, at least one day a week, like ravenous royalty.

There were huge roasts of pork or duck with bread or potato dumplings drowned in rich gravy, and bowls of sauerkraut laced with sweet brown sugar and peppered with caraway seed. Fruit-filled dumplings, slippery with melted butter, sugar and poppy seeds—as heavy as softballs and almost as big.

Neighborhood ovens overflowed with pork hocks and greasy, succulent pig's tails, sweet potatoes glazed with brown sugar and chopped walnuts. Out of their woodstove ovens came roast chickens, turkeys, and great pink hams, or smoked butt with cabbage and parsley-boiled new potatoes. In the crisp, clear days of autumn, men and boys armed with walking sticks and burlap bags left the neighborhood and the city, trudging through the Illinois woodlands. Their eyes were trained on the ground, searching for wild mushrooms that would be carefully picked, dried, and later used to season stews.

Summer or winter, huge pots of beef noodle or liver dumpling soup simmered on the tops of stoves.

And the bakery! Pastries and deserts, apple pies and apple strudel, prune and apricot-filled *kolacky*—light and flaky, and sprinkled on top with powdered sugar.

All this food was washed down with steins of beer or water glasses filled with homemade dago red. On Sundays, they reaped the rewards of the week's hard work, and nobody in Lawndale went hungry.

They weren't perfect people. They still harbored Old World resentments and quickly adapted to New World bigotry. They themselves were a long way from the top of the socioeconomic ladder and they understood that. But they also suspected their status was higher than the Irish or Italians, and they were convinced that it was far above Chicago's Negroes.

Jews were beneath them too, dismissed as *sheenies* and found either on Maxwell Street or driving horse-drawn wagons in the alleys, collecting old rags and junk.

The children of Lawndale played softball or tag in the streets and alleys and went to Mass regularly. Still true to the customs of Europe, many belonged to the Pioneers, a youth-oriented arm of the SNPJ—the Slovene National Benefit Society—formed in 1904 to sell low-cost life insurance to early immigrants. Some were enrolled in *sokol*, a quasi-military youth club dedicated to the European culture of drill, gymnastics and physical fitness.

Everyday customs and traditions were inherited from parents. On the street, at school, and among themselves, the kids spoke English—but around the supper table, they spoke Czech, Polish and Slovenian.

In 1923, at four years of age, Otsie entered kindergarten at Gary Grammar School. His report card graded him as excellent or good throughout eight years of grade school.

He and his buddies—Bob Jensik, Rudy Zamrzla, Eddie Riha, Ray Svejda, and Lou Vasik—were street kids. They spent summer days and evenings exploring the neighborhood, shooting marbles and playing mumble-de-peg, hide-and-seek, and 16-inch softball on Hamlin Avenue, the game's bases and home plate drawn on the street with great chunks of chalk that were tossed to the kids from passing railroad cabooses.

At Farragut High School, in the middle of the Depression, Otsie's record was surprisingly poor compared to his grades at Gary. In September of 1935, after only two years, he left Farragut to go to work—perhaps to make up the income that was lost when his father left the house.

Ots in front of Brachtl's Drug Store—late 1930s.

As he grew older, like a lot of boys raised in the alleys and on the concrete sidewalks of the city, Otsie began to find his pleasures in the outdoors. He loved to hunt and fish, and every chance they had, he and his sister Erma's fiancé, Milt Peknik, along with a few other friends, would clamber into somebody's old Ford or Chevy to make the long trip north. Up Wisconsin Rte. 12 through Tomah, Eau Claire, and Chippewa Falls, to the Spooner area in northern Wisconsin—known for its deep, clear lakes and flowages filled with pike, muskie, and walleye.

Chicago is a neighborhood town. To come of age on its streets meant being part of one. Lawndale stretched roughly from Hamlin Avenue on the east to Cicero Avenue on the west. 22nd Street represented its northern edge and to the south, the neighborhood ended at the railroad tracks and the wide, sluggish Sanitary & Ship Canal just beyond them. One of the local hangouts was Jim Brachtl's drugstore on 31st and Hamlin, just kitty-corner from Gary Grammar School.

Otsie would meet his future wife there. Born in Radnice, Czechoslovakia on August 15th, 1920, Zoe Nemacek had come to America with her parents when she was still a child. She was seventeen when she met Otsie, and remembered that: "We met at the corner drug store, where I always went with my girlfriend for ice-cream sodas. This is where all the dates were made—to go dancing, or to movies and parties."

Movies were at the Atlantic or California theaters on 26th Street. Before settling in their seats to hold hands and watch "You Can't Take It With You," "Gone With The Wind," or "The Philadelphia Story," Otsie and Zoe could stop at the Greek's little soda fountain next door to the Atlantic. At the Greek's they might treat themselves to chocolate malts or Cokes and buy ten-cent bags of fresh popcorn, covered with melted butter.

The big dances were at Pilsen Park, where legendary Frankie Yankovic often came down from Cleveland to play polkas and waltzes, where the beer and pop were cheap and roast beef sandwiches were served steaming hot and drowned in gravy.

During the late 30s, a special occasion was Riverview Park, on the far-off, unfamiliar turf of the North Side. Opened by Wilhelm Schmidt in 1904, the rambling 74-acre amusement park was hit hard by the Depression. But even strapped for cash, most young West Siders managed to find ways to dig up streetcar fare to get there—then spent everything that was left on carnie games, riding the *Bobs* or the *Parachutes* and eating cheap foot-long hot dogs on the loud and colorful Riverview Midway.

Zoe remembered Ots as being a great ballroom dancer. Beside hunting and fishing, his interests centered on music and handyman projects around the house.

He was a fine dresser, and he never looked better than on the day they were married at Blessed Agnes Catholic Church, May 20th, 1941.

They would live in the same house in which Ots was born and raised. "He was very close to Erma, Millie, and his mother," Zoe said. "They were a close knit family and easy to get along with."

Happy and thankful to have a decent job, Otsie worked at Automatic Electric, making telephone equipment. Zoe recalled that his ambition was to become a department supervisor so he could afford to buy a car.

But events occurring overseas had different plans for him and a lot of other young Americans who were just beginning to live their lives.

In Europe two years earlier, the world began to go insane. War had officially been recognized with the signing of a nonaggression pact between Nazi Germany and Soviet Russia.

Adolf Hitler quickly and easily occupied Bohemia and Moravia. His foreign minister, Joachim von Ribbentrop signed a pact with Stalin, and the German war machine attacked Poland on the first of September 1939, setting off the long, grotesque nightmare that would soon engulf the world.

Bohemia, Moravia, and Poland had fallen, and with their small radios announcing events overseas, the people of Lawndale soon learned of the sweep of war into the Balkans.

Unable to resist, Hungary, Romania, Bulgaria, and Albania had allied themselves with the Axis countries. Yugoslavia soon joined them, but when anti-Nazi Serbian radicals took over the Yugoslav government in 1941, the German Army invaded. The Yugoslav Resistance—including the local Communist Party, or Partisans, led by Josip Broz, known as Tito—would stubbornly fight against German occupation for the rest of the war.

The middle-class burghers and working people of Lawndale could relate to the horror that was sweeping across Eastern Europe. Most still had parents, brothers and sisters, cousins, aunts, uncles, and friends in those small towns and villages that were being methodically overrun by Hitler's *Wermacht*. They huddled in front of their radios, whispering among themselves, frightened of the approaching storm.

In October 1940, the first peacetime draft in U.S. history began.

But Otsie and Zoe considered themselves to be first generation Americans. Bad news from the Old Country meant less to them than to their parents. "Chattanooga Choo-Choo" was hot that autumn, as was Duke Ellington's "Take the A Train." A year earlier, Roosevelt had beat Wilkie for an unprecedented third term, and FDR was promising an end to hard times.

The war across the ocean was Europe's war, the president insisted. The United States would not involve itself again—not for the second time in a century.

Otsie and Zoe, like young couples all over America, breathed a sigh of relief. They had lives to live—furniture, appliances, and automobiles to buy—families to start. Things would soon be getting better.

President Roosevelt had told them so.

2

As an increasingly troubled America went about its business with nervous eyes on Europe, across the ocean in the Far East, Japan was on the move as well.

Ever since 1931—while Otsie was still a kid at Gary School—events in Japan had been taking ominous turns. It was in a state of apprehension and turmoil that Japan entered the *kurai tanima*—the dark valley of the 1930s.

Political tensions were rampant within the Empire, and militant reaction to them was widely held in the army, especially among the younger officers who tended to be hot-tempered and ambitious.

Throughout the country, a network of state-sanctioned Shinto shrines provided a solid base for the return to *bushido*—the ancient "Way of the Warrior" and an almost religious belief in Japan's historical superiority over the rest of Asia and the world. The Empire's armed forces were independent of civilian control, and were becoming a powerful force for the eventual application of these concepts in both domestic and foreign affairs.

The army's growing independence was made possible by Japan's system of government. It dated back to the *Meiji* days of a century before, and required that army and navy ministers had to be officers on the active duty list. Consequently, without a minister of the army or navy's choice, no cabinet could be formed, and none could remain in power. The generals and admirals soon learned that they needed only to withdraw or threaten to withdraw their ministers, to bend the cabinet to their will.

In turn, the generals and admirals were themselves under unrelenting pressures from increasingly fanatical junior officers, finding themselves, in effect, being blackmailed by young turks rarely above the rank of colonel.

And when thwarted in their fanaticism, the radical officer fringe resorted to assassination or civil disobedience.

All through the '30s it was the army that was making Japanese foreign policy, and the civilian government was helpless to do anything but serve as an embarrassed and unhappy apologist before the world.

Fearing Communism, the Japanese took advantage of China's civil war. Japan's army, virtually unopposed by either the Chinese Communists or the Nationalists who were busy fighting each other, occupied all of Manchuria.

In 1937, they moved again. This time the invasion turned into full-scale war—a Far Eastern preview of the blitzkrieg that Hitler was soon to visit upon Europe.

In the first six months of that year, Japanese troops poured across the Great Wall. They took Peking and sacked Shanghai and the Nationalist capitals of Nanking and Hankow. By the end of the decade, Japan held an area of Eastern China larger than France, Germany, Spain, and Italy combined.

The central instrument of Japan's political aims was the concept of the Greater East Asia Co-prosperity Sphere. Long feeling exploited by the western powers, the Japanese formulated a policy that saw an Asia united "in the spirit of universal brotherhood" under the leadership of Japan, with each nation allotted its "proper place" by the Emperor. It would lead to prosperity, the Japanese were convinced, and it would induce millions of Asians to cooperate in a war against the west.

Across the ocean, life on Hamlin Avenue remained largely unchanged. Otsie and Zoe were living in his mother's home. At Automatic Electric, he was working hard to build a life for them. By now, both his sisters, Millie and Erma, were married and raising toddlers, and Otsie too, was looking forward to a family of his own.

Then, on that clear, cold Sunday in December, his life was abruptly altered. Across the world that morning, three hundred and sixty carrier-based Japanese planes attacked the American base at Pearl Harbor. They crippled the U.S. Pacific fleet—sinking the battleships *Arizona, Oklahoma, California, Nevada,* and *West Virginia,* damaged three other battleships, three cruisers, and three destroyers, destroyed two hundred U.S. warplanes, and killed almost 2,500 American soldiers and sailors.

The news of Pearl Harbor came to Hamlin Avenue over the radio. It was the crisp, cold, final day of the year's professional football season. Chicagoans were listening to Coach George Halas and his Bears beating their arch rivals, the Chicago Cardinals, with the Bears on their way to another world championship.

But throughout the country that Sunday, Americans heard only that the Arizona was sunk, and the Oklahoma capsized. What stunned them all, was the sudden and devious manner of the attack—on a peaceful Sunday morning—in Pearl Harbor, Hawaii, a place few people had even heard of.

In Guilford, Connecticut, far from anyplace that Otsie knew, George and Edith Townsend, along with a friend, were listening to music on the radio—Ella Fitzgerald doing her light-hearted, wonderful rendition of "A Tisket, a Tasket"—when the program was interrupted and the news was broadcast.

"Pearl Harbor? Where's Pearl Harbor?" George asked, and no one could tell him. After temporary duty at various bases in India, George would finish out the war as an aircraft armorer with the 490th in Burma and China.

All across the country, other young men who would in time be a part of the same outfit in which Otsie was eventually assigned, were hearing the news.

Harry DePew, who'd wind up a 1st Lieutenant, flying B-25 Mitchell bombers over some of the worst jungle in the world, was still a high school senior in Atlanta. Harry had no idea of how fast he was about to grow up.

Frank Peter and his fiancée were driving over Western Hills Viaduct in Cincinnati, on their way to the Cincinnati Symphony's Sunday Concert. When the news broke over the car radio, they could only look at each other, dumbfounded, not quite knowing what to make of it.

Tom Quinlan had just finished an all-night pinochle game in Yonkers, New York. He heard the news at 8:00 a.m. Sunday morning, and went to see Humphrey Bogart in "The Maltese Falcon" that night. Turned down by the Coast Guard because of his eyesight, Tom would eventually wind up in the Air Corps as Squadron Operations Chief in India, Burma, and China. His job was to assign enlisted men—the radio/gunners, engineer/gunners, armorer/gunners, and tailgunners to specific missions. Most came back alive. Some did not. It was never an easy job.

Ken Shugart first heard about Pearl Harbor after church that Sunday. His first thoughts were *why would a backward country like Japan attack a country as powerful as the United States?* His hunch was that the war in the Pacific would be over in a short three or four months. But soon the dominos began to fall: Hong Kong, Guam and Wake Island first. Then the desperate struggle in the Philippines, and the fall of Singapore and New Guinea. Like most other once-confident Americans, Ken soon realized the Japanese were neither weak nor backward

Line chief Clyde Dyar had just turned eighteen. He'd never heard of Pearl Harbor, had no idea where it was. In Detroit, he overheard some guys making a joke of it. "Hey, the Japs bombed a whorehouse in Hawaii, owned by some gal named Pearl Harbor."

Of all the momentous events that would galvanize their lives over the next four years, Pearl Harbor was the one that most Americans would remember most vividly. It was as if a Kodak camera had suddenly clicked in their minds, freezing in place every motion and thought at the instant they heard the news of the attack.

There were 120 million Americans who were old enough to understand what was happening, and each reacted in their own personal way, mixing astonishment, outrage, and disbelief with his or her own particular concerns.

Roosevelt declared war the next day, even as American outposts in the Pacific began to fall like tenpins before the weakly opposed Japanese advance. Two days after Pearl, Imperial Marines landed on Luzon in the Philippines. A day later, Guam fell in the Mariannas. Then Wake Island, and Hong Kong, and two days before Christmas, eighty thousand troops of Gen. Masaharu Homma's 14th Army came ashore at Lingayen Gulf.

Four months later, on April 9th, 1942, the seventy-six thousand American and Filipino troops on Bataan yielded to Homma's forces the mountainous peninsula they'd held for fourteen stubborn, bloody weeks. Reading their newspapers, Americans learned with sadness that the surrender marked the largest capitulation of a United States military command in history. A month later, the thirteen thousand ragged defenders of nearby Corregidor heard Gen. Jonathan Wainwright broadcast a surrender order, instructing his command to give up their rocky little island at the entrance of Manila Bay. Except for scattered guerilla resistance, the fall of the Philippines was complete.

Not too long afterwards, news of the Bataan Death March filtered into America's consciousness, showing the nation what the enemy was made of, and what kind of war it was to be.

3

Americans were outraged, and a lot of young men raced to join up. At first it was thought the Japanese could be beaten quickly, but with the dismal news of Bataan, Corregidor, and Wake Island, initial euphoria and confidence of victory began to quickly fade during the first months of the new year, 1942.

Although jukeboxes throughout the country were playing "Goodbye, Mama, I'm Off to Yokohama," and "You're a Sap, Mr. Jap," these indeed were the darkest days of the war.

All over the country, buses and trains were suddenly full of men in uniform. Waves of newly inducted servicemen shuttled between training camps, shipped out for overseas, or were on leave and traveling home to wives and sweethearts. In the two weeks following Pearl Harbor, the railroads moved more than 600,000 troops.

The destinations of the trains and buses were stateside camps with names like Dix, Benning, or Leonard Wood. Arrival at these places thrust the recruit into a world he'd never known before. Often, the climate, the culture, and almost everything else seemed hostile. Boys from the cold weather climates of Duluth or Buffalo sweltered in the Georgia heat and humidity of Fort Benning. Many of those from the gentle, mild southern states shivered in the cold and wind that howled across the drill fields at Great Lakes Naval Training Center on the shores of Lake Michigan, or at Camp McCoy in southern Wisconsin.

Within each camp, recruits found themselves in a strange, rushed world of inch-long doctor's needles and half-inch crewcuts. They were issued unfamiliar equipment and given drab uniforms that usually didn't fit. Once in training, they exchanged their civilian identities for a rank and a serial number, surrendering themselves to a series of predictable rituals—morning calisthenics, marching in cadence, endlessly practicing drill, and performing the drudgeries of cleaning and kitchen work.

"Chow" was food. "SOS" was an acronym for the chipped beef and gravy that was served over toast and fondly characterized as shit on a shingle. And when nothing went as planned, things became SNAFU'd—"Situation normal—all fucked up."

Otsie managed to stay a civilian until almost the end of April 1943, but the draft finally caught him. He reported to Camp Grant and was there for two days—a willing but reluctant soldier, wishing against all that was happening in the world to be back with Zoe in the old neighborhood he knew so well—no different than any other young draftee.

The first letter his sister Millie received was from Clearwater, Florida. Her kid brother had been temporarily bivouacked there. He and other recruits were waiting to be sent to more permanent quarters in nearby St. Petersburg.

Dear Sis...

Sorry I couldn't write you any sooner, but I'm sure you understand how things are when you first get in. No time and always on the go, from morning to night. Well, I'm going to start from the beginning and tell you what I've been doing. I was at Camp Grant for two days for shots, uniforms, and aptitude tests. The Tuesday of the 13th we were put aboard a train and our destination was unknown.

We found out we were going to the Air Force at St. Petersburg, Florida, and during the trip we ate in dining cars and were served by waiters—saw many beautiful sights on the way, but when we reached camp, we were the most disappointed group in the whole army. We were in a section that they call The Jungle...plenty of snakes, crocodiles, lizards, and other reptiles. The camp was not so hot but we were only there for seven days. I went out for radio and made it, so I was pretty lucky.

Now let me describe the place we are staying at. It is the former Belleview Biltmore Hotel on a high bluff overlooking the Gulf of Mexico. Civilians had to pay as high as $25 per night to stay here! Shower, bath, toilet and sink in each room. We have an 18-hole golf course, tile swimming pool, tennis courts, badminton courts, and the most beautiful winding roads lined with palm trees. Grass all over the place and it is very clean. There are two theaters in the hotel, we eat four to a table in the dining room and every flight has its own day room, which includes pool tables, ping pong tables, record players, and games. We also have golf clubs, fishing tackle, bats, balls, and all sports equipment.

However, all these things can never take the place of Zoe, for I certainly miss her an awful lot. Have you seen her lately?

Well Sis, I have about twelve letters to write so I guess I'll quit for now. Mom has a picture of the hotel—ask her to show it to you. Write soon, hello to everybody.

At this point, he was Pvt. Adolph Malovich, Squadron 515, Flight C, 601st Training Group, 63rd Training Wing. He wrote a second letter to his sister Erma and her husband, Milt, the same day:

Hello—

How are you people? Sorry I couldn't write sooner. So, today being Sunday I thought I'd write to everybody...

This life isn't so bad, but it is pretty tough. The trouble is that it's too far from home. I haven't had any KP or guard duty yet, but I think my time is coming pretty soon. I'm going to be here for about 28 days and from here, I will go to a radio school. New York, Chicago, or Scott Field...

A week later he wrote to Millie again:...*I will truthfully tell you I was depressed while at St.Pete's. The place was like a jungle. Hot as hell during the day and cold at night. We were there for seven days and removed our clothing only when we showered...some of the most deadly snakes in North America shared the camp with us.*

However, that was good experience, as they say that anyone who can live in "the jungle" for a week will make a good soldier.

We live in such a clean place now that it makes us mad because we are always cleaning. We have to scrub the floor, tub, sink, and toilet every morning, and wash woodwork every week. The neighborhood is clustered with millionaires and you should see some of the houses here...

If Otsie was a reluctant draftee at first, he eventually became comfortable with the routine of army life. His outfit stood retreat on Wednesdays and had review on Saturdays. The color and ceremonies impressed him, and in a letter to Millie, he observed that they were finally *"beginning to look like soldiers, not the rookies we were a few weeks ago.*

"Things are becoming easier now, he wrote. *And they are really pushing us through. Basic Training used to be thirteen weeks, but the Air Corps gets only eighteen days, so you can imagine how hard we're working..."*

Ots went out blue-water fishing once or twice in Florida. He came home skunked, and wrote his sister about alligator hunting on one of the small islands offshore from the base. They had two that were kept as pets, he told her, with sergeant's stripes painted on their tough hides.

Once finished with Basic he was assigned to go back north—to radio school at Scott Field in Illinois. It wasn't very near Chicago nor was it close to his wife, but it was a lot closer than Florida—close enough to get home on leave, and close enough for Zoe to visit him.

From Chicago to Scott Field, near Belleville, was a long, boring ride by bus down Route 66, south through Springfield, and with stops in more than a dozen other little towns.

Scott was an old base, established in 1917 and named after Cpl. Frank S. Scott, an Army aircraft mechanic. Corporal Scott was flying as a passenger in a Wright Type B biplane that crashed five years earlier at the Army Flying Field in College Park, Maryland. He was the first enlisted person to be killed in an airplane crash.

In 1921, the War Department made Scott Field a "lighter than air" station for dirigibles and balloons, but these operations came to an abrupt end in 1937 when Air Corps policy switched from airships to airplanes. Four concrete runways, each a mile long, were constructed at Scott after the great airship hangar was demolished in 1939.

The base was originally selected as a potential site for the Air Force General Headquarters, scheduled to be relocated from Langley Field in Virginia. But as the scope of the war in Europe rapidly expanded, Gen. George C. Marshall elected to keep HQ GHQ close to the center of power in Washington, D.C. Although Scott never became the center for the Army's air combat arm, it did assume the important wartime mission of training radio operators/mechanics, and soon the school became known as the "Communications University of the Army Air Forces."

While he was at Scott, Ots and Zoe made as many trips to see each other as they could. In those days of war, travel was anything but easy. Virtually every train station, bus depot, and airport in the country was overflowing with military personnel on the move between training camps, military posts, and points of embarkation for overseas. The railroads carried ninety-seven per cent of the traffic, moving two million men a month. Troop movements required half of all Pullman space, putting weary civilians into cramped coach seats.

Riders often endured cattle-car conditions and were grateful for just standing room. A brisk black-market in Pullman reservations developed. Throughout the country, scalpers sold tickets at markups of $10 to $50. Even legitimate travel agencies began tacking $20 "service charges" on to the price of a ticket.

In addition to the discomforts of travel, people on the West Side of Chicago, and in other large cities and small towns throughout America were feeling the war. During the icy winter of 1942-43, fuel rationing was begun, and consumers were allotted only about two thirds of their 1941 consumption.

Josephine Malovich, pulling a red wagon behind her, would scour the nearby railroad tracks, scavenging the loose coal that fell from the passing coal cars as the trains roared past. Each wagonload was carefully hoarded and fed into the basement furnace to heat her home.

Everyday items of convenience or self-indulgence, long taken for granted, were suddenly hard to come by—liquor, laundry soap, facial tissue, cotton diapers, thumbtacks and haircurlers. Nylon had "gone to war" too, and Zoe, Millie and Erma went back to stockings of rayon and cotton.

The shortage that hurt most was meat. Beef supplies were way down. Housewives in Chicago and every other U.S. city found themselves with plenty of meat ration coupons to spare, but nothing to buy.

The alternatives were to go to the black-market butchers, who got an estimated twenty percent of available beef—or to local substitutes. The Czech butchers along 26th and 31st Streets began to offer unrationed horsemeat at twenty cents a pound.

But the most stubborn shortage was housing, with ninety-eight percent of U.S. cities reporting insufficient single-family houses and ninety percent unable to meet apartment needs. As more and more workers streamed into booming defense towns, they were greeted by "No Vacancy" signs. The lucky ones shared rooms with other new arrivals or moved into rows of jerry-built boxes of plywood and plasterboard, while the unlucky ones resorted to tents and even shelters nailed together from packing cases.

Ots had left.

Millie's husband, Joe Vesely, was gone—taking flight training at Thunderbird Field in Glendale, Arizona.

Erma's husband, Milt, was in the navy, and Milt's brother, George, was in the infantry—destined to be killed during the Battle of the Bulge twenty months later.

Now, no different than her sisters-in-law, Zoe found herself alone and soon made the decision to move back home to 33rd and Springfield, with her own parents, Emil and Anna, and her older sister, Julia.

Like so many other young wives, she would just have to put her life on hold, and settle in to wait out the war.

Part Two—The Squadron

4

In February 1942, with the world at war on two fronts, the Japanese overran Burma and took full control of the critically important 700 mile-long Burma Road that ran from the Burmese railhead at Lashio to Kunming—the capital of Yunnan Province in China. By early March of that year, Japanese troops also took control of the strategically vital Burmese cities of Rangoon and Myitkyina.

By May, Mandalay fell and Burma was lost to Japan.

An old China Hand—Joseph "Vinegar Joe" Stilwell was the officer in charge of American forces in the China-Burma-India theater.

A proud man, Stilwell was nevertheless forced to lead a grueling, bitter, twenty-day retreat out of Burma and back into India to lick his wounds, swallow his pride, and settle down to plan a counteroffensive that was to eventually wrest Burma back from the Japanese.

The Burma Road had been built by the Chinese five years earlier as a military supply route. It was used by Allied forces during the early months of World War II, with supplies for China landing in Rangoon and then being carried by rail to Lashio. From there, they were hauled by truck to Kunming, over rugged mountains almost nine thousand feet high.

Until he held a press conference in Delhi on May 25th, the world had viewed Vinegar Joe Stilwell's flight from Burma as a glorious strategic retreat, but Stilwell made it a point to set them straight.

"I claim we got a hell of a beating," he said. "We got run out of Burma and it is humiliating as hell. I think we ought to find out what caused it, go back and retake it."

With Stilwell gone and forces of the Japanese Imperial Army now straddling this part of Asia—it was only the American Tenth Air Force, under Maj. General Lewis H. Brereton, that was still active in the defense of Burma and India.

When Brereton arrived in Ceylon to take command almost a year earlier, he had one LB-30, five tired B-17s, and firm orders to shape the fledgling Tenth into an effective, efficient fighting unit.

Part of the Tenth, the 341st Medium Bombardment Group was activated in India on September 15th, 1942. The new 341st drew much of its personnel from the tattered remnants of the 7th Heavy Bombardment Group—a bloodied and decimated unit that had seen many of its own killed or captured in the fall of the Philippines eight months earlier.

The Seventh had earlier been diverted to Australia and ordered to begin preparations for operations in Java, but at this point in the war, the Japanese were showing themselves to be unstoppable, eventually overrunning Java, too.

The weary Seventh finally straggled into Karachi in March, orphans of the war, to be taken under Brereton's command. Along with remnants of the Seventh, a few of the surviving members of the famed Doolittle raid on Tokyo also joined when the new Group was formed.

The 51st Fighter Group, having gone through an odyssey similar to the Seventh's, also arrived in Karachi to be added to Brereton's small organization. This bunch was in bad shape, too, having only ten operational P-40s that were rather the worse for wear—the rest having been lost at sea to Japanese surface action.

With the 341st soon to be divided into four squadrons, and equipped with new B-25C and D medium bombers, the 11th, 22nd, 490th and 491st squadrons would begin training that fall, in India.

On September 16th, 1942, the afternoon sun hung in the sky like a scorching white ball, casting waving shimmers of heat over the Sind Desert just outside Karachi. Sweat ran like small, salty rivers down the drawn and tired faces of a small group of officers and enlisted men as they stood at rest and listened to their orders being read. They were newly arrived—pilots, bombardiers, mechanics, clerks, cooks, gunners, and through the vagaries of chance, these few were present at the creation, dutifully listening as the 490th Bomb Squadron was activated into being.

The 490th would be assigned to the 341st Bombardment Group, along with the 11th, 22nd and 491st Squadrons. Prior to this point, the WW II history of the 490th was the history of the 11th Bombardment Squadron, which was split in half to form the 490th. The new unit received personnel and equipment and trained with B-25Cs and Ds from September through December 1942.

A tight, professionally rendered version of the 490th's Skull and Wings. A cruder, but more accurate version is below.

Their distinctive insignia was designed by Eugene Clay. Clay was an artist, engineer, and friend of Col. James A. Philpott, the new squadron's first commander. The winged skull was painted on the nose of the Lockheed Hudson that Colonel Philpott had ferried to China soon after the attack on Pearl Harbor. The 490th would need an identity and the Skull and Wings seemed a natural choice. The emblem was approved in late 1942 and used on the forward fuselage of the 490th's Mitchells, as well as on flight jackets, throughout the time the squadron saw action in India, Burma, and China.

At Karachi, one of the first things Sgt. Ivo Greenwell remembers seeing was a camel pulling a wagon with American tires on its wheels. He was soon to learn that it was about as modern as things got in India. Newly arrived airmen were loaded into British trucks and taken to Malir Airforce Base, just north of Karachi at the edge of the Sind Desert. Their British-built billets were small, adobe buildings that housed five or six men. This was to be the temporary HQ of Ivo's outfit—the 1106th Ordnance Group.

Many years later, Ivo would write as an introduction to the squadron's first newsletter: *"Remember those heat-oppressed natives languishing somewhere between an ethereal existence and death itself? Who doesn't remember how they dozed in shop entrances, along sidewalks, and even in the streets—and how the freelance cows roamed through open stores sampling food without hindrance? Who doesn't remember the skinned goat carcasses hanging, dehydrated and flyblown, from a tree? Who doesn't remember skinny-legged men in dingy dotis carrying their brass pots? Who doesn't remember the disease and filth that kept them sickly and afraid? Who doesn't remember how they chewed their red "pan" and endured famine, pestilence, and finally death? And do you remember Mother Ganges with her dolphins and crocodiles, and little brown men bathing in her bosom?"*

They had East Indian *wallahs,* or hired servants, to keep their floors swept and their water hot for shaving, along with any other chores that needed doing. The wallahs were paid by British Army Command, and the American airmen were both surprised and happy that, with the wallahs bustling about, they themselves had few boring or unpleasant chores to do.

They had to walk about a quarter of a mile to mess, Ivo recalls, and one hot evening as they approached the mess hall, an odd smell hung heavy in the air. Moving closer it was soon evident that the smell was coming from the kitchen.

"It's camel," a Brit told them. "On the menu tonight."

"Jesus, a camel?" Somebody asked, unbelieving.

Most of the Yanks walked in anyway, just hungry and curious enough to try it. "It was stringy," Ivo says. "It was gamy and it stunk to high Heaven. Our breath smelled bad for three days afterwards."

There were days when they could go into town and attend tea dances at the local British version of the USO club. A few of the British girls, most of them young secretaries and clerks, would regularly show up to dance with everyone, and their presence caused more than a few fights between the Yanks and the Brits.

Sometimes, Ivo and his buddies would head for the beach and go swimming in the Indian Ocean. Six of them rented horses one day and because he was from Oklahoma, Ivo was elected to ride the lead nag. The others hailed from New York or Massachusetts and were convinced that anybody from the far, Western frontier of Oklahoma had to know how to ride.

Ivo didn't, but no one believed him.

"The animal didn't even want to leave the corral," Ivo remembers. "It didn't want to be ridden. It was hungry and its ribs were sticking out. The owner had to lead him out of the corral before I could get him to go."

The rest of the bunch followed. They went for a long ride down to the beach and into the surf before it began to rain. Finally deciding to head back, Ivo turned his horse's head toward home and the beast immediately broke into a fast walk, then a trot, and finally a gallop.

"I couldn't rein him in," Ivo says. "He wanted some oats, or a mare, or something. I hung on for dear life, but there were small brick culverts over little streams that had to be navigated. It was pouring rain and they were slick. Going over the first, the horse slipped but kept his balance. On the second one, he went down hard on his belly with his legs splayed wide. His head harness slipped, his belly strap broke, and I was still hanging on—astride his head and clutching his neck as we slid through the gate."

As the others rode up, Ivo was picking himself up off the ground, his dignity shaken and bruised. One of the GIs from Boston was excited. "Did you see that? Okie rode him all the way in and stayed on him when he fell. What a rider! Nobody but Okie could'a done that!"

To the eastern boys, Ivo was a hero, but he was through with horses and decided to let his buddies think whatever the hell they wanted.

South of Malir, near a British army camp, was a small theater. There was little else going on that could serve as entertainment, so the Yanks often walked down to take in a movie. At first, they were usually British films but as more and more GIs kept appearing in the audience, the theater managed to get a hold of a few American movies.

Yank cheers went up the first time one was shown, as the theater darkened and the screen was filled with "A Day at the Races" with the Marx Brothers. It was an old film, released in 1937, and most of the guys had seen it years before. But hell, it was a Hollywood product, and Hollywood was California—and California was the good old USA—home.

Groucho and the boys never played to a more appreciative audience.

But each night, before the projector flickered on, the theater management played the British National Anthem. Both Yanks and Tommies would stand as the recording began, but the Americans stood awkwardly silent as the Brits gave voice: *God save our gracious King, Long live our noble King...*

After awhile, the GIs got tired of standing like dummies while the British sang out their fealty to King and country.

"God save my ass," one of the Americans finally said, reflecting most of their feelings. "How about some rockets red glare and bombs bursting in air? Maybe the Limeys don't know it, but we're stuck in this shithole, too."

After listening to a howl of complaints, the theater finally agreed to play the Star Spangled Banner as well as God Save the King. But even this concession didn't satisfy the Yanks—their anthem was always played second. As more complaints were heard, the weary East Indian theater owner shook his head, shrugged his shoulders, and the following night played the Star Spangled Banner first.

"Bloody hell!" A Cockney voice shouted, and soon punches were being thrown. The two groups of Allies waded into each other, pride in their outfits and countries at stake.

The theater manager stood aghast as he watched the young Tommies and GIs make a shambles of his establishment. With the help of military police, the fight was broken up and the movie house was closed until discipline could finally be restored.

A wary truce prevailed, but not for long. The next night, the theater didn't open, but blood was still running hot and a fight broke out anyway. Now the MPs, becoming tired of the game, stepped in and closed the place for a week.

Things stayed quiet until a café opened up next door to the movie. Since the British camp was closer, the Tommies had first crack at whatever the café offered and everything was eaten up by the time the Americans could get there. A few days of this and the lads were at it again, busting up the café and each other until everything was screwed down tight while British and American officers decided what to do.

"They worked it out," Ivo Greenwell remembers. "Americans one day and Brits the next."

Peace, order, and harmony prevailed.

5

Soon afterwards, Ivo and his unit received orders to move. Less than a week later they were loaded into narrow gauge railway cars and headed east to Allahabad in central India.

Each car was filled to capacity, every seat taken by soldiers and East Indian civilians alike. Thin-legged children with pop eyes and protruding bellies squatted in the isles. Indians hung out every window and door. Atop each screeching, jerking car, more passengers clung, carrying pitifully small sacks of bread and fruit to sustain them on the journey.

The Indian trains moved relatively slowly, giving the GIs a good look at all sorts of animals. Large bands of monkeys screeching in the trees, great, dirt-caked elephants, ears twitching, grazing in the tall grass. The elephants would stop and raise their trunks as the train rumbled by, then lower their heads to graze again. Nothing seemed to make any permanent impact on this strange, ancient land.

The East Indian train crews had grown up with British ways and customs, and one of these was tea-time. The train would come to a screeching halt in the middle of the bush or in a small village along the route. Steam from one of the engine taps would be used to brew tea. Time meant little. Schedules would keep. The train crews sipped slowly and enjoyed their break.

When the cars pulled into a station at night, the weary GIs would wake to the sound of screeching brakes, and strange voices crying out "Char walla! Char walla!" while the smell of hot tea steeping in unglazed earthen pots wafted through the crowded cars. Eerie strains of music filled the darkness and chants to Krishna could be heard.

When the thin and ragged platform children spotted American uniforms, the scene was one of pleading eyes, small, outstretched hands, and insistent cries of "Baksheesh, Sahib, baksheesh?"

Once at Allahabad, the GIs were quartered in the old Bengal Lancer barracks there. The parade grounds were carefully kept and beautiful, and the Ganges River flowed nearby. The land was fertile, green, and lush—a far cry from the stark emptiness of the Sind desert.

They finally settled near Ondal, where a large British steel mill was in operation. That meant British girls to look at, along with a fine Officer's Club and a good NCO Club open to the Americans.

With this move, Ivo's crew had also acquired a bomb dump full of British and American ordnance. The dump was located at the bottom of a hill and below a medical clinic for leprosy. The dump even included a misfit Russian bomb that no one knew how to fuse or disarm.

Sergeant Greenwell's introduction to the 490th came two weeks after he arrived at Ondal. The 490th, a small squadron of B-25s—each bearing the insignia of the Skull and Wings on its nose—had settled in at the site of a larger runway at a nearby British airfield.

Ivo was called into HQ one morning to learn that he was to accompany Major Shore to the 490th's orderly room, where the two of them met with the new squadron's CO, Maj. James A. Philpott.

"Flamboyant Phil" was a hot pilot and former test pilot with TWA, sporting a pair of pearl handled Colt revolvers similar to those worn by Gen. George Patton.

Major Philpott had been the subject of an unusual article in the Atlantic City Press five years before: "An Army air cadet interested in seeing if his aerial bombs hit the target in practice today," the article read, "leaned over the edge of the big bomber to watch each bomb speed earthward. Cadet James A. Philpott, 22, of Pomona, CA. fell from an altitude of 2,000 feet—in close pursuit of his bomb. Halfway down, he recovered from his surprise and jerked his parachute ripcord. Rolling up his chute, he walked to Mather Field to report his mishap and learned that his pilot hadn't even missed him."

"Pick twenty men, sergeant," Shore told Ivo. "Major Philpott's outfit needs ordnance people. You'll be transferring into this squadron within the week."

Out of Camp Moire in Ondal, Ivo's new outfit—the Skull and Wings—flew their first combat mission on the 18th of February, 1943.

Ivo remembers it well. "After us twenty ordnance men had settled in to the new squadron, we began to learn bomb loading techniques—specifically, how to load them safely and accurately on a B-25. Within a few days, orders came for the 490th's first bombing attack. It was our first job and we were nervous."

Six Mitchells went to Argatella and loaded bombs, then flew their first sorties of the war. They busted up the rail terminal at Sagaing, then went on to smash anything they could find that might delay the movement of supplies from southern Burma to the Japanese troops fighting in the northern part of the country.

The daily missions continued relentlessly, and the squadron was beginning to get some press. A routine mission that took place about the middle of March 1943, was written about by Associated Press War Correspondent, Toby Wiant, who went along for the ride: *"With U.S. Medium Bombers over Mandalay Area.* The Japanese, who were stubbornly defending Myitnge Bridge, got the surprise of their lives last month, but few, if any, are probably now living to tell about it.

"The largest formation of U.S. Medium Bombers ever assembled over a single target area in Burma wiped out ack-ack batteries surrounding a bridge six miles south of Mandalay, then followed through on what appeared to be several direct hits on a span and nearby installations.

"It was the greatest exhibition of mass bombing that I have been privileged to witness during the past six months in the Middle East and in this theater. It climaxed a dramatic two-day series of raids on the repeatedly bombed bridge, one of the most important targets in Burma because it's located on the vital railway connecting Rangoon, Mandalay, and Lashio.

"All of our planes returned safely. Total damage consisted of two small ack-ack holes in one plane."

But it was at Ondal that the squadron suffered its first loss.

All through the night on the 5th of May, ground crews and armorers were down on the field, busy preparing twelve aircraft for the morning mission. At dawn, the first flight taxied into position.

The Wright Cyclones were run up, switching from one mag to the other, checking for drop in rpm's. Each plane in the first flight left the runway and when airborne, circled above, waiting for the rest of the bunch. They were scheduled to go after rolling stock and railroad targets near Mandalay that morning.

In the second flight, 1st Lt. Bill Stephens, brought his Mitchell into line, then gave it full throttle down the Ondal runway. His wheels never left the ground. For some reason never learned, Stephens' Mitchell careened off the runway and smashed itself into a drainage ditch.

With tears streaming down their faces, the ground crews swore in shock and disbelief as the crashed aircraft was ripped apart by the dull blasts of its own exploding bombs.

By the time they reached the plane, there was little anyone could do. One of the crew, still strapped in his seat and burned beyond recognition, hung in a nearby tree. After almost two lucky months, the grim reality of war had finally come to the 490th.

The day after, with the entire squadron attending, Lieutenants Bill Stephens, Rex Bevins, and Karl French—along with Sergeants Walt Czerwinski and Carl Temperate were buried in the Asansol British Cemetery.

The rest of the month was casualty-free, but on May 2nd, an assistant crew chief changed out the port engine plugs on one of the squadron's planes and then went up for a test flight with its pilot. The Wright ran smoothly and everything checked out. That night, the planes for the next morning's mission were loaded with bombs and armed just prior to takeoff.

Just as Capt. John Christy lifted his aircraft off the runway, his port engine failed—the same one that had received new plugs the night before.

Before he could belly the ship into a wet, soft rice paddy off the edge of the runway, Christy's left wing dug into the ground and the plane almost cartwheeled. 1st Lt. Hank Groninger, the bombardier, was thrown clear before the fuel tanks and armed bombs began to explode. Half dazed, Groninger picked himself up and raced back to the burning Mitchell, pulling out Sergeants Jim McAuliffe and Bill Harbes, who were both badly hurt.

Once again, with three Mitchells flying overhead, taps were played at Asansol Cemetery as Captain Christy and Lieutenants Bill Hennessey and Bob Plagens were laid to rest next to their comrades. The rest of the squadron stood at attention, with the maintenance group standing withdrawn and silent, wondering if they were somehow to blame.

Goddamn it, each of them thought. Christy's aircraft had tested fine, what the hell went wrong? The war was not generous with answers. They would never know.

But missions continued each day and life went on. After awhile, both the Officer's Club and Enlisted Men's Club at Ondal were fairly well organized and established. The whiskey and beer rations arrived on time more often than not. Carew's Gin was plentiful, if not exactly favored, and the East Indian cooks had learned to put together fairly decent Spam omelettes.

Even though the men liked to crack that "the longer you're here, the whiter they look," life was bearable—even without women. Craps and low stakes poker games were popular, but the "old men" of the squadron: "Mac," "Ozzie" Southworth, "Doc" Livingston—a pediatrician in civilian life—and Russ Herre, a former Kotex salesman, preferred Monopoly at a dollar a game.

The quarters at Ondal were similar to those at Karachi. The stucco walls of the *bashas* were set on concrete floors and covered by thatched roofs, with wooden shutters in the windows.

At Ondal, each basha had a native bearer to make the beds, see that the laundry was done, and make sure that the sweepers, or "shit wallahs," did their jobs. The head bearer was always called Babu and most of the Babus proved to be cunning bastards who often lashed out fiercely at their underlings just to prove who was top dog.

At chow time, aggressive, scavenging kites circled the mess, often swooping down to pick up any leavings on the ground—or sometimes right out of the mess kit of a startled GI.

Once, irritated by the marauding birds and without anyone seeing him, Sgt. Doug Knokey fished a hot coal out of the charcoal burner and tossed it high into the air. One of the kites immediately grabbed the burning coal in its talons and flew off—promptly dropping it on the thatched roof of a barracks.

Hastily recruited bucket brigades were unsuccessful in preventing the complete destruction of the roof.

Knokey kept his mouth shut about the entire incident and his buddies never learned what really happened until thirty years after the fact.

6

With the ebb and flow of events on the ground, the 490th was soon slated to move. In late March of 1943, they received orders to relocate to a new base at Kurmitola, located near the ancient town of Dacca in the populous and flood-prone Ganges-Brahmaputra delta. The air echelon would begin staging from there on May 19th.

Once again, slow, rickety trains transported most of the ground personnel. They took along their supplies, tools, rolling stock, a few rag-tag coolies, and even a number of screeching little monkeys that had since joined the squadron as dubious pets.

The trip took most of a week, and while the ground crews were on the move, the flight crews and planes staged out of a secondary base at Chakulia, until the ground crews at Kurmitola were settled in and ready to service them again.

Although not completely finished, the new base at Kurmitola was much larger than the squadron's operation at Ondal. Each group was given crews of Indian laborers who, it was thought, were used to working in the brutally hot and humid climate. But the Americans soon learned that malnutrition had rendered the Indians much less suited for physical work than the GIs. So the Americans worked together with them, and although not as strong, the East Indians proved themselves a willing, loyal workforce.

During this time, the aircrews pounded bridges, locomotives, railroad yards, tracks and rolling stock in the Monywa-Mandalay-Gokteik region, ranging as far north as Myitkyina and as far south as Thazi.

The pilots and crews of the Skull and Wings soon learned that the skies over Burma were a terrible place to be. The high, rugged mountains were unforgiving of mistakes or sloppy flying. The weather was treacherous and unpredictable. Japanese ground fire was well established and usually heavy, and the jungle itself seemed a dark, malignant thing—steaming humidity and filling the air with the fetid stink of rot and decay.

And it was a thankless job to boot. The CBI was primarily a British show, and demanded only a limited amount of attention in the American press. There were no George Pattons or Douglas MacArthurs in this war, no great, sweeping campaigns. There weren't any Iwo Jimas, Tarawas or Guadalcanals to sear their names into America's memory.

It was a war of misery and monsoon, of jungle rash, dysentery, and malaria, poisonous snakes and stinging insects—a war of boredom, death, and slow attrition—and aside from Stilwell and Chennault, a war of little-heralded commanders. It was a backwater war, important only to the men who fought it, but what those men quickly learned was that you could die here just as easily as anywhere else—even easier if you were flying B-25s over Burma in rotten weather.

But the Mitchells they flew were marvelous birds.

In 1938, the United States Army Air Corps had issued a proposal calling for a twin-engined medium attack bomber.

North American Aviation, based in Inglewood California, initiated a design proposal they designated as NA-40-1.

It was the birth of the Mitchell bomber.

Number 810—typical equipment of the Burma Bridgebusters. This B-25J went down on May 30th, 1945, while strafing the Sincheng Bridge in China. The entire crew was killed.

North American's design called for a twin-engined, twin-tailed, tricycle landing gear equipped monoplane of clean aerodynamic configuration. In January 1939, the prototype was rolled out and tested. Between the test flight of NA-40-1, and the first of the B-25Js—the last Mitchells to roll off the Kansas City assembly line in 1944, a total of ten major design changes would take place, along with countless field modifications by squadrons and ground crews throughout Europe and the Pacific.

The later models had two Wright R-2600-13 Double Cyclone fourteen-cylinder air-cooled radials, rated at 1700hp each for takeoff and 1500hp at 2400 rpm. The airplane had a maximum speed of 275mph at 15,000 feet, and a 230mph cruising speed. Carrying 4,000 pounds of bombs, it had an effective range of 1,275 miles. The Mitchell medium bomber was a rugged, dependable aircraft that crew chief Ed Branning compared to the venerable wristwatch that "took a licking and kept on ticking."

Throughout its service, changes in armament, fuel capacity, bomb carrying capacity, and other items of equipment were necessitated by constantly shifting tactical requirements. Losses in one area of performance were more than equaled by increased versatility and combat effectiveness.

The B-25 was structurally sound, a fact that was proven by countless crewmen throughout every theater of the war—air combat veterans who performed a multitude of creative armament experiments on the tail, fuselage, and engine nacelle positions.

Various Mitchells in North Africa ripped through surprised Italian and German fighters with additional guns jerry-rigged to the fuselage and nose. Other models sported ball socket joints supporting a single .50 caliber gun in the tail. Some types had open or enclosed waist gun positions firing either .30 or .50 caliber weapons. Still others boasted four fixed forward-firing package guns attached to the sides of the fuselage.

They operated in the freezing Arctic cold and snow of the Aleutians and Iceland, the blistering sand and desert heat of North Africa, and the soggy, corrosive climate of the South Pacific and Burma.

Radioman/gunner Dick Goodwin, now retired and living in Daytona Beach, remembers that when he reached India in early 1943, the squadron was flying C and D model Mitchells—without waist guns.

"The bombardier had a single .50 in the 'greenhouse' nose," Dick recalled. "While the armorer/gunner was in the top turret, just aft of the bomb bay, with twin .50s."

But the radio operator manned a virtually useless lower remote turret with twin .50s. To operate his guns, he had to kneel on the floor and try to sight through a periscope that offered only a 20-degree cone field of vision.

"As you might imagine, it was pretty tough to swing the turret around and pick up any enemy fighters coming up under the belly of the ship."

Because of these limitations, the 490th ground crews decided to tear out the lower turret, leaving a 30-inch hole in the Mitchell's belly. They rigged a length of angle iron across the hole and mounted twin .30s on a ball joint that was attached to it.

Not content with this setup, the crews turned their attention to the two small waist windows on the C and D models, cutting holes in them and installing ball sockets which held two more .30 caliber machine-guns without recoil adapters.

"We attached a bungee cord to a support inside the fuselage," Dick remembers. "And when the pilot told us to test fire the guns, the radioman would unhook the port gun, put a burst through it, and then reattach the bungee. Then he'd fire the belly guns, and move on to the starboard .30.

"The .30s gave very little recoil, so even without adapters they wouldn't usually cause a problem.

"But once I had what was called a 'runaway gun'—I'd taken my thumb off the trigger and was ready to refasten the bungee when the whole gun came out of its socket. I was hanging on to it by the handgrips while the .30 was bouncing around like crazy and putting rounds through the belly of the ship."

Fortunately, the errant gun soon jammed and Dick was able to get it remounted in its socket. Aside from a lot of bullet holes in the floor no serious damage was done—luckily for the crew, all the B-25's cables and hydraulic lines were routed along the sides of the fuselage.

Within the 490th, a secret classification procedure codenamed the Mitchells *gulls*. Each member of the crew carried the standard army Browning .45 automatic—either on his hip or in a shoulder holster. And packed safely away inside more than one of the gulls was a .45 caliber Thompson sub-machine gun for use in the jungles of Burma if its crew went down and survived the crash.

Escape and evasion kits were also issued to each airman, part of which was the famous "blood chit" made famous by Claire Chennault's American Volunteer Group—the "Flying Tigers."

The blood chit was basically an exchange token which would reward the bearer for returning a downed American airman alive.

Starting with the Flying Tigers, the first such token was a Chinese flag painted on silk with a brief text in Chinese promising a reward for assistance to any individual presenting it. The offer was authenticated by an official "chop" or stamp. Called a "life token," the nearest English translation was "blood chit."

In the languages of each specific theater, the message read: *I am an American and do not speak your language. I need food, shelter, and assistance. I will not harm you. I mean no malice toward your people. If you will help me, my government will reward you.*

Along with the blood chit, every airman went up with a money belt that could be used to bargain for assistance with the natives in the event of going down in the jungle.

In the 490th, Cpl. Frank Peter issued them to the crews before each mission. Frank was sometimes known as the "Money-belt Wallah."

"Each belt," He remembers. "Was a sealed canvas affair much like a carpenter's apron. It held a hundred rupees of .999 silver, along with a hacksaw blade, a tiny compass, and a silk map of Burma."

Also inside every newly built plane was a plaque that bore the names and hometowns of approximately thirty American citizens. It read:

To The Crew
Signifying their patriotic desire to ride in spirit with you
in this North American B-25 bomber, these Americans
have given us the serial numbers of War Bonds they have
purchased, and have requested that their names accompany
the crew on every mission. Wherever your duties take you
in this B-25 bomber, let these names be a token that the
Americans for whom you are fighting wish you good
hunting and happy landings, and are doing their utmost
to "Keep 'em Flying."

Occasionally surprises were in store that went beyond the patriotic. As Capt. Ed MacKay was flying a brand new Mitchell overseas from Morrison Field, he took out the oxygen mask and attached to it was a note bearing the red lip prints of a woman, and reading: *From the sweetest lips in the world, to the sweetest guy flying.* Unfortunately, the note was unsigned.

Even now, almost sixty years later, the Mitchells are fondly remembered by the men who flew and worked on them:

Pilot Clarence Reynolds says: "The B-25 Medium Bomber took me over the target sixty times and brought me safely back home. A wonderful piece of equipment."

George Townsend, whose job was loading them with bombs: "The Mitchell was a superb plane…versatile and dependable."

Pilot Harry DePew: "B-25s were a rugged and dependable airplane…I know of no other bomber that carried as much firepower."

Ken Shugart, who specialized in pulling old, worn-out engines and installing new ones, as well as prop removal and replacement, remembers the Mitchell as: "An extremely well-built aircraft…a flying gun platform."

But if the planes were good, it was the skill and courage of the men who flew them that made the squadron great.

They were given tough targets. The Japanese had been in Burma a long time and were well entrenched. Their troop positions, lines of supply, and newly built airfields were heavily defended, and they had air power of their own.

Capt. Bob McCarten of Fargo, North Dakota, assumed command of the 490th soon after Major Philpott was reassigned as 341st Group Exec Officer.

It was a good match. McCarten was tactically smart, and popular with his men. His first baptism as CO came quickly. In May, he led nine Mitchells on a raid to the Thazi railroad junction, and after they'd unloaded their bombs, they came under fire from ten or more Zeros and, strangely enough, a single German ME 109 with the Japanese "meatball" painted on its wings.

With a good pilot at the stick, the Zeros were formidable foes. The Japanese fighter's airframe was light and streamlined. Its two 7.7mm cowl mounted machine guns were manually charged from inside. Two 20mm Type 99 cannon were mounted in the wings, and more than a few Zero pilots carried a good luck teabag hanging from their gunsight.

Although it didn't really apply to Mitchell bomber crews, American and British fighter pilots were repeatedly warned against trying to turn with, or outmanuever a Zero—it just couldn't be done—and those who had tried were mostly dead.

This day, the Zeros and the oddball Messerschmidt first came in from the front, then from the sides and rear. McCarten's lead Mitchell had its top turret torn up in the first attack—with his turret gunner badly wounded by an exploding cannon shell.

Sgt. Vern Cook grabbed the bleeding gunner and pulled him down into the relative safety of the fuselage, then Cook repaired and manned the turret guns himself, until a second hit put them out of commission for good.

Still unhurt, Vern Cook took up the fight from the waist guns. He was a little fellow—120 pounds of fight—whose service record listed him as being "physically unfit for combat."

The Zero pilots over Thazi that day might have disagreed with that assessment, but they went on to press the fight.

The lead ship of Flight B, piloted by Capt. Lou DeLapp was hit hard and fell away. DeLapp regained control at about 500 feet and attempted to rejoin the fight, but his Mitchell disappeared again and the plane and crew were later listed as missing in action. In the hour-long running fight, four Zeros were confirmed and one gull was lost.

On returning to base, a determined Captain McCarten took off again on a solo mission to locate the wreckage of DeLapp's plane and possible survivors. As would be the case so many times, nothing was ever found.

On May 19th, as the ground crews were boarding trains to a new base, the air echelon had begun temporarily staging out of Chakulia. Two days after their arrival there, nine Mitchells again led by McCarten, pounded the Ghauk Workshop Buildings from an altitude of ten thousand feet. On their way home, just south of Mt. Victoria, the flights were intercepted by more than two dozen enemy fighters.

The skillfully flown Zeros and Oscars bored in hard, raking McCarten's Mitchells with heavy cannon and machine gun fire. Lt. Bob Coons and his crew were badly hit. His plane left the formation with a gang of enemy fighters swarming all over it.

At two thousand feet, the crew bailed out—only to be shot to pieces as they drifted down.

"Ah, shit," cursed the American gunners who watched their buddies die, not altogether certain that they might not do the same to Japanese bomber crews if the situation were reversed. War was war, they knew, and an enemy killed today, helpless or not, was one less that would come at you tomorrow.

Lieutenants Coons, Horeen and Van Schaik, along with Sgt. Herb Miller died that day. The only crewmember to survive the slaughter was Sgt. Martin Beckman who sideslipped his chute to avoid being machine gunned.

Beckman survived the drop, landed in the jungle, and despite the loss of blood from four wounds, managed to find his way back to an advanced British base four days later.

The last two scheduled missions out of Chakulia were scrubbed because of weather, and shortly after that the air echelon left to reunite with the ground crews at their new base at Kurmitola.

The monsoons had started and would last into October. Flying over northern Burma during this period, the Supreme Allied Commander in Southeast Asia—Admiral the Lord Louis Mountbatten—peered out the window and asked for the name of the muddy, rushing river below them.

"That's not a river, sir," said an American officer aboard the plane. "That's the Ledo Road."

During the four or five-month monsoon season, it often rained as much as three hundred inches in some places. In India and Burma, valleys became lakes and rivers rose as much as thirty feet in a single night.

At Kurmitola, the ground crews slogged through porridge-thick mud. Disease and biting insects were rampant. The men suffered from dysentery, malaria, and dengue fever. Cholera appeared occasionally, as did scabies, yaws, and typhus. Swarms of black flies drove the crews inside as much as possible, and after heavy rains the trees and bushes became infested with fat, bloodsucking leeches.

After the rain stopped, the temperatures would climb and the humidity was like a shroud over everything. Fungus and bacteria multiplied—spreading rot, mildew, and disease.

At night, the ground crews suffered in the heat, exhausted from the day's work. The air crews tried to sleep, too, but the oppressive heat and humidity, combined with apprehension about the next day's mission conspired to keep them awake and worn down.

The land was low and much of their supplies would mildew or rust. Trucks would get mired-down in knee-deep muck. Ivo Greenwell remembers they often had both their bomb service trucks stuck in the monsoon mud. A winch truck would arrive and it would get stuck, too. Once, the squadron had six trucks bogged down at one time.

The Kurmitola monsoons, both in summer and winter, piled misery on top of misery. Often the ordnance crews worked all night, plodding through mud to load bombs—only to have the mission order changed, and with it, the chore of reloading different sized bombs.

The base was occasionally without a mission due to weather during the monsoons. It was impossible for planes to fly when it rained so hard—often ten to fifteen inches a day. The men learned that the record at Kurmitola was forty-three inches in a twenty-four hour period!

It was as hot and suffocatingly humid at night as it was during the day. Once the sun had set, the jungle bogs began to steam, rising thick into the same air being breathed by the working crews.

When they did get to rest, and to sleep, it was a fitful sleep. Mosquito netting had to be tucked in under the sheets, but even with this precaution, malaria was common.

And buzzards were a hazard to the flight crews. More than once, on takeoff or landing, a Mitchell would smash into one of the big, ugly birds. One crashed through a windshield, knocking the pilot senseless, but the copilot was able to land the plane.

Between the monsoons, the poisonous snakes, malaria-carrying mosquitos, and low-flying buzzards, many of the men voiced the opinion that the Japanese might be hard-pressed to be considered enemy number one.

India offered exotic creatures, too. "Strange looking frogs were in the vicinity," Ivo Greenwell recalls. "Some with balloon necks, some with tails, and some with knots all over their bodies—all in bright colors and shades."

And snakes. In Karachi they had *kraits*—about the size of a large worm—but very deadly. Steel blue or black in color, the different species were often referred to as 5-step or 100-step kraits, with the names referring to how many steps a bitten man might take before he died. Even with antivenom, the bite of a krait was said to produce a 50 percent mortality rate. At Kurmitola, there were cobras, too—the dread hooded cobra in particular. Nervous GIs would blow them apart with their sidearms, much to the dismay of the Indian wallahs who considered the reptiles sacred.

A few guys from the squadron killed a cow once, Ivo recalls, because all they had were cans of Spam and some corn willy. They were meat hungry, and once the cow had been skinned and gutted, they roasted her on a spit all night long.

The East Indians immediately ran screaming to the Brits, complaining that the Yanks were barbaric savages, killing and devouring the flesh of a sacred animal. Looking down their noses, the high-ranking British officers sided with their Indians and condemned the Americans for what they'd done.

The Yanks generously offered meat to their wallahs, who quickly declined. Although a few were Christians, most were Hindu and looked upon the American habit of eating beef as foul and repulsive. But they were earning high wages and most looked the other way as the bovine was consumed. For many, the belief in sacred animals seemed to wither before the might of the American dollar.

And there were the monkeys. While the ground crews and ordnance people were off working, hordes of monkeys would often descend on the squadron's grass-roofed, bamboo bashas. The monkeys tore the mosquito netting to shreds and after one too many simian raids, the 490th was forced to post an armed guard who shot in the air to frighten them away. It worked with the females and the youngsters, but the big males showed little fear. Some were as tall as a man when they stood on their hind legs, and with their harems in tow, the evil-tempered males would protect them to the death.

"Not that I ever tried to steal one," Ivo says. "But they just stood there, daring anyone to try."

7

Mac McCarten—who'd been recently promoted to major—was proving to be anything but a desk-bound CO.

Out of Kurmitola that August, he led three of his Mitchells on a low-level sweep along the muddy Irrawaddy River, searching for enemy shipping. The gulls came in at five hundred feet just south of Pakokku and then split up—each aircraft sweeping in on scattered targets of opportunity.

McCarten's ship attacked a boat near Monywa and began getting hammered by intense, accurate anti-aircraft fire. His plane was smashed with four 40mm and fourteen 14mm shells, but everybody aboard escaped injury.

But, leaking oil, fuel, and hydraulic fluid—and with most of his instruments not functioning, McCarten dropped the remainder of his bombs on another boat and then climbed to sixteen thousand feet—hoping for enough fuel to make it home.

Before reaching Kurmitola, their fuel tanks went dry. The major and his crew bailed out of the falling Mitchell at 4500 feet. Along with McCarten, the men who parachuted into the jungle that day were Capt. "Ozzie" Southworth, Lieutenants John Perdue and Bill Ziedler, and Sergeants Earl Tischendorf and Al Chibnik.

The Chittigong Hill Tract Police, with the help of native scouts, found all them within five hours. Two days later, hunkered down in a small boat run by two somewhat dissolute natives the crew had nicknamed "Big Syph" and "Little Syph," they were delivered bone-tired and dirty to the nearest British garrison at Rangamati.

The Brits listened to their story and checked the Yanks out, then put them aboard an old diesel motor launch bound for Chittigong, where they managed to climb aboard a C-47 back to Kurmitola.

Three other stories that have become legend in the annals of the 490th include one that received nation-wide publicity:

Lt. Bill Gallimore was returning to base with his bomb bay loaded full with American canned beer. Gallimore, a Texan and a former FBI agent, buzzed low over the area in the traditional pilot's greeting. Pulling out of his shallow dive, the laws of physics took over and his jerry-built platform holding the beer came apart. Case after case of the amber brew fell from the sky and crashed down over the entire area. The thirsty GIs down below couldn't believe what they were seeing—cases of beer falling from the heavens.

The suds flowed freely among 490th personnel that night, even though some of it was beyond salvaging.

Another time, Lt. John Schrader managed to get a Japanese airfield named after him. Navigator Schrader inadvertently took the flight he was leading off course on a night raid against Heho airdrome.

Instead of Heho, the Mitchells unloaded on an airport that nobody even knew was there.

At the post-mission briefing, the reports were taken with more than a few uplifted eyebrows—and for the lack of any other name, the target began to be referred to as "Schrader Field." A check of all coordinates and a thorough examination of all available enemy airfields revealed nothing at that location. But a few days later, pictures from a photo reconnaissance squadron indeed proved the existence of the field and Schrader began to get credit for putting an authentic enemy airfield out of commission before it even had time to become an accredited target.

Finally, there was Lt. Charley Powell of San Diego, who ran into heavy flak and was forced to salvo his bombs before reaching the assigned target. It was later learned, through reconnaissance photos the next day, that Powell's bomb load had been inadvertently dumped squarely on a Japanese army divisional headquarters.

And although it never became well-known, radioman Dick Goodwin remembers another story: "We were approaching a railroad bridge on a low-level mission and I was looking out through the belly hole of our aircraft, trying to find something to hit with the twin .30s. We were still quite away out, but as we closed on the target, I began to feel water hitting me in the face. It was a nice, clear day and I ruled out rain."

Puzzled, Dick finally stood up and peered over the top of the bomb bay only to find himself watching their bombardier urinating into the relief tube.

Not all the hazards of combat flying were Japanese.

The squadron settled in for what was to be a fifteen-month stay at Kurmitola, and after spending months hitting railroad yards, river boats, enemy barracks areas, and supply dumps, Major McCarten's squadron began receiving orders to go after new targets—bridges.

McCarten and his men soon learned that bridges were one of the toughest targets built. Pilots and bombardiers groaned about them. To the 490th and the other bomb squadrons in CBI, bridges usually spelled failure, but they were high on the priority list because any destroyed bridge was difficult for the Japanese to rebuild.

In Burma, most bridges were usually located in river valleys or narrow canyons—relatively easy for the enemy to defend. The squadron's low level approach would usually tip off the Japanese gunners and more often than not, the attacking gulls would find themselves flying through a hornet's nest of anti aircraft fire, smoke, flak, and sometimes even cross-canyon cables designed to bring a bomber down.

Above all, bridges were difficult to take out. The squadron was frustrated by bombs that either bounced off the targets or bounced off the closely surrounding terrain at different angles, rather than imbed in the ground so that on explosion they took down both abutments and supports.

But McCarten was a determined man, deciding to wrestle with the problem until he'd solved it. During the last months of 1943, the 490th concentrated on their bridges, struggling to find a way of knocking them out and knocking them out to stay.

Everything was being tried; high and medium altitude bombing, "on the deck" bombing at extremely low level, "dive" bombing, "skip" bombing, and dozens of variations on these techniques.

McCarten knew that in Europe, bridges were blown to pieces by sending huge numbers of bombers over the targets and saturating them with hundreds of tons of bombs. He also knew that the same method wasn't feasible in Burma—simply because it was just such an unheralded, low-priority war, and great numbers of bombs and bombers were pure wishful thinking.

The men grumbled that bridges were a jinx, but on New Year's Day of 1944, something different happened.

The target that day was the Mu River Railroad Bridge, connecting the Mandalay-Sagaing district with the Chindwin River area. On this first day of the New Year, the squadron's operations officer, Capt. Bob Erdin, from Paterson, New Jersey, was getting in some flight time. Erdin disliked bridges, too, but he'd decided to try a new approach to them today.

Wanting more time over the target, he was going to forget about approaching the Mu River Bridge diagonally or at right angles like they'd all been doing in the past. This time Erdin would make his run straight down the railroad tracks and over the bridge lengthwise, reasoning that he'd have the entire length of the span to hit instead of just a small portion of its width.

It made sense, but as he made his low-level bomb run, a tree suddenly loomed in front of him. To miss it, he was forced to pull up and when he brought the Mitchell's nose down again he was already on the target and it was time to release his eggs.

After trailing a neat string of five hundred pounders along the bridge's length, Erdin climbed, banked, and looked back. Two trestles of the 480-foot long Mu River Bridge were a memory—lying sunken in a twisted heap in the muddy river.

"Hot damn, look at that sorry sonofabitch," somebody called out over the intercom. Erdin himself could barely believe it. *That's it,* he thought, *that's what McCarten's been looking for!*

The shallow dive just prior to releasing the bombs, Captain Erdin told his CO once the group returned to Kurmitola, had sent them in at such an angle that they didn't skip or fail to detonate on impact.

An experimental bombing range was hastily built, with Captains Erdin and Harry Sutphen put in charge. They were given the job of perfecting the new technique. After weeks of trial and error with different combinations of bomb loads, fusing, approaches, speeds, altitudes and simulated targets, the two officers found that a low-level approach, combined with a slight dive just before the payload was released would prevent the bombs from skipping once they hit the bridge.

The 490th had found their specialty.

8

In the weeks to come, the 490th began asking for bridge missions—and they got them. Capt. Angelo "Boots" Boutselis, one of the squadron's hottest pilots—with a brash attitude and a ten-inch handlebar mustache—nailed the Myitta River Bridge, a target the entire squadron had missed on a previous mission. Using the new technique, Boutselis and his crew dropped it into the water with only two bombs. Captain Boutselis was so pleased with himself that he conducted prayer-meeting hymns over the intercom as he twirled the tips of his mustache all the way home.

"Boots" Boutselis received recognition in a 1950s comic book and later, when he had a small part as an Air Force flight instructor in "Air Cadet," a war film starring Rock Hudson. Here, Boots (r) and a photographer chat with beautiful film star, Paulette Goddard.

The mustache and the man behind it became well known in CBI, and when popular movie stars Keenan Wynn and glamorous Paulette Goddard stopped at Kurmitola on their India itinerary, the first person the gorgeous Goddard asked to see was the "B-25 Brushmush, Boots."

Not long after, the Skull and Wings blew apart the Meza Railroad Bridge—eight hundred feet in length—over which had passed almost ninety percent of the supplies and reinforcements from the Japanese supply lines in northern Burma. And exactly a month after Captain Erdin accidentally stumbled onto the "skip" bombing technique, sixteen gulls destroyed three bridges on a single mission. A few days later, six 490th Mitchells blasted two more spans, and before the week was out, the squadron had accounted for eight bridges.

In February, 1944, Gen. Howard C. Davidson, commanding general of the 10th Air Force sent a telegram to Colonel McCarten: "To you, your Burma Bridge Busters, and all the boys on the ground who keep 'em flying, on their successful accomplishments, my personal congratulations. Your devastating results have been received with glee."

Burma Bridge Busters! The Skull and Wings squadron now had a new name.

By now, the Central Burma Campaign was in full swing. On the ground, Allied forces were pushing on toward Lashio and Mandalay after the capture of Bhamo and Katho. Because of the 490th's distinguished low level bombing record, and in addition to their regular combat missions, the squadron was picked to drop propaganda information and materials to the Burmese people still under control of the Japanese.

The operation would come to be called the "Burma Mail."

Once each week or so, a single Mitchell bearing the Skull and Wings insignia of the 490th would take off, reach altitude and turn toward Japanese occupied Burma.

Although its .50 ammunition belts were loaded and ready, this aircraft carried no bombs. Instead, its bomb bay was filled with bundles of paper leaflets to be dropped over native villages deep in still-occupied territory. These news leaflets, printed in the Shan language, told native villagers news of the war throughout the world, but concentrated mainly on news of the Burma campaign. Each contained pictures, photos, and simple maps showing the positions of American, British, and Chinese Nationalist troops, as well as the advances of loyal native units down the valleys into central Burma.

The lone Mitchell would roar low over a small village, its bomb bay open as the load of leaflets scattered in the aircraft's slipstream and fluttered slowly down to earth. At the first sound of the bomber's engines the villagers scattered and fled into the dark jungle. Remembering how the Japanese had indiscriminately bombed their villages in 1942, they would watch intently from the bush, bewildered, frightened and suspicious.

But no bombs were dropped. Only sheets of paper. Curiosity eventually overcame fear. They came out of the jungle in twos and threes, muttering to one another and gathering the leaflets.

Then a meeting would be called by the village headmen. The elders were quickly summoned. People chattered excitedly as they gathered in small groups and read of the fall of Bhamo, the progress of the new road from Ledo to China, the Allied advances in far-distant Germany and the bombings of the Japanese home islands. Can all these things be true? The people asked each other. Only a few days before, Japanese Military Police had told them that New Delhi had been taken by the Emperor's troops and that Imperial Japanese forces were driving on to Bombay.

"Bhamo captured by the Allies?" A man would ask his neighbor. "This must be a lie. Did not the Japanese soldiers who collected our rice quotas tell us that the last American forces holding out in India had been annihilated? Bhamo cannot have been captured."

A week later the American plane would be back. This time, thousands of small packages were dropped. The villagers gathered them up and tore them open, barely able to believe their good fortune. Sewing kits with fine steel needles, brightly colored spools of thread and small packages of salt. Above all else, there were seed packets. When planted, one packet alone might produce eighty-seven pounds of radishes and almost seven hundred pounds of tomatoes.

The people would laugh and dance about. This American airplane with the Skull and Wings upon its side was providing them, for the first time in years, some of the necessities impossible to get during the long, hard Japanese occupation of their country. The news would spread to other nearby villages and people would come from miles around to buy or barter for these gifts.

The Japanese came, too. Tough, wiry little soldiers—some of them bare chested and laughing—even making jokes with the villagers. Others harsh and cruel, barking orders as they pushed and prodded the Burmese with rifle butts and bayonets.

The Japanese took whatever seed packets, salt, and sewing kits the people had failed to hide. Then an edict was read to the assembled crowds by a Japanese officer who spoke passable Shan: "All articles dropped by the enemy will be turned over at once to the Imperial Japanese authorities. The seeds and salt are poisoned. They will not be used. All leaflets will be turned over to the authorities. Anyone found reading leaflets or hiding them will be severely punished. By order of the Imperial Japanese Commander."

Japanese soldiers were posted as guards to watch the village and wait for anything else that the Americans might drop.

A week later the drone of a twin-engine aircraft was heard again. The people and their guards looked up to see another B-25 dropping more packets of leaflets. The Japanese quickly scurried about, gathering the leaflets up and burning them in the village bazaar. The Burmese could only stand back, reading the large boldface headlines as the leaflets were carried past them. "Namhkam Captured by Allied Forces."

A few days later, some Shans from Namkham stopped at the village. They were bullock cart drivers until they'd abandoned their carts. In hurried, whispered voices, out of earshot of the guards, they would tell the villagers of the Japanese retreat from Namhkam, and how the Japanese had forced them to haul supplies that aided the retreat.

"Then it's true," an old man whispered. "Namhkam has been taken. The British and Americans are advancing into our Shan states."

"How can the Japanese be in New Delhi, then?" Someone else asked, shaking his head. "These things the Japanese tell us are lies. The Allies are truly coming."

Days later, more leaflets were dropped. "Stay away from roads and trails used by the Japanese," they said. "Do not retreat with the Japanese. They cannot feed you or protect you. When the fighting comes to your area, take your possessions and hide in the jungle."

Another warned them bluntly: "Shans! If the Japanese force you to haul their supplies, abandon your carts and run away. Your carts may be bombed! From the sky, Allied planes cannot tell Shans from Japanese."

Much later, when the retreating Japanese forces came to the small settlements to recruit forced labor to help in their retreat, they would find only empty, abandoned villages. The Burmese had taken all they owned and gone into the jungles and the hills to hide. Some were later credited with killing Japanese stragglers they stumbled upon, while others provided up-to-date information to Allied patrols, and assisted downed Allied airmen to find their way back to friendly territory.

Week after week, the squadron flew its "Burma Mail"—a payload of hope, goodwill, and friendship to the Burmese down below—while at the same time, as the war raged on, daily flights went out each day, bombing and strafing targets selected by 10th Air Force Headquarters.

The squadron soon settled in to their new home. The quarters at Kurmitola had bamboo walls, thatched roofs, and were set on concrete slabs.

Back in May, 1943—until the air echelon arrived from the temporary base at Chakulia—engineering officer Capt. Howard Bell remembers having a hut all to himself and sleeping uneasily, with his .45 Browning automatic close by and handy. The pistol was a cheap insurance policy against the hungry and unpredictable jackals that wandered through the still-empty camp each night.

Kurmitola was near Dacca, and down the road at a place called Tezgoan, there was an ATC maintenance base and a few units of the 7th Heavy Bomb Group with B-24s and some B-17s. A British hospital, a South African medical unit, and the Red Cross were nearby as well, and the 490th soon learned of the presence of nurses.

Even war must sometimes step aside for love. Major Philpott, the squadron's first CO, would eventually marry Beverly Brown—one of the Red Cross nurses. Miss Brown endeared herself to the major, and to virtually everybody else who learned of it, when she unofficially accompanied "Flamboyant Phil" on an impromptu strafing mission over Burma.

One day at Kurmitola, a jeep pulled up with Red Cross girls in it. Ken Shugart was pulling an engine for replacement when one of them called out—offering coffee to anyone that wanted it. It was too hot for coffee and Ken didn't drink it anyway—but this was a white girl—so he hurried over to the jeep. The pretty American nurse poured coffee into a cup and turned around to scoop sugar out of a ten-gallon kettle in the back of the jeep. As she did, her elbow hit the back of the seat and she spilled sugar all down the front of her slacks.

Feeling foolish, Shugart stood there, not knowing what to do. The girl looked up him with a cute smile and a sexy wink. "Just like sugar on a doughnut, isn't it?" She said, casually brushing herself off.

Ken still remembers that day.

But if the presence of nurses added spice to the life of the squadron, it was soon to be replaced by tragedy. In August, two of the Red Cross girls hitched a ride back from Calcutta aboard one of the gulls. As they landed at Kurmitola and scrambled down the Mitchell's aft access ladder, the girls noticed only a jeep full of young airmen eagerly waiting to drive them home. Laughing and excited, the nurses were careless and rushed unsuspectingly into a still-spinning prop. One was killed instantly and the other severely injured.

It was a tragic incident—the worst sort of bad luck, and the men silently, secretly hoped it wouldn't rub off on the missions ahead.

9

When Stilwell, who'd been licking his wounds long enough, reckoned his forces ready to punch back in and retake Burma, his plan was to fight his way across the northern Burmese mountains to the village of Naga. From that spot, they'd gather strength and push down the Hukawng Valley toward Japanese-held Mogaung, whip the enemy there, and then press on to Myitkyina.

At the same time Stilwell and the Allies were making plans, the Japanese were also preparing two offensives of their own: Tokyo had given authorization for Operation U-Go in early January. It was to be carried out by Gen. Renya Mutaguchi's veteran Fifteenth Army.

Mutaguchi was to push westward out of Burma and into India's Imphal Plain, while a second offensive would strike eastward into China. A determined man, Renya Mutaguchi held much more ambitious notions, however, and with the encouragement of Subhas Chandra Bose, the leader of the Free India Movement, the Japanese general had his sights set on nothing less than the invasion of India itself.

Bose's units, made up of Indian prisoners of war who'd been released by the Japanese, had formed a ragtag, uninspired force that he called the Indian National Army. Along with these dubious fighters, Bose believed that once the Japanese entered India, the East Indians would willingly and happily rise up in bloody revolt against the British.

Now, with the level of warfare in CBI ratcheting up, the Allies quite rightly viewed logistics and supply to be the number one priority in achieving a successful campaign against the Japanese.

Lord Mountbatten gave his approval for the final plan of the offensive, codenamed *Operation Thursday*, on January 14th, 1944.

Stilwell was to push his force from Ledo to Shaduzup and then into the area surrounding Mogaung-Myitkyina. From here, the plan had him heading east toward China, building the supply road as he went. Actually, Stilwell had been on the move since October of the year before. He'd already reached the Hukawng Valley.

Now, three things were planned by the Allies: British Gen. Orde Wingate and his "Chindits" would cut the communication of those Japanese units facing Stilwell, and establish permanent areas of occupation behind Japanese lines. The Chinese would move into Burma from Yunnan, driving the Japanese defenders before them; and British Gen. William Slim would take his troops west, from Arakan, India into Burma.

At the center of this three-pronged attack was the town of Myitkyina, called "Mitch" by the pilots flying over Burma.

Near the end of 1943, in their thrust to occupy India, the Japanese had managed to overrun and capture communication points around Imphal and were laying siege to that city and the entire Imphal Plain. In doing so, they'd also surrounded General Slim's army, and with Slim in a box, the planned third prong of the Allied offensive had been effectively nipped in the bud. Every commander in CBI understood that if Imphal fell, the door to India would have been effectively blown open for Japanese occupying forces.

By early spring of 1944, the Allies were in a desperate battle to keep the Japanese from overrunning them at Imphal and Kohima, and things soon turned even darker. On a flight to visit his troops there in late March, Gen. Orde Wingate was killed in a crash of the B-25 in which he was flying.

Even as the Imphal fighting was raging desperately, in Burma to the east, Stilwell was laying his own dogged siege against the Japanese at Myitkyina, and by the middle of May the Allies finally had their hands on "Mitch's" vital airstrip.

Realizing the critical need for all the air support he could get and remembering a past promise from Franklin D. Roosevelt, Theater Commander Lord Mountbatten now called in his markers and requested it from the American President.

So, from Kurmitola, the squadron was ordered to move again near the end of May. This time to Chittagong with orders to temporarily cease combat missions and act as a supply carrying unit to the Allied troops besieged at Imphal and Kohima, two places that were now seeing some of the heaviest fighting since the British evacuated Burma two years earlier.

Between May 20th and the end of the month, with only one day of downtime due to weather, the Bridge Busters flew a total of 380 tons of ammunition from Chittagong to Allied units fighting on the ground.

If the crews thought that carrying supplies would be a cakewalk compared to bombing targets, they soon found out how wrong they were. Four days after these operations began, two of the squadron's Mitchell's found themselves in trouble.

On a routine mission to Imphal, 1st. Lt. Carl King was jumped by ten Zeros near Bishenpur. King succeeded in evading the enemy fighters and got his ship down undamaged. One of his gunners, Sgt. Don Morgan, was later given a confirmed kill in the brief dustup.

And later on the same day, another Mitchell—this one piloted by the 490th's Commanding Officer, Lt. Col. Bob McCarten—ran into seven Japanese fighters in the same area. Twice the Zero pilots pressed determined attacks but McCarten managed to lose them without receiving damage.

Fifteen minutes later, McCarten had five more fighters after him. Two Zeros crossed his flight path and one dropped an aerial bomb. A third came screaming in from two o'clock, both its 20mm cannon and 7.7mm guns tearing into McCarten's Mitchell and setting one engine on fire.

Despite a shot up aircraft and a smoking engine, the commander once again lost his attackers and made it back to base where he was forced to make a crash landing. Parts of his hydraulic system had been shot to pieces and McCarten's copilot soon found out that they could lower their landing gear, but couldn't lock it in position. The wounded Mitchell hit hard and skidded down the packed-dirt runway, raising great clouds of dust, and tearing itself apart in the process. But it didn't burn, and McCarten's crew all scrambled out unhurt, except for Sgt. Bill Elders who suffered superficial injuries.

Two days after McCarten's close call, another B-25 piloted by 1st Lt. Harry Mesnik failed to return to base. The burned-out wreckage of Mesnik's plane was later reported to have been located in the Shillong Hills, but no details of the crash were known. The others who died with him that day were navigator Lt. Phil Blumer, Sergeants Al Germaine, Herb Miller, and Cpl. Earl Quigley.

Two days after Mesnik failed to get back, 2nd Lt. Frank Potwine and his crew took off from Chittagong and were never seen again. Reports later came in that the plane had gone down near Dighinola, in the Chittagong Hill Tract.

This time, due to the location of the crash being relatively close, Maj. "Ozzie" Southworth, the squadron's exec, and flight surgeon Capt. John Wadsworth were sent into the bush to search for the missing plane and crew. They left Kurmitola by air and landed at Chittagong, where arrangements were made for a small boat and outboard motor. Early the next day, they fired up the little Evinrude and proceeded up the Karnaphali River to Rangamati and Langdau Bazaar where, sunburned and tired, they spent an uncomfortable night trying to get some needed sleep.

Out of Myanimukh, they tried to push their way up the Myani River, but the current was too much for the small outboard. Storing their gear where it might stay dry, Southworth and Wadsworth hired a guide and two bearers, taking just necessities and three day's supply of K-rations. The five men then began hiking, 36 miles over crosscut streams and rugged terrain, until they reached Dighinola. On arriving there, the two American officers were given a note dropped by Col. McCarten's plane earlier in the day—advising that a crashed aircraft had been sighted near the village of Khagrachari.

"There is a good trail to Khagrachari," they were assured.

"Good enough for bicycles?" The Americans asked hopefully.

"Oh yes, sahibs, good enough for bicycles."

Relieved that they wouldn't have to walk Southworth and Wadsworth set out for Khagrachari the next morning. They soon found the charred remains of the aircraft to be another plane—a different one that had crashed nine days before Potwine went down. Its crew had survived and burned the plane themselves.

Disheartened and exhausted by a trail that was nowhere close to "good enough for bicycles," the two returned to Dighinola to learn that the crash site they were searching for was located near a village called Babuchara.

After resting for a night, they again arranged for a guide and bearers and slowly made their way over five miles of tough ground before finally reaching the scene of Potwine's crash.

Along with the pilot, those who went down here were Lt. Herb Jewett, Sergeants Clay Ewing, Jim Cowie, and Pvt. George Dobbins, Jr.

The Mitchell had gone in on a ridge about a hundred feet down from the summit of a rugged hill. To the American officers, it was obvious that the aircraft had hit the ground at a high rate of speed, burying its engines and heavier parts eight to ten feet into the surrounding earth. Demolished and burned, there were few parts left that even identified it as an airplane.

Three of the crew had been dismembered and burned beyond recognition, and had already been buried by the natives. From the smell and the swarms of flies, Southworth and Wadsworth suspected that the other two bodies had been crushed into the ground by the weight and impact of the wreckage.

Wearing bandanas over their faces, the searchers sifted through the charred wreckage looking for evidence that it was the plane they were after. First they found a scorched Ray-Ban sunglasses case with Potwine's name on it, and then a shoulder holster etched with the name "Cowie" on the inside of the holster flap. Two .45 automatics were also found. One carried a serial number that had been issued to 2nd Lt. Francis H. Potwine, the other wasn't registered in the squadron's files.

The natives told them that a number of smaller airplanes, probably enemy fighters, had been all over the B-25 while it was still in flight, and that Frank Potwine's Mitchell was already burning before it crashed.

There was no attempt made to exhume the two remaining bodies. They lacked the proper tools, and as a seasoned medical officer, John Wadsworth knew that whatever they might find would be impossible to identify.

With the help of the natives they raised mounds of earth over the three already buried bodies that had sunk because of heavy rains, erected a simple marker, and took photos of the wreckage and the gravesite.

What they were able to do wasn't much, but the two American officers hoped that the photos might someday bring a measure of relief and closure to the grief of five families back in the States.

Nine months afterward, on April 10th, 1945, Maj. Ozzie Southworth would himself be lost. Flying on a routine administrative flight out of Warazup, Burma, his aircraft was reported missing and never found. Ozzie Southworth was the last remaining ground officer from shipment 2299G—that small group of original officers and enlisted men who'd been present at the 490th's activation near Karachi, in the Sind Desert three long years before.

10

As the squadron was perfecting their low-level bombing techniques, Ivo Greenwell was given a different sort of a mission—one on the ground, but still carrying its share of risk.

Three P-51 Mustangs had recently been jumped by a gang of Zeros. The Mustang was a fast and powerful fighter, but it didn't have the Zero's moves. To gain more manueverability, the P-51 pilots had had to shed some weight—fast. They quickly salvoed their 500lb wing bombs, took up the fight against the Japanese, and eventually ran them off.

But the salvoed bombs, dropped unarmed, were a threat to a small Indian village near the drop site. They had to be either detonated or brought back by the Ordnance Section, and Ivo was Ordnance.

He took four men, requisitioned a jeep and a bomb service truck. They loaded everything that might be needed to blow the bombs or winch them onto an Indian barge to be floated home.

Ivo and his little convoy met an East Indian leftenant and his crew at a wharf on the river at Narangange. The Indians knew the location of the village, the ordnance crew was told. They had a small barge and a tug, and it was midday by the time everything was loaded and they were chugging north upriver toward the Chin Hills that divided India from Burma.

"Any Japs left in your area?" Ivo asked the Indian officer.

"No," the leftenant answered happily. "All Japs gone. After the fighting at Imphal and Kohima, the British have secured the area, you see."

The men relaxed the best they could aboard the barge, smoking cigarettes at the rail while watching the brown, muddy water move sluggishly past. They often saw the dead and bloated bodies of men and animals rolling in the current, floating slowly downstream toward the delta and the Indian Ocean several hundred miles to the south.

Night on the river was spooky and strange. Ivo and the crew tried to sleep on the barge's filthy deck, surrounded by some of their gear, but sleep was hard and fitful. The Indians aboard the tug were awake all night, chanting their religious mantras. Other boats passed quietly in the darkness, small oil lamps hanging off their gunwales. The GIs saw no other lights except campfires on shore and a few dim, flickering lamps in the small villages they passed.

At the barge's stern and three steps down from the deck was a small outhouse. The men relieved themselves while squatting two feet above the lapping water and the floating bodies.

As the sun rose over the trees the next morning, the barge was beached on a broad sandy shore edged by heavy thickets of bamboo.

"Jesus," somebody whistled. "Where the hell are we?"

"There's some trees further inland," one of the other ordnance men said, pointing off into the distance. "But I don't see nobody around."

"OK, let's unload the jeep," Ivo suggested. "We'll all get in it and find somebody around here who knows the score."

They made their way along the beach until they found a small village. As they looked around, they saw little faces—curious kids—peering out at them from behind stands of thick bamboo. When casually approached, the children ran away.

"Well, we need to find somebody who knows where those bombs are," Ivo said, suspecting the children might be of help if they weren't so shy. The GIs unpacked the American soldier's secret weapon—Hershey Bars—and one by one, the children approached the jeep for candy. Soon, two or three of them climbed aboard for a ride, and eventually the ordnance crew was mobbed by dark, skinny little Indian kids with wide eyes—all hoping for some chocolate and a ride in the strange looking cart that no one had to push or pull.

In time, they were meeting with the village constable, weaving their rudimentary knowledge of Hindi with his sparse command of English. They learned where the bombs—four of them—were located, buried in the dirt around the settlement. Two more had landed in the river, the constable said, pointing toward the beach they'd landed on.

"We can write those two off," Ivo tried to tell the official. "No way to find them, and it won't take long before they're waterlogged and inert."

They spent the rest of the day carefully digging out the other salvoed bombs and screwing nose fuses into them. With warnings to everyone in the village to stay clear, the plan was to blow the bombs the next day.

That night they ate their field rations back on the barge and turned in early. Again, sleep was impossible. On the small tugboat, the Indian sailors were at it again, chanting far into the night.

"Jeez," somebody observed. "The Andrews Sisters they ain't."

Weary of the incessant singing, Ivo's crew got up and began to explore the area. A half mile away, they stumbled onto a pagoda and a large statue of Vishnu, the Hindu deity of cosmic order. All around the imposing statue were burning candles, perfumed flowers, and colorful gifts. They soon learned that a wedding celebration was under way and they were invited to attend.

"Sarge, maybe we oughta bring some presents, too," one of Ivo's crew suggested. "I think maybe it's expected."

They returned to the jeep and brought back all the empty ration cans they could carry. These were highly regarded as cooking utensils by the practical East Indians.

That night, there was dancing and revelry in the pagoda. After being politely but firmly asked to remove their shoes and leave them outside, Ivo and his men placed their presents at Vishnu's base.

"I'm takin' bets we never see those shoes again," one of the GIs said.

The villagers danced and sang first, then asked the Americans to reciprocate in kind.

"Hell, ain't the ration cans enough?" The crew asked as they took the stage and began to chorus: *"God Bless America, land that I love…stand beside her, and guide her…"*

"We ain't the Andrews Sisters, either," one pointed out in a whisper. But the natives, immensely pleased with their foreign guests, seemed to love it.

"Where are the bride and groom?" Ivo asked the village elders.

They are alone, he was told. In small, separate tents. They would not be united in marriage until dawn. The celebrations and festivities were mainly for the parents of both.

Back on the barge in the wee hours of the morning, the Indian sailors were still dutifully chanting their mantras. Finally, Ivo gingerly approached the leftenant: "My men are tired and need some sleep," he explained. "But the chanting of your men is keeping them awake."

The Indian officer was visibly distressed. "All of my men," he said. "Are praying for your success in discharging your dangerous task with the bombs, and also for safety from the greater danger of the Japanese invaders, who not so long ago, entered India only to be chased back into Burma.

"My men are not sleeping either," the leftenant continued. "But they are willing to sacrifice their sleep for the greater welfare of you and your men."

Ivo found himself hard-pressed to counter this argument and went back to the barge. Soon afterward however, the chanting stopped, and in the glow of a burning cigarette across the water, the GIs saw one of the sailors grin and wave. The men suspected that their East Indian allies were relieved as well.

Over the next two days, with one of his men assigned to keep the kids happy riding in the jeep and with all the villagers watching from a safe distance, Ivo and the rest of the crew blew two of the five-hundred pounders. They rendered a third inert by fracturing its casing to let in moisture. The cracks would let in enough water to mix with the amatol and make the bomb pretty much harmless.

The fourth bomb was never found. The Americans could never find anyone who could pinpoint its location, and Ivo came to believe that it, too, was probably underwater, buried deep in river mud. Early the next morning, the ordnance crew bid the villagers farewell and sailed south again, back to Narangange.

For four young Americans, it had been an adventure in a strange, exotic land, and a brief respite from the otherwise grim routine of war.

As the fighting in CBI dragged on, the 490th was getting lost or badly damaged planes replaced regularly, but new personnel to fly them were proving more and more difficult to come by. The word was that the war in Europe and the Pacific was eating up available flight crews and the CBI being mainly a British show, remained a low priority.

With this shortage of manpower, ground personnel were unofficially allowed to man planes and fly missions, and many quickly volunteered—eager to find out what air combat was really like.

Ivo Greenwell was curious, too. Up to this point, he'd only been on the loading side of the bombing process.

He volunteered and his first two missions exposed him to a strange situation. They were carrying supplies of .50 caliber ammunition into the airstrip at Myitkyina, recently taken by the Allies—at least most of it had been taken.

Although one end of the field was secure in allied hands, the other end was still in dispute. At first, the Japanese stubbornly held ground very close to the runway, allowing them to pop away with their 6.5mm Type 96s—raking any American aircraft taking off or coming in on final approach for landing.

No planes were lost, but Mitchells kept returning to Kurmitola with holes in their fuselage. It hadn't been the worst introduction to combat flying, Ivo thought, but it wasn't any picnic either.

His third mission took him over a target where the Japanese had concentrated ground troops—protected by small bunches of Zero fighters that came up to fight the mediums of the 490th.

The Japanese pilots seemed reluctant, Ivo recalled. The four Zeros and twelve Mitchells both exchanged ineffective fire during a fifteen-minute running fight. The fighters came in and around, but never close enough to pose any real threat.

"Jesus, I think those little bastards were just as scared as us," somebody offered as the flight returned to Kurmitola. The air crews began to suspect that there were no supermen in the skies over Burma—just a lot of shit-scared men on both sides, trying to do their jobs without getting killed—hoping against hope to get back home again someday, whether home was Brooklyn Heights or Niigata Prefecture.

Ordinarily, most of the men cared little about knowing the enemy, while a few others often wondered about the Japanese pilots they were flying against.

The basic Japanese air combat unit was the *sentai*, which was equivalent to a British or American group, though with only half the aircraft. With an effective strength of between thirty or forty planes, the sentai was commanded by a major or lieutenant colonel, himself a flying officer.

In turn, the sentai was divided into three *chutai*, or squadrons, usually commanded by a captain. Occasionally a chutai might be detached for service in an isolated area, or an "independent chutai" would operate on a continuing basis outside the usual command structure, moving from place to place as needed with its own HQ and attaching itself to whatever group was already there.

Moving up the chain of command, two or more sentais—often a fighter group, a heavy-bomber group, and a light bomber or ground-support group—made up a *hikodan*, equivalent to a British wing and commanded by a colonel. Two or more hikodans made up a *hikoshidan*, equivalent to an air force and commanded by a general officer.

It was widely believed both before and during the war, that in loyalty, courage, and willingness to follow orders, Japanese pilots were second to none. But towards the end of the war in CBI, with their air forces depleted and short of supplies, ammunition, and equipment, many of the enemy fighters that came up to challenge the Mitchells and other Allied pursuit planes seemed to do so half-heartedly.

One morning a few missions later, his aircraft flying solo, Ivo's pilot spotted four bogies below them at one o'clock and flying in the opposite direction. "Maybe they won't see us," the pilot said hopefully.

"I was flying tail gunner," Ivo says. "And when the Zeros were far enough away they climbed to altitude and came back at us from behind. I was busy reporting their positions to the rest of the crew and when they got fairly close I touched off the twin .50s in short bursts. Every tenth round was a tracer bullet and they could see we weren't surprised and had them in our sights. Four to one and they decided against pressing the attack. I think they knew they were losing the war in Burma anyway and didn't want to risk getting hit."

The next day was another solo mission, and this one turned a little tense. Two Japanese fighters jumped Ivo's ship and these two seemed as stubborn as dogs on a bone. There was a lot of cloud cover and the single Mitchell was staying above it. The Zeros had spotted the American plane earlier on and were following at a distance, taking cover in and out of the clouds, until they finally climbed high and attacked from above.

"The engineer gunner and I took one Zero each and began hammering away. As they came in, we gave them burst after burst. They didn't seem daunted by it and it was plain to see that they were pressing to get in close."

Once they did and began firing, Ivo's pilot tucked it in and flew into the clouds, barely missing the side of a mountain. They hid in the clouds for awhile, circling the mountain, watching for the Japanese. Once they chanced coming out of the clouds and running for home, but the Zeros were soon on them again. It was back into the clouds, until fuel began to be a problem, and then back out again. The Mitchell couldn't outrun the smaller fighters, its crew knew. They'd just have to fight their way back home.

After another pass and exchange of fire, the Japanese suddenly broke away and flew off, probably low on fuel themselves.

Back at Kurmitola, Ivo was sweating. He hadn't had time to be scared earlier. He was too busy firing his .50s. But when the relieved crew climbed down from the Mitchell, they began counting holes in the fuselage and Ivo felt his knees buckle and go all rubbery.

"I couldn't help it. I had a hard time walking for awhile, and I wasn't the only one who had that problem."

In all, he flew seven missions as a gunner and when he got back to his regular job of ordnance, Sgt. Ivo Greenwell had seen all he wanted to of the air war over Burma.

On June 23rd, the Brits regained the offensive at Imphal. Both that siege and the crisis were over. A week later, MacCarten's Bridge Busters were ordered to cease their supply operations and five days after that, the ordnance crews were loading bombs into the Mitchells once again.

Although Stilwell had taken the airfield at Myitkyina in May, his forces there still remained under siege until the first few days in August. When the Japanese stranglehold was finally broken, those GI engineers who went in to clean up were to learn just what sort of enemy they'd been fighting.

Pvt. Robert Paglucci was part of a cleanup squad and he wrote about it this way: "After you've captured a place, you have to clean it out if you plan to remain there. In the case of a place like Myitkyina, cleaning up means considerably more than just burying the dead and repairing the damage to the town. It's necessary to locate and detonate the many dud bombs, shells, and cartridges that litter the landscape and can make day-to-day life a hazardous proposition.

"One item that gives us a fair amount of trouble are Jap booby traps. The two types we've run into operate like this: one is the pressure type. The Jap hand grenade is ignited by hitting the cap on a helmet or a rifle butt. In the pressure-type booby trap, holes are dug in the ground to fit two grenades, with the caps sticking out about an inch above the ground. The pins are pulled and a plank placed over the grenade caps. When you step on the plank it breaks the caps and six seconds later…boom! The crack of the caps isn't much of a warning. They sound just like dry twigs.

"In the trip-cord trap, a cord is strung out in the grass and across a path. The cords run to a rock hung on a small bush or limb. When you trip over, or touch the cord, the rock falls on the cap of the buried grenade.

"We've had a few close calls. One day, detonating three heavy artillery shells, we were hunkered down behind our jeep, hanging on to the detonation wire. When the shells blew, the base plate of one hit the front bumper and smashed it into the radiator.

"One day, we blew a Jap aerial bomb and after the smoke cleared away we discovered that the blast had opened up a Jap tomb of sorts. Nine of them, all rolled up in blankets. One had committed hara-kiri. He had a knife stuck in his heart and his hand was clutched around the knife handle. In the other hand was a note to his wife: *Dear Wife, I am writing this note to let you know that I am going to kill myself. I can hear the sun goddess Ameterasu calling for me. I will be waiting for you in her kingdom. Goodbye, dear wife.*

"Interesting people, the Japanese."

11

By January of 1944, the 341st Bomb Group HQ, with its 22nd and 491st squadrons was moved to China, leaving the 490th behind in India with the principal responsibility of causing havoc on the Japanese-held bridges in northern Burma.

Now the 490th became part of the 10th Air Force, while the 341st came under control of the 69th Composite Wing of the 14th Air Force.

The 341st, increasing the tempo of its activities, threw its weight behind the Chinese forces defending American bases, but despite their efforts the Japanese kept hammering away. Changsha, Hengyang, Kweilin, Liuchow, Nanning all fell in rapid succession. By December of 1944, the Japanese had achieved their objective, an overland route from Korea to Singapore. Now they could transport the wealth of natural resources of their southwestern empire via land to their industries in Manchuria and Japan.

One of his last times home on furlough. With his sisters and nephews, Left: Erma and Tommy. Right: Millie and camera-shy "Jimmer."

Back in the States, overseas duty was coming closer for Otsie. But In addition to the fact of being shipped overseas, he was now facing something he worried more about than fighting Japanese.

Zoe was seriously ill. For a time, she'd been losing weight. Her appetite was poor and she found herself facing each day with less and less energy. Eventually she developed a fever and a nagging cough.

At Billings Hospital in Chicago, the doctors had shaken their heads and told her she was suffering from tuberculosis.

Now when he came home on leave, Ots spent most of his time at the hospital, at Zoe's bedside, urging her to keep her spirits up. They both knew that tuberculosis was deadly. He loved her and was afraid for her, but at this point, words of encouragement were all he could offer. The two of them may have been mercifully unaware of it, but somewhere in any library were written the words of Hippocrates, who identified tuberculosis, or "consumption," as the most widespread disease of his times. It was almost always fatal, the ancient Greek physician had noted, warning colleagues against visiting victims in the late stages of the disease, lest the patient's inevitable deaths damage the reputations of attending physicians.

Soon after seeing his wife for the last time, Ots was sent to the Combat Crew Center at Hunter Field, Savannah, Georgia—to be part of a medium bomber crew destined to ferry a new Mitchell somewhere overseas—where the war was being fought.

Hunter Field, Combat Crew Center
Savannah, Georgia
September 10th, 1944

Dear Mil and Jimmer:

Better late than never, right? Sorry I didn't come around to say goodbye but I just couldn't make it. I spent what time I had at the hospital so that was the reason.

I suppose by now Pep is on his way to his new station. Let me know how it goes. Has he any idea of what he's going to do now?

I got here Tuesday morning all set to kill a lot of Japs as we were to stay here only long enough to get our equipment and plane, but something snafu'd and here we are. Fighting spirit all gone and we may sweat the war out here for the duration. All kidding aside, we'll be here for perhaps three weeks. But do you think they'd give us a furlough? You guessed it. All we're doing here is nothing and it's a shame. I'd rather spend this time at home.

This part of the country is hot as hell. I'd give anything to go back to Greenville and some of that cool Carolina weather. There's nothing like it.

Trying to kill this Sunday writing letters. This is my fifth and my fingers are pretty tired already. But the Air Corps never says die.

Tonight I'm going to see Dorothy LaMour in something or other. You ought to slip in this show sometime, you get a bigger kick out of the wisecracks the guys pull off than anything else. It's really a scream. The boys sure are cocky around here. Well Mil, don't be like me when it comes to writing letters. It isn't nice. So when you have a little time, write your lonesome bro.

Love,
Otsie

Hello to the Vesely's

In the meantime, the 490th Bomb Squadron was gaining a well-deserved reputation as a "hot" outfit. Their new 'glip' bombing technique—derived from the components of 'skip' and 'glide' bombing, had already earned them the new name "Burma Bridge Busters."

Otsie wouldn't learn about it for a few more months, but the tactic's effectiveness depended upon an approach along the axis, from one end or the other of the bridge. The double glide angles of the attack compensated somewhat for this headlong flight into the guns of the enemy. To successfully 'glip' a bridge, a deliberate passage through the concentration of small arms, machine gun and automatic weapons fire, and often blossoming, white puffs of time-fused mortar shells, was essential.

The pilots soon learned that the amount of enemy opposition varied with every individual bridge, but its gut-churning intensity could usually be relied upon at the big ones like Phu Lang Thuong, Hai Duong, Yen Xuang, Phu Ly, Ninh Bibh, Dap Cau, Ba Trung, and Song Rang.

And, of course, some level of opposition was likely at every bridge target attacked. In addition, there was the ever-present hazard of being caught on the deck by bunches of Zeros who also knew which targets were vulnerable to American attack. But even without enemy fighters, there were more than enough hazards involved in low-level work.

On a night mission, April 8th, 1st Lt. Bill Cook and four other Mitchells left Kurmitola on a twelve hundred mile round trip strike against the formidable, heavily defended Sittang railroad bridge, fifty miles from Rangoon—considered by the Japanese to be the most strategically important bridge in Burma.

Cook was from Fullerton, California and only eighteen years old. With a full moon shining white, the small flight picked up the railroad tracks at a point five miles from the target. Using the bright glint of moonlight on the steel rails as their guide, Cook and the others came in low, boring down on the bridge at almost three hundred miles an hour. Bill Cook's was the second ship in and he lined up on the black steel girders two hundred feet below. When his bombs were released, two of the bridge's spans were blown to pieces, but as he pulled up sharply to avoid heavy ground fire, his right wing sliced through the tall spire of a pagoda on the river's bank and neatly sheared off six feet of wing tip.

Struggling to maintain altitude, Cook nursed his crippled ship and nervous crew to a Royal Air Force base three hundred miles from the target, where he finally managed to bring it in safely.

Bill Cook and his crew were killed a month later, on another mission just after the young pilot had celebrated his nineteenth birthday.

On June 14th, three days before Stilwell's troops completely recaptured the airfield at Myitkyina, Mac McCarten was reassigned to 10th Air Force Headquarters as Operations Officer and Maj. Bob Erdin assumed command.

Under Lt. Colonel McCarten, the 490th had flown a total of 226 missions and scored more success than any other medium bomb squadron in the CBI. At the time of his departure, McCarten was one of the theater's ranking pilots—having 89 missions and 429 combat hours on his ticket.

At the Kurmitola base four days earlier, the 490th gave a farewell dinner for McCarten. His tenure as CO was recounted by a number of fellow officers and at the end of the speeches he was presented with a wristwatch by all the men of the squadron. The watch was a gift he was to wear his entire life, until his death in the early 80s. He'd been a fine commander, greatly respected by those who'd served under him, and when he stood to speak, a hush fell over the men. Aside from a few muffled coughs, the room was silent.

"One of the highlights of my life," Lt. Colonel McCarten said with simple sincerity. "Will always be the fact that I was once Commanding Officer of the 490th."

12

Between late May and the end of June, during the Japanese offensive thrust into India, the Bridge Busters under Bob Erdin, who'd been promoted to Lt. Colonel, had been carrying supplies and ammunition from Chittagong to Allied units at Imphal. During the 1944 Allied summer offensive against the Japanese in Burma, they assisted the ground troops by providing low-level air support, bombing and strafing enemy troop concentrations, and in particular, blowing apart the bridges which led into Myitkyina.

No crews were lost during July, but at Kurmitola and Myitkyina Airfield, two planes were forced to crash land—one due to hydraulic failure and the other to engine trouble.

Going into August, the squadron nailed ten bridges that were located along the strategic railway connecting Myitkyina and Nabajet—all these missions were led by Capt. Walter Allen and Lt. Gari King.

On the 11th of August, during a strike against a Japanese camp area and underground stores at Kadu, weather forced three out of nine Mitchells back to base still carrying their bombs.

Of the remaining six planes that reached the heavily wooded target, one was lost enroute. 1st. Lt. Howard Erickson and his crew were last seen losing altitude on the way to Kadu. It was later learned that engine trouble forced the aircraft down and that the crew was forced to bail out over Burma, but very near the border with India. Although the entire crew exited the stricken ship, only Lieutenant Erickson, Lt. Bob Lundin, and Sgt. Jim Clayton survived. Clayton returned to Kurmitola after an odyssey of two weeks in the jungle. The two other crewmembers, Sergeants Lou Corradine and John Pomphrey were listed as MIA and never found.

While Sergeant Clayton was fighting to get back to his outfit, the 490th was once again ordered to move. On August 18th, an advanced echelon was flown to Dergaon in the Bhramaputra Valley to establish a new station. A week later, crammed into C-47s, most of the squadron was brought into Dergaon while those few remaining at Kurmitola were taken out by rail.

When the 490th got to Dergaon, a Chinese-American B-25 composite squadron was already there as they arrived. These composite squadrons usually had one American pilot and one American flight engineer to every three aircraft. At Dergaon, these pilots and engineers had become heavy drinkers—claiming it was the only way they could fly with the Chinese aircrews.

"When this bunch moved out," Doug Knokey remembers. "They loaded the B-25s heavy in the tail, and when they took off, more than a few bounced their fuselage on the ground. But they all managed to get in the air and headed for China. I don't know whatever happened to that outfit. We never ran across them again."

At Dergaon, Capt. Sig Krostue, the 490th's adjutant, was sent back to Dacca on a noncombat mission. He was flying with Capt. Andy Squire and acting as copilot and engineer—two jobs that Sig knew little about. Andy Squire, an ex-race driver, was widely regarded as a hot pilot and carried more than his share of self-confidence.

In Dacca, they got to drinking stateside liquor and stayed too long. It was already dark on their way back to base and they managed to get caught in a sudden storm. As Squire and Krostue approached the strip at Dergaon, the squadron's CO, Bob Erdin, was waiting for them with his jeep lights on.

Squire made his approach and at the last minute was forced to go around again because of Indian cattle grazing on the field. Lt. Colonel Erdin chased the cows off and Squire finally brought his ship in safely.

"We got our butts chewed out," Sig Krostue remembers. "Both because we overstayed our leave in Dacca, and then I took extra heat because the emergency landing lights weren't working. Most of their engine generators had been stripped for use in home-made motor scooters."

It was also about this time that the Bridge Busters acquired a mascot of sorts. Flying a new B-25 across the ocean from Morrison Field, Capt. Gerry Hannaford had managed to smuggle a small dog in an ammunition box on the aircraft. The nondescript little pooch was called "Bombsight" and stayed with the squadron most of the time that Hannaford was overseas. Sig remembers that somebody actually built a small parachute and Bombsight was strapped into it whenever he went along on a mission with Hannaford.

On missions out of Dergaon, the Mitchells flew SSW towards the Dimapur-Kohima-Imphal area, climbing as fast as possible. The land was flat here and gave them a chance to gain altitude before turning ESE into Burma.

Normally, their missions consisted of twelve aircraft. If it was to be a low level operation, the planes would take off two at time, spaced at fifteen minute intervals. This would put six separate flights over the target and keep it under sustained attack for an hour and a half. If the first flights succeeded in destroying the primary target, the rest of them would go on to hit a wide variety of secondary targets.

If the raid was to be at medium altitude, all twelve gulls went out together, in tight formation.

During monsoon, the Naga Hills were socked in up to fifteen thousand feet and the flights usually hit the soup before reaching ten thousand. Flying blind, pilots sweated and hoped their navigators were on the ball and had picked a clear course between the hills. Once past them and into Burma, the weather cleared enough to drop down to seven thousand. Each airplane carried enough fuel to get from Dergaon to Mandalay, go east to the Salween River, up toward Myitkyina, or anywhere else in that wide area.

Sig Krostue remembers that flying in India, one of the crew's favorite sports after a successful mission was to spot sampans, come in low and buzz them, watching the prop wash knock over the little boats. It infuriated the ordinarily friendly natives who would try to throw their paddles into the Mitchell's props, but it relieved tension for the crews.

And there was usually tension in spades. Not every 1st Lieutenant was a hot pilot and some crews were much better than others:

Engineer/gunner Tom Murray remembers a flight he made on September 3rd. "The last mission I flew was a real lulu. It was my forty-eighth combat mission, including the ones I flew in the 491st and with the Air Commandos.

"I volunteered for the mission, trying to get my time in. The rest of the crew were all combat greenhorns. The pilot did everything ass backwards from what we were told at the briefing.

"We were after the railroad bridge at Tajamal—just two B-25s alone. We were told to make only two passes at the bridge, but my pilot—I can't remember his name—made about ten, and we really caught hell. To this day, I don't know how we made it back. I think they counted over fifty holes in the fuselage, cables all shot up—we had two one thousand-pound bombs stuck in the bomb bay and we had to get them out by hand. The hydraulics were completely shot out and we had to use all emergency systems.

"The radioman said that he didn't know how to wind the flaps down so I did it. I was the engineer aboard that plane. To top it all off, on the bomb runs the nose guns wouldn't fire—we found out afterward that they hadn't been charged by the ground crew.

"I guess I went kinda nuts when we finally got down, screaming and cussing at the pilot. I went to the commander and raised hell with him, too. He wanted to court martial me, but Flight Surgeon Wadsworth stepped in and said that I was combat weary, and due to be rotated home.

"Of all the missions I flew, that one was the worst."

By mid-August, Taungi had fallen to the Allies, and the Japanese advance was halted, but across the border, Chinese air bases were still falling like dominos to the Japanese.

On the 15th of September, two hundred miles of the newly built Ledo Road was opened to allied convoys traveling between Ledo and Warazup in Burma. The following month saw General Stilwell resume his offensive on Bhamo, only to be recalled to Washington because of worsening personal relations between he and Nationalist Chinese leader, Chiang Kai-shek.

Before the month was out, Stilwell had been replaced by Gen. Daniel I. Sultan, who was made Commanding Officer of the India-Burma Theater, while Gen. Albert C. Wedemeyer was appointed Chiang Kai-shek's Chief of Staff and Commander of American Forces in China.

Bhamo would crumble to allied pressure on December 12th, 1944, and S/Sgt. Ed Laytha, *CBI Roundup* Staff Correspondent, was there to provide an eyewitness report in grim detail:

"*General Sultan's Headquarters, Myitkyina*—It's all over now. The flags of the Chinese wave over the cadaver which once was the lovely town of Bhamo. Its sudden fall, after 28 days of siege, was the collapse of a typical Japanese suicide garrison. To the Nipponese it was a human tragedy, sad and humiliating. To us it was an anti-climax, for we planned the final showdown for last Sunday.

"Friday afternoon, however, the Jap garrison was no more. A squad of Chinese engineers with mine detectors led the party (correspondents) through the rubble from one end of town to the other. Two enemy machine guns were still active. Here and there snipers were rounded up and shot. Once in awhile a hand grenade exploded in a dugout—that was *hara kiri*.

"Bhamo resembled a blitzed cemetery. No building remained intact. This picturesque town of golden roofed pagodas and spacious monasteries suffered a much harder fate than Myitkyina.

"Gilded Buddhas of clay and Buddhas of marble were blown into a thousand pieces from their pedestals and littered the ground. Only the massive jewel-studded idols of bronze and brass withstood the carnage, sitting motionless on their golden thrones in the open air, with the stench of rotting Japs all about them.

"The smell of death came from the dugouts which were deep, solid, and elaborate, for the enemy had been digging in for weeks before the siege. The Jap at Bhamo knew that his chances for escape were extremely remote. He knew that he was being sacrificed in order to delay the Chinese 38th Division and that he was building his last shelter on earth…

"…many an enemy's chest was blown wide open by his own grenade and his arms lay far away. These were the stragglers who couldn't escape and paid the consequences.

"The jubilant Chinese were clearing the debris, counting the bounty. The smallest Jap item gave them pleasure. At a road crossing we passed, they had proudly piled up dozens of rifles, helmets, machine guns, small howitzers, a couple of Samurai swords, and stores of ammunition…

"…such was the end of the once-strong garrison. How many Japs lived there during the siege, nobody will ever know. They burned and buried their dead the first opportunity after action. Those couple of hundred who succeeded in breaking out have been surrounded and annihilated by the Chinese. A couple of dozen who finally escaped will roam the forests in search of their countrymen. They will be a nuisance to our patrols and a menace to the natives."

In late October, on one of the 490th's frequent missions against the bridges north of Lashio, an observer and recording team was sent along—their bulky equipment shoehorned into the nose of mission leader Andy Squire's aircraft.

In connection with the Blue Network, and a weekly series called "Yanks in the Orient," a recording of the entire mission was to be made and narrated by Lt. Bert Parks, who later gained fame as the long-running host of the popular Miss America Pageant. The recording was scheduled for replay in the United States on Christmas Eve, 1945.

The destruction of the Lashio bridges, Parks told the audience, was to be a Christmas present from the 490th Bomb Squadron to all the folks back home.

But by the end of the mission and the close of the recording, American listeners would learn that this particular mission against the Lashio bridges had cost one Mitchell bomber and its crew of five. In closing, Lieutenant Parks offered: "The price of Christmas presents is a little high this year."

Late that month, the 490th would move again. This time, they'd be staging from Moran, in Assam Province, edging ever closer to Burma itself.

Back in the states, Otsie had been sent to the Combat Crew Center at Hunter Field, in Savannah, Georgia. Here, he and the five others that made up his crew awaited operations orders and the delivery of the new airplane they'd ferry overseas.

Waiting was hard and the days passed slowly with little to do but wait. Ots was edgy. His wife was ill back home, and he faced a future he knew nothing about. But he'd come this far. He'd trained to do a job, and even though hesitant about admitting it even to himself, he could feel a certain anticipation of adventure ahead.

Hunter Field, Combat Crew Center
Savannah, Georgia
September 18th, 1944

Dear Sis—

Having a lot of time to myself now, I decided to start a new policy and that is to answer my mail more promptly than before. Although there isn't anything to write about as we aren't doing anything. I must go through with my plan, as you know letters do not come if one does not write.

It's been raining for almost five straight days and I just love it. Just right for the sack. I'm afraid I'll have to get me a bottle of alcohol soon and start using it, otherwise I'll get bed sores.

No kidding, this is the life. There isn't a day that I got up before 9:00 since I've been here. But you know as well as I that this is the lull before the storm.

We are obviously waiting for a CBI shipment as all the boys we came here with have gone out Saturday night. We saw our pilot and he said we can plan to be here till the fifth of next month. But try to get a furlough and they'll beat your head in.

I haven't seen the town of Savannah yet, outside of the ride we had through it on our way from the railroad station. I don't like these Rebel towns at all and have no desire to go in. When we want a little diversion we go right out the gate, have a chicken dinner and a couple of beers and have enough. No travel worries or financial worries.

I understand that everything in town is double the price we pay at the (unreadable). Then too, they have a midnight curfew throughout the south, so as soon as a guy gets into town he's got to worry about coming back.

Thanks for the $2.00 you sent. Seeing as how it was a birthday present, I won't moan about it, but don't ever do it otherwise. To tell you the truth, I spent my last fifteen cents yesterday, so you can imagine how much this gift is appreciated.

You see, I haven't been paid last month. I missed payday on account of being on furlough, and then I missed the supplementary payroll due to shipping out. God only knows when I'll get paid again. However, between you and me and one more person I've negotiated a $15 loan. I should get it through the mail tomorrow or the next day.

You see, I've got to stock up with soap, blades, and a few miscellaneous things before going over, 'cause these things are impossible to get out there. Our pilot tipped us off. He should know 'cause he's been there before. Well

Mil, I think I've written more than I thought I could. It probably isn't too interesting but it makes conversation.

Write when you have time. Hello to Jimmer and the Vesely's, and to Mom, of course. Till we meet again.

Love,
Otsie

Back in the old neighborhood, his sister Mildred had put together a package of everything she could find that might be useful to her brother—wherever he was going. Razor blades, bars of soap, toothpaste, gum, cigarettes, and a little cash. All the men in Millie's life were away now, her husband Joe, her brother Otsie, and her brother-in-law Milt. She followed the war news as best she could, and based on her brother's letters, began to learn all she could about what was happening in the far-distant, little-publicized war in Burma—a country she barely knew existed.

Mildred and her sister were typical of the young wives in the neighborhood—both trying to earn a living and raising their children alone, working at whatever jobs they could find while the Grandparents babysat. Their daily excitement was the mail, and hopefully a letter from their men. It was much the same in every city and small town in America.

Hunter Field, Combat Crew Center
Savannah, Georgia
September 28th, 1944

Dear Sis:

Your letter came two days ago and the package came yesterday. Thanks a lot, everything was practical and I'm sure will come to a good use. Should I go to the South Pacific maybe I'll be able to trade a bar of soap for a great big nigger woman—to do my laundry, of course. I'm only kidding, The boys did make a few suggestions, but you know how boys are. We are still sitting around doing nothing at all and believe me I'm getting pretty tired of it. I'd just as soon go off to war than have this war of nerves. We had a chance to go to Alaska this morning for coastal patrol, but our pilot turned it down as he has his heart definitely set on going to China-Burma-India. This would have been a good deal but then too, it would mean doing nothing again. If he keeps fooling around like this, there's no telling what will happen to us.

Halfway through this letter and already I'm stuck. No, there's nothing that I'm holding back. These letters are not censored and I'm free to write what I please, but the fact that I'm doing nothing makes it hard to find things to write about.

You asked me what I think of Mom working. Well, I don't like it so much, but due to her short hours and the place she works at, it isn't so bad. But you know Mom, I think she'd die if she didn't have anything to do.

Well, I hope Pep gets a good deal out of his new assignment. Perhaps he'll like it a bit better now. Satisfaction is the most important thing, I guess.

I guess this is about all for now. Write again when you have time. Maybe I'll have more interesting things to write about in my next letter. Between you and I, I hope so. You see, I'm an eager beaver. Hello to Pep and the Vesely's, and thanks.

Love, Otsie

On the 17th, their airplane arrived—#111, a brand new B-25J, still unpainted. The crew walked around it, looking the new ship over. It was the full-bore strafer model—the first the squadron was to receive. In addition to its blister packs, #111 had eight fixed .50 caliber guns bristling from its solid nose. None of them knew it at the time, but this was to be the final production version of the Mitchell, now being built exclusively at North American's Kansas City plant.

After having been given many modifications, the J Model had now returned to its primary function as a medium bomber. This model sported the tail gun position with the deeper rear fuselage, bay-window model waist guns, and the forward-mounted dorsal turret that had been first introduced on the H. The blister gun packs on the sides of the forward fuselage had also been retained, and the copilot position was restored.

The bomb racks and bomb bay doors were now all electrically operated, and Ots made a mental note of the 50,000 BTU surface combustion heater now provided at the waist gun station.

Hunter Field, Combat Crew Center
Savannah, Georgia
October 13th, 1944

Dear Sis,

Got your letter this morning and thanks very much for the $2.00. You've no idea how handy it came in at the present time. However, please don't do it anymore 'cause I realize how things are and besides, I'm sure Milt could use it first as much as I can, and then too, you could get something extra for Tommy. Understand?

Well, as far as my going back to Greenville was concerned, it turned out just as I thought. Purely rumor.

We were called out yesterday for another shakedown and we were to leave today, but again something is snafu'd and we are still here. Perhaps tomorrow will tell the tale.

We've got our airplane and are all packed up. We will be headed for India, traveling by way of South America. If I know my pilot well enough, I think we'll have another vacation in South America. By the way, we will be paid $7 per day while traveling, with an expense account of a large amount. It won't be so bad.

I'm sorry to hear that Milt was hurt, but the rest will do him good and I'm sure he doesn't mind being in the hospital for awhile. There were many times when I tried to figure out a way to get in myself.

Georgia is turning cool now and it's time to pull out if we want to miss winter this year. I understand it gets cold here at times.

Well, we're here five weeks now, and it's been a vacation with nothing to do. Sleep as late as we want to, no formations, roll calls, PT, or anything. The whole day is entirely our own. I've seen every picture that came to this field for that's about all there is to do.

We go outside the gate once in awhile for fried chicken and beer, and that consists of our nightlife. I guess the rest is well deserved, for we certainly flew our pants off at Greenville.

Well, I've got other letters to write so I'll close. Keep writing to Georgia until you get my APO. Thanks again for the $2.00. My engineer and gunner thank you too, for we've been sharing all we've got for the last few weeks.

Love,
Otsie

Hello to Mom, Tommy, and Milt.

Hunter Field, Combat Crew Center
Savannah, Georgia
October 13th, 1944

Dear Sis:

Your letter came yesterday and as usual was very interesting and long. Just the way I like them.

Nothing much has happened lately. We've been taken off the New Guinea shipment and have been put on a CBI shipment. We all thought we'd go to China, but lately the 14th Air Force in China have been losing their bases, so evidently we'll go to India.

We were to leave today, but as usual things have been snafu'd lately, and we are still sticking around, wearing the seats out of our pants. When we do go, we will hit the POE at West Palm Beach, Florida where we will have our plane modified and from there we will go to South America.

The captain figures on taking his sweet time going over so I imagine we'll get to see a lot of South America.

While traveling, we will be allowed $7.00 per day for expenses and we also will get a lump sum for same. You can see it's a pretty good deal considering most everybody else goes across by boat.

Sorry to hear Pep has shipped, but it really isn't so bad. Don't you think the both of us did a pretty good job staying here as long as we did? I'm sure everything will turn out OK.

Tell Jimmer thanks for the buck, from all of us, but please don't do it again. Don't get me wrong, it's appreciated, but if I knew you had more than you could use it would be different. Understand me?

I'll see if I can pick up some nice souvenirs during my travels, and in that way I'll try to repay you for what you've done—because I want to.

Georgia nights are becoming very cool lately, and I can imagine what the weather at home is like. Truthfully, I'd rather have the good ol' Chi weather.

I guess you know that I spoke to Zoe on the phone the other day. It sure was swell, but I certainly hope she can come home for good one of these days. I feel so sorry for her being cooped up the way she is.

Well, time to go, so I'll close again. You can write to this same address unless you get my APO in the meantime. Thanks again for everything and I'll see you soon.

Love, Otsie

Their operational orders were finally cut.

Otsie's original crew was made up of pilot Paul Taylor, from Providence, Rhode Island, copilot Ken Schaible and navigator Orville Christensen, both from Chicago. In addition to Ots, the two other enlisted men included engineer/gunner Bob Hyde, who hailed from Tarbere, North Carolina, and tailgunner Harold Peppard from Fort Worth, Texas. They took charge of their new B25J in Savannah, flight checked all the controls, calibrated the instruments, compasses, and drift meter, and installed the bombsight. With its eager crew, the new Mitchell took them south to Morrison Field in West Palm Beach, Florida.

West Palm was their Port of Embarkation for overseas. It involved two days of overseas briefing, receiving flight orders, maps, radio codes and identification, and a supply of K-rations. Then they were off at last, climbing into the clear, blue skies over the Straits of Florida on October 21st, 1944, with Andros Island off their starboard wing and tiny Nassau off to port. Their destination was to remain sealed until they were flying a hundred miles out to sea, but the crew already suspected it was to be India, and probably the CBI.

Again, sealed orders for their final base of operations would be issued in Karachi, and not before.

Before leaving the States two months earlier, navigator Don Harkins had gotten a different tip off on where he might be headed. "They took away all my heavy winter flying suits and an old top kick said he hoped I could speak Chinese."

If Otsie thought he'd seen a lot of new country since being drafted, he was about to see more of the world than he'd ever thought likely.

Out of West Palm, their first stop for refueling was at Borinquen Field, the military airbase in Puerto Rico. Approaching the large island, the crew marveled at the rugged mountains and lush, tropical landscape—all surrounded by a lovely blue sea.

Flying south again from San Juan, they had a short stop in Trinidad, and then almost an eight hour haul down to Atkinson Field near Georgetown, the ramshackle little capitol of British Guiana, just below the mouth of the Demerara River, on the northeast coast of South America.

A long, long way from 32nd and Hamlin Ave. Ots relaxing on the beach at Accra, Gold Coast, in late October 1944 on the way overseas.

After refueling and a brief rest, they continued southeast for almost five and a half hours to Belém, flying above the rugged jungle vastness of northern Brazil. Once the Mitchell touched down in this chief port city on the lower Amazon, they were already a good distance south of the Equator.

From Belém, it was five hours down along the East Coast of Brazil to Natal at the mouth of the Potengi River. There, they'd gas up again, rest awhile, and then head out due east across the South Atlantic, flying over open ocean for seven hours until they touched down again at tiny Ascension Island.

This was the strategic refueling base for U.S. aircraft, midway between South America and the sprawling sub-continent of Africa.

With no bombs or supplies aboard and carrying only crew and fuel, the Mitchells had an approximate ferry range of 1,500 miles, cruising lean. Another seven hour push across open ocean brought them to Africa's old Gold Coast, where the airmen had a few days to relax on the white sand beaches of Accra, along the Cape Coast of the Gulf of Guinea.

After some time on the beach at Accra, they took off again, on a heading along the coast to Lagos, Nigeria and then northeast to refuel at Kano. From there, they put down at Wadi Sedna, in the Sudan, at Aden, Yemen, and over to Masira Island off the coast of Oman, in the Arabian Sea.

From Masira it was more than three hours over water again, crossing the wide expanse of the Arabian Sea and finally into the old seaport and trading center of Karachi, India. In Karachi, they had their longest rest, waiting once again for sealed orders.

Once a tiny settlement of poor fisherman, Karachi sat on the finest natural harbor of the entire southern Indian coastline. Here, Corporal Malovich and the rest of the crew stared at men in long white robes and turbans, almond-eyed women whose dark brown faces lay hidden beneath veils.

This India had mountains up to twenty five thousand feet high, they were told, with lakes washed pink by the massed bodies of flamingos. It was a land over a million and a half square miles in size, with a population of 400 million souls speaking twenty major languages. One out of every five people in the world, they learned, was East Indian.

To Ots, thinking of his wife and family back home, it seemed as far away as anyone could get from 26th Street and the life he'd always known.

But if there was the sweet smell of apricot trees in the countryside, Karachi's streets offered no such pastoral vision. Crowded and dirty, knotted with people all going somewhere, the streets were jammed with trucks and jeeps, water buffalo, donkeys, camels and goats.

A few days later, when their final base orders arrived, the crew learned they were being sent to the 490th Bomb Squadron, currently operating out of Moran, India, in far eastern Assam Province. Now they flew over the width of India, with brief touchdowns at Agra, Dinajpur, and Tezpur—before entering the great wide Valley of the Brahmaputra River and finally dropping down on final approach to the steel-mesh runway of the small base at Moran.

It seems their destination had been a secret to everyone but pilot Paul Taylor. To this day Taylor is a bit of a mystery. For reasons known only to him, he wanted to return to CBI for a second combat tour. He must have had some considerable clout, because Chicagoan Lt. Ken Schaible was originally scheduled to fly them across, but Schaible was bumped into the copilot's seat in favor of Taylor. And yet, Ken Schaible remembers, just two days after landing at Moran, India, 1st Lt. Paul Taylor was ordered to report to the CO and quickly disappeared from the squadron. Ken still doesn't know what happened to him.

Other information on Taylor is contradictory. Howard Bell seems to remember him well. Howard recalls that Taylor returned for a second tour in CBI because his girlfriend in the States had married someone else. According to Howard, Taylor was made a copilot the second time around, just to learn how things were being done. Bell says that Paul Taylor went on to become a pilot, flew his minimum amount of missions and then rotated home again.

Although Don Harkins didn't remember Taylor by name, he did recall a pilot that came back for a second tour about that same time. Don says that they wanted him to fly copilot for five missions as was customary. The man didn't want to do it and talked them out of it. He went down on the first mission of his second tour.

Along with his buddies, Bob Hyde and Harold Peppeard, Ots was living in a British desert tent, with either three or four men to a tent. The Brits had already dug five foot-deep slit trenches between each tent, so that job of work was already done. The base was pretty much surrounded by rice paddies and large tea plantations. At Moran, the Bridge Busters shared the airfield with the 58th Fighter Squadron, a P-47 outfit known as the "Red Gorillas." When the 490th had left Dergaon for Moran, Don Harkins remembers landing at the new field and spotting a familiar name painted on the fuselage of one of the Thunderbolts. It turned out to be a boyhood friend who he hadn't seen in years, and they enjoyed a fine reunion.

In addition to the rice paddies and tea farms, the men soon learned that the entire area was surrounded by deadly hooded cobras, but with the progress of the war, there were rumors that Moran was to be only a short-term deal, before they packed their bags and moved again.

Next time, the rumors said, they'd be staging out of Burma.

But Otsie would begin his first combat missions from Moran. He was finally in the war, and about to put everything he'd learned to use. They had little in the way of recreation facilities, and most of his free time was spent writing letters home. It would be the first that his wife and sisters had heard from him since he'd left Savannah a month earlier.

Part Three—
Assam Province

13

Staging out of Moran, November 8th proved a memorable date in the squadron's history. It marked the destruction of the 100th enemy-held bridge since the Bridge Busters were activated.

A day before—the same day that #111 landed at Moran, the first strafer model of its type in CBI, Franklin Delano Roosevelt had been re-elected to an unprecedented fourth term. But it made little difference to the men of the squadron. The luxury of caring about American politics was far-removed from the daily realities of war in India and Burma.

The milestone target of November 8th was the Bawgyo Bridge, a target previously attacked by the squadron, but never seriously damaged. This time they got it right, and it brought a lot of recognition in the press of the CBI Theater:

"EAC HQ—Eastern Air Command aircraft last week kept up their unrelenting attacks against Japanese rail, road, and river routes throughout Burma, at the same time furnishing close air support to Allied ground forces as they advanced on the North Burma and Tiddim-Chindwin fronts.

One of the week's outstanding accomplishments was the destruction of the Bawgyo Rail Bridge by 10th AF B-25s of the 490th Bomb Squadron. This bridge was one of the keys to the Mandalay-Lashio Railroad, and marked a hundred bridges knocked out by the squadron since they began operations over Burma…"

Along with the cobras, it didn't take long for the new men in the squadron to learn about the treacherous Naga Hills they'd soon be flying over, and of the strange and primitive people who lived in them. To the veterans, it was a never-ending source of amusement to watch the "greenhorns" as they listened to stories about the headhunters of Assam Province.

Otsie and his tentmates were no exception. They were soon hearing tales about the *Nagas*—the savage tribes that lived and hunted the rugged hill country in the eastern portion of the Brahmaputra Valley in Upper Assam and Manipur.

The Nagas, they were told, still relished fierce, murderous feuds among themselves, as well as with the Japanese who occasionally blundered into their territories, and headhunting was the Nagas' specialty.

Ots had known tough guys at Farragut and along 26th Street—guys who'd just as soon fight you as look at you. But Jesus, cutting off heads was taking things to a whole new level. He briefly wondered what Zoe and his sisters would think about such matters.

The largest of the Naga tribes were the *Angami*, who considered their culture far superior to that of their neighbors. Aside from the family, the basic unit of Angami society was the Khel, and each of these groups of brothers by blood was constantly at war with the rest of the world. Other groups of Nagas included the *Aos*, and the *Semas*, each of who were as savage as the others. They were totally ignorant of the use of money, and the bloody custom of headhunting was popular among them all.

Among the Naga tribes, the Semas were especially notorious for cruelty combined with treachery. Their trick was to feed and entertain a guest, and then to slay him when he was drunk or off his guard.

But all the Naga tribes were headhunters, and they used every treachery in securing their trophies. Every head counted, whether it was a man, a woman or a child, and the heads entitled the man who took them to wear special ornaments.

Every tribe, almost every village, was at war with both its neighbors and with outsiders. No Naga dared to leave the vicinity of his village without knowing that his life was hanging by a single thread.

The strange scars and tattoo marks that every successful headhunter was permitted to wear, differed in pattern with each tribe, and afforded a quick means of recognizing strangers.

Warriors of distinction wore the hair of slain enemies hanging from their heads and forming a fringe around the face. The eastern Naga warrior also wore a special collar on taking his first head.

"But if you go down out there," an increasingly nervous Ots was finally told. "Those little brown buggers can sometimes save your ass. Uncle Sam pays 'em for every American or British soldier they bring out alive. The Japs haven't figured that angle out yet, and a lot of the Nagas' cut heads are buck-toothed and squinty-eyed."

Until the outbreak of the war, the world knew little of the primitive tribes in the Naga Hills of Northeastern India, but American and British soldiers—the airmen in particular—came to know them well.

The Nagas became valuable as guides for military operations, and later on were even more valuable in air rescue work. Many a downed flyer would owe his life to the survival skills of a Naga headhunter.

Otsie began combat flying on November 11th, 1944.

Ten gulls took off that morning, the mission being led by 1st Lt. Ed Tengler. The three flight leaders were men Otsie would come to know and admire from a distance: 1st Lieutenants Don Karschner, Dick Johnson, and Rollin White.

The flight plan was one that was to become familiar. From Moran, they flew ENE, going just south of Ledo, then banked south toward Burma at Pangsau Pass. The pass was forty-five hundred feet high and the flights could usually clear it with no weather problems.

Turning south again, they flew down the Hukawng Valley and on to the target areas. The usual altitude was seven thousand feet until twenty or thirty miles out from the target area, when they'd drop down to fifteen hundred or two thousand feet on their initial approach.

Otsie's first raid was one of the toughest targets the 490th flew against—Lashio—the strategic railhead at the end of the Burma Road.

This day they weren't after bridges, but rather the Japanese airdrome north of town. Otsie was more excited and curious than scared. Like most of the new men, his level of fear would ratchet upward with each mission flown. At the start, they were ignorant of what awaited them around the targets in Burma. But as each mission passed and they witnessed friends killed or lost, the fear grew stronger, knotted in their stomachs like some slow growing, malignant thing.

They didn't go in low on this strike, bombing instead from between eight and nine thousand feet. Ots was on the radio, but as a waist gunner he had little else to do at these altitudes but watch for enemy fighters.

The three flights unloaded almost a hundred and sixty hundred pound bombs and over two thousand small incendiaries. Otsie stared down as they banked away from the target. Smoke and fire covered the entire area and would still be visible when they were sixty miles away and headed home. A plume of greasy black smoke rose almost seven thousand feet in the air over Lashio.

Nobody was hit. All went smoothly except for two dozen hundred-pounders that malfunctioned. Half of these were salvoed a little way south of the target, and the others five miles west of Namp Khi Bridge.

Ots took a deep breath and relaxed on his fold-down bench, feeling the soothing vibration of the Mitchell. He'd been in the war. He hadn't fired at anybody, but he'd done his job and they were on their way home.

His first combat mission was behind him.

That night, all those replacements who were new to the game and who'd flown against Lashio that day were in a mood to celebrate—almost like a high school football team after an easy win. The beer and Carew's gin flowed.

"What's it like?" A few of the new guys who hadn't flown yet asked, self-consciously, almost in a whisper, yet hoping to sound casual.

"Not too bad," those who'd gone up for the first time that morning told them. "Long haul out, drop the eggs, long haul back."

But that night Ots didn't sleep well. The day's mission had been almost a cakewalk, and deep in his gut, he suspected that every day wasn't going to be as easy. Most of the others suspected it, too.

"We're on the deck," somebody mumbled just before briefing the next morning. "All low level shit today." Ots was scheduled to fly again, and this time they had orders for a sweep along the Irrawaddy River from Singu to Katha. And then, along the rail lines in northern Burma—bombing and strafing locomotives, shelters and rolling stock as far south as along the railroad line from Tantabin north to the Meza bridge.

This morning, the weather officer reported only patches of low hanging fog and mist in the valleys of the Naga Hills. But they'd be flying high over that. Weather at all targets was reported as clear. Their mission leader was veteran pilot 1st Lt. Charley Powell, and flight leaders were Lieutenants Bob Cole, Elden Cross, Bob Knowlton, and Andy Squire—the former race car driver from Albans, Long Island—in New York City.

All attacks would be at three hundred feet.

Again, the mission went well. As they'd been briefed, it was all low level work and this time Ots was busy on his guns, putting to practice everything they'd taught him in gunnery school at Fort Myers. *Hell*, he thought as his .50s pounded away at trains, buildings, and parked trucks, *this is kind of fun. We're like bulls in a china shop with a green light to bust up everything we can.*

They came in low north of the railroad yards and tore apart a number of locomotive revetments, of which only half of one was left standing. Their .50s, 75mm cannon, and five hundred pound bombs then smashed a locomotive that was hidden in its shelter.

Rolling stock on a siding was strafed with cannon and .50s, and a length of track leading into a revetment was torn apart. More rolling stock north of Zigon was bombed and a few of the freight cars were blown off their tracks. A few small buildings that adjoined the tracks were demolished.

Hits on tracks at Zawchaung tore gaps in rail lines and cars at the station were strafed and hit.

Between the gunners, almost ten thousand rounds of .50 caliber were expended, along with over thirty 75mm cannon rounds, and sixty-eight five hundred pound bombs.

This time, the Japanese shot back. At Kanbalu, the flights encountered some ineffective machine gun fire, but they took accurate anti-aircraft fire from a position south of Wuntho. One plane was hit twice, receiving minor damage but no casualties.

The low attack altitudes the Bridge Busters were flying gave the Japanese gunners a few problems. Aside from the raw terror of watching these gunships bear down on them at three hundred miles per hour, and right on the deck, it wasn't that easy to hit a target moving so fast and so low. The ground defense gunners were usually hidden, their field of fire often blocked by leaves and branches as the fearsome Mitchells howled down upon them. Many of the Japanese just judged the direction of attack, aimed their barrels straight up in the air and held the triggers down. More than one Skull and Wings pilot likened it to trying to run through the spray of a hose without getting wet. It wasn't an easy thing to do.

But once more, the crews were returning happy. Nobody hurt, mission judged a success, and the next day was a day off. Otsie felt great—a small part of the damage done today had been done by him. On the way back this time, at the pilot's suggestion, Ots let the outside antenna trail out behind the aircraft and the long-range radio picked up some American pop music from a radio station at Imphal. The station was playing "Moonlight in Vermont" and he piped it in to the rest of the crew over the intercom. Interspersed with static and announcements in a weird mix of Hindi and English, the next two selections were "Sentimental Journey" and "You're Nobody Till Somebody Loves You."

Ain't that the damned truth, Otsie thought, thinking of Zoe back home in Chicago—almost as far away as the moon.

But many times, nothing went right. Don Harkins remembers well a number of his missions out of Assam.

On one of them, flying navigator with pilot Capt. Walter Allen to the rugged mountains just east of Mandalay, their targets were train tunnels that had been bored through the sides of the mountains. Operations had given them an interesting task—to come in low and head on, skip a thousand-pound bomb directly into the tunnel and then pull up at the last minute to avoid flying into the side of the mountain itself.

"Well, we managed to pull it off," Don recalls. "Through Walter Allen's flying skill. From the tunnels, we then went on flying low over the old Burma Road looking for secondary targets—enemy trucks, trains, boat, whatever.

"But we got too close to the Gokteik Bridge which had been closed to us as a target. The British-built Namtu and Baldwin ruby mines were right there, and the Brits wanted them back in good shape after the war. The Japs wanted them working, too. They were pulling out rubies for future trade, so the whole area was heavily defended.

"We pulled away from Gokteik and managed to fly right over an unmarked Jap airfield where we got the stuffing shot out of us. There were two purple hearts out of that one, but nobody killed."

On an attack against Lashio, as Don's plane started its run on the target, another B-25 came in firing behind and below them. This pilot's navigator saw their mistake and was screaming for him to break off, but the pilot didn't understand. "After taking that terrible thing—friendly fire," Don remembers. "We broke off our bomb run and got out of there."

On a two-plane mission against the Hsipaw Train Bridge, they lost their wing man in heavy fog, then found the target to be completely socked in. The pilot asked if Don could get him in anyway, so they traveled a hundred miles south, got a break in the cloud cover, headed back flying on the deck and dropped four thousand-pounders on the bridge, blowing it apart. They got shot up again and came home. Don and his pilot were recommended for the Distinguished Flying Cross, but they never got it.

"They were pretty stingy with medals over there," he says.

On his last mission to Lashio, Don and pilot Capt. Don Karschner were sent in ahead of the rest of the flight. It would be their job to go in and reconnoiter, deciding if the others could go in at low level. Karschner and Harkins circled the target for the better part of an hour, taking ground fire all the time they were there. They finally decided that it would be a medium altitude mission and returned to join the rest of the flight on the bomb run.

After they'd bombed, Karschner—who Don describes as a good pilot, a great friend, but a little crazy—decided to go down low on the deck to check out the damage they'd done.

It was a bad decision, Don recalls. They got their airplane shot to pieces, but fortunately none of the crew was hit. "Karschner and I have laughed about that mission ever since," Don says. "But it wasn't funny then."

Otsie had only been at Moran for a few days, when a returning Mitchell taxied up to where Doug Knokey and two other armorers were waiting. As the plane came to a stop, its agitated pilot dropped down from the forward ladder and began yelling that his plane was carrying a live bomb that hadn't dropped.

"It's laying on the bomb bay doors," the keyed-up 2nd lieutenant insisted. "My release switch wouldn't work. We had to salvo the whole damn load, along with the bomb racks and everything else."

"That'd be a helluva trick, lieutenant," one of the armorers pointed out, as they tried to calm the excited young pilot. "You'd need to have taken out about five hundred bolts to have done that."

Knokey and the others decided that one of them would have to climb into the airplane, open the doors and let the bomb drop out. They drew straws to see who'd get stuck with the job.

Jim Osterhout, a corporal from Auburn, New York, drew short straw. While he crawled up into the fuselage and into the bombardier's position, the rest of them hunkered down in a ditch.

Osterhout took a deep breath and pushed the door release handle. As the doors flew open, out dropped an old, dried up peanut butter and jelly sandwich that one of the gunners had tried to slide over the top of the bomb bay sometime earlier.

"That don't look to be much of a bomb, sir," Osterhout called out.

The lieutenant, embarrassed but still shaken, just stood up, shrugged his shoulders and sheepishly made for his tent.

They soon began to hear rumors of the squadron's next move—this time across the mountains and into Burma—where the Japanese were taking a beating and pulling out of one base after another. The word was that the squadron would be going to a place called Warazup, with an airfield right alongside the newly built Ledo Road.

But until that time came, there were more missions to fly.

On the 14th of November, they hit Lashio again—this time from low level. Three supply areas were hit hard by twelve gulls led by Don Karschner—who'd flown as a flight leader on Otsie's first mission. This time, the other three flights were led by Lieutenants Harry Fisher, Bob Lundin, and George Hayden.

As far as pilots were concerned, Ots was partial to Ken Schaible because they'd flown together in training, and many of the combat missions he flew were with Ken at the stick. He hadn't been there long enough to learn the pros and cons of one pilot over another, but it often didn't make much difference. As an enlisted man, and a new one at that, Ots and his tentmates usually had little to say about whom they were going to fly with.

Navigator Don Harkins, on the other hand, had strong feelings about it: "Yes, I had favorite pilots like Ed Tengler, Dick Johnson, George Chapman, Walter Allen, and Maurice Graves. Then there were a couple of veteran pilots that I refused to fly with—and I'm glad I did, because they later killed their entire crews."

Again, the gulls lost altitude after passing over the Naga Hills, and came in low at Lashio. Again, Otsie was busy. First radioing Moran with their time on target, then working the waist guns, pouring out round after round of .50s as they skimmed the trees approaching the supply sheds. The tail-gunner was firing too, and the entire area from back of the bomb bay to the tail position carried the sweet, heavy smell of burnt cordite.

Each Mitchell that came in was a howling messenger of destruction. From its nose it spit either .50s or devastating 75 mm cannon rounds, and from fixed packages on either side of the pilot, a rotating dorsal turret, two waist positions, and the tail—a steady stream of .50s raked everything and everyone in its path. It was literally a "flying gun."

Over a hundred three hundred pound bombs were dropped on Lashio that day, plus more than fifteen hundred incendiaries. The raid blasted storage buildings and set some on fire. At the railroad station, more buildings were strafed and burning, along with damage to rolling stock.

Some anti aircraft fire came at them from four scattered gun positions around Lashio, and heading home they took some concentrated fire from just south of a little place called Hkai Hee, but once again everybody got home safe and in one piece. Only one aircraft received damage enough to keep the ground crews busy the next day.

It was Ots' third mission and even though this time things had gotten a little exciting up there, so far he hadn't felt in much more danger than if he'd been walking down 26th Street on a Saturday night. Maybe this whole show wasn't going to be as bad as he'd thought.

Some of the other rookies were beginning to feel the same way—they were getting a little cocky, like fighters who'd gone three rounds without having a glove laid on them.

And their luck was to hold for awhile.

The following day, the squadron went after the storage and personnel areas at Kawlin airfield, setting fires, tearing things up, and returning home untouched. Piece of cake. Break out the gin.

On the sixteenth, lousy weather kept everybody home. The weather was either their worst enemy or their best friend. Bad weather grounded everyone, and except for those really "gung-ho" few, most everybody else was glad to see the mission scrubbed. To the older hands, it meant that they were at least sure of one more day of living.

But there was always the next day, and this one was another "on the deck" job against Lashio—this time they were after the bridges there. Nine gulls left Moran, led by Bob Lundin. 1st Lt. Bob Cole led one flight, with Ed Kitta and Bob Knowlton leading the others.

The Lashio Bypass Bridge, still under construction, and the Lashio east Bypass Bridge were both destroyed, while the Lashio main and pontoon bridges were heavily damaged.

Over this target, they spotted two machine gun positions and the strafers put them out of business. The gulls took heavy fire from a total of six positions but came back none the worse for wear.

Ots flew again on the eighteenth. This time, nine B-25s went after the railroad station, locomotive shelters, rolling stock and warehouses in the Mongwe area.

With the mission being led by 1st Lt. Harry Fisher, and the flights led by Charley Powell, Rollin White, and Herb Schwarz, the bombers came in low, attacking Mongwe from three hundred feet over the trees. Many boxcars were destroyed or damaged, and blast shelters protecting rolling stock were blown to pieces. The Mitchells were tearing long lengths of track apart. As Ots fired the .50s out the waist gunner's window, his memory flashed back to the 32nd Street railroad tracks a half block from his house, where he and the other kids used to catch large chunks of chalk thrown out to them by the train crews.

At the warehouse area north of the yards one warehouse was completely destroyed and four others badly damaged. The main locomotive shelter in the center of the yards was destroyed. Several small fires were started north of the north storage area.

All through the attack, they took moderate antiaircraft fire and two of the Mitchells came back to Moran with minor damage.

Three days later, he was up again. This time, after the important Hsipaw Railroad Bridge and the Bawgye Road Bridge. Both were destroyed as the squadron hiked its bridge-busting total to a hundred and five. Six aircraft attacked Hsipaw Bridge. Four spans were destroyed, an approach severely damaged, and a lot of track was torn up. Four other Mitchells dropped thirty-two five hundred pound bombs at Bawgye, destroying the entire north half of the structure and damaging both approaches.

Ots and the other gunners poured rounds of .50s into five Japanese machine gun positions at both targets, silencing all of them, but not before two planes were slightly damaged and a fellow radioman, Sgt. Al Hurlbert, was hit. After returning to Moran, Hurlbert was taken to the hospital at Chabua for treatment of his wounds.

This had been Otsie's sixth mission, and that evening after chow was the first free time he had to sit down and catch up on his letter writing.

China-Burma-India Theater
Moran, India—Assam Province
November 21st, 1944

Dear Sis…

Thanks for your letter of the 23rd. Took a long time reaching me, and it sure was a welcome sight.

Well, I'll try and tell you all I can.

We left the states on the 21st. Flew our own plane over and had a pretty nice time doing so. We covered approximately 20,000 miles and stopped at places such as Puerto Rico, Trinidad, Brazil, Ascension Island, Africa, Arabia, and India.

I'm finally settled now, assigned to the hottest bomb squadron in the CBI Theater, namely the 490th. Naturally, I can't tell you exactly where we are, but I can go as far as saying that we're somewhere in Assam Province.

I made my sixth mission today. They are quite something which I won't even try to explain. I don't want Zoe to know that I'm actually a part of this war yet, for she'd only worry. So I tell her that I'm still in training. Keep that from her, will you? I'll get around to telling her when I add a few more to my list.

Well, I guess that's all for me right now. I don't like the idea of Mom working so hard, so do what you can to make her quit. I know it's too much for her.

I'm glad to hear that everything is okay at home. I still can't help worrying about Zoe, however. I sure hope she can come home soon. Well, I'm going to quit now, so tell everybody hello. I'll write as the letters come in.

Otsie

Part Four—Warazup

14

Operating out of Assam, on missions where the 75mm cannons of the H-model gunships wouldn't be used, Doug Knokey and a few of the other armorers had stumbled on to a practical use for their big 75s.

During the first two years of the war, beer had been almost non-existent in the remote East Indian bases. There was never any ice to be had. But late in 1944, the squadron began to be occasionally issued two or three cans per man.

Someone quickly realized that when the flights were returning from their missions into Burma, they had to fly at high altitudes over the Chin Hills to get back home. The waiting armorers found that after the planes had landed, condensation would cause water to pour off their ice-cold guns.

From that point on, when they knew the 75s wouldn't be used, the armorers would secretly slide cans of warm beer into the long barrels of the cannons. When the planes returned to base in the afternoon, they'd unload both unused ordnance and cans of ice cold beer.

"We didn't do it very often," Doug Knokey recalls. "And only for a short period of time, because ice later became available. But this was one of the best-kept secrets of the war, because if the aircrews had happened to open the breech of any one of those 75s, our beer was gone!"

More than fifty years later, at a squadron reunion in Colorado Springs, Doug told pilot Harry DePew about how those 75s were used.

DePew could only laugh and shake his head. "I was flying into Burma, risking my hide, just so you guys could cool your damned beer!"

The end of November 1944 saw the squadron move once again. Crews were busy stuffing many of their excited Indian wallahs and tent boys into B-25 bomb bays for the flight over the Naga Hills into Warazup—on the banks of the Mogaung River—their new base in Burma.

After hard fighting, the airstrip at Warazup had been recaptured from the Japanese eight months earlier. The squadron's first day there was hot and humid, and the enlisted men were put to work digging slit trenches.

A little Burmese boy wandered into camp reporting that while swimming in the river, he'd found hand grenades lying about. Later, a small, heavily-armed recon patrol was sent eight miles up one of the jungle trails and found live 105mm shells scattered all over the place.

"The Japs sure argued a little over this area," mechanic Ken Shugart recalled somebody saying.

So, they thought, this was Burma.

For three years, the flight crews had seen it from the air, yet at ground level it was an ancient, eerie land that surrounded them.

The country's history was the history of a people who migrated down along the Irrawaddy River from Tibet and China, and who were influenced by social and political institutions that had been carried across the sea from India. First came the *Mon,* perhaps as early as 3000 BC.

They established centers of settlement in central Burma, in the Irrawaddy delta, and farther down the eastern coast of the Bay of Bengal, constructing irrigation systems and developing commercial and cultural contacts with India, while maintaining loose ties with other Mon civilizations in the Chao Phraya Valley of Siam.

The *Pyu* people followed much later, moving down the western side of the Irrawaddy and founding a capital near present-day Prome in 628 AD. The Burmans entered the Irrawaddy River valley in the mid-9th century, absorbing the nearby Pyu and Mon communities. Later waves brought in the *Shan* and *Kachin,* who, along with the native *Karen,* all played a part in the country's development.

Pagan was conquered by the Mongols under Kublai Khan in 1287. This was the beginning of a turbulent period during which northern Burma led an uncertain existence between Shan domination and tributary relations with China, while southern Burma reverted to Mon rule.

In the late 1800s, under British Rule, Burmese culture was submerged beneath a colonial overlay. Under colonial rule the linkage of government and religion was lost, the monastic orders fell into disarray, and the monastic schools, which had actually given Burma a higher rate of male literacy than Britain, declined as English became the language of social advancement. The indigenous culture nevertheless persisted in the magical world of the *pwe,* a type of folk opera, in the practice of Buddhism and *nat* worship, and in the language of the peasantry.

The British moved the capitol from royal Mandalay to the port city of Yangon in 1886, developing it as a substation of the British Empire in India. This led to large-scale Indian immigration. Yangon thus became the hub of a "steel frame" of administration spreading out into the hinterland, where district officers maintained law and order, collected revenue, and administered justice. As the country was opened up to the world market, it became the world's major exporter of rice—from 0.5 million metric tons before the fall of Mandalay, to two million in 1900, and three million before the war began in 1939.

But for the most part, the history and economics of Burma were irrelevant to the men in the air and on the ground who were fighting to wrest the country back from its Japanese invaders. To them, it was a place as foreign and as far away from home as they'd ever known—and surely no place a man wanted to die.

Meat on the table.

When he wasn't flying or servicing his guns, Otsie had a lot to write home about.

The boys did a lot of hunting and fishing in Warazup. But these sports didn't involve the tried and true techniques Ots was accustomed to using in the duck blinds of Illinois or the pike waters of Wisconsin's Chippewa Flowage.

Operations clerk Tom Quinlan remembers some of it this way:

"I was on the buffalo safari. We had a personnel carrier with a battery-run searchlight. Around midnight, we all sat near the Mogaung River for an hour or two and then turned on the searchlight and pointed it across the river. Then everyone let go.

"It sounded like the fireworks after the 1812 Overture. I think they stewed the buffalo for three or four days before we could chew it—and our teeth were in good shape in those days."

Clarence Hill says: "I was the one who shot the water buffalo. Myself and several others shot a lot of deer and tried to keep the mess supplied. The buffalo was so tough we ground it up."

Shugart recorded one of the squadron's famous fishing trips in his diary: *The maintenance crew went fishing today, also some of the crew chiefs. Charles Hawks, Harry Briscoe, Walt Clements, Sergeants Dave George, Jim Frost, Jerry Bakunas, Don Chamberlain and Jud Reynolds. We caught 310 fish, using three cubes of plastic explosive. The "bait" is tossed into the river, while the party on shore, with one end of the wires, touches them to the jeep battery. The fish really bite at that instant!*

These were the pilots that Ots flew with at Warazup. FRONT ROW L to R: Harry Depew, James Richards, Ken Schaible, Holden Kuhns, Bill Dugan, Ray Wakeland MIDDLE ROW L to R: Val Verutti, Word Payne, Bob McFann, Bert Snow, Bill Short, Gerald Hannaford, L.P. Bloodworth, Don Wegner TOP ROW L to R: Ed Kitta, Orville Fjeldheim, Ed MacKay, Ralph Everett, Ed Tengler, John Thomson, Walter Pierpont, Dick Johnson

The squadron was getting a bit of publicity back home, too. In addition to the nickname "Bridge Busters," The 490th was also called the "Burma Dental Clinic" and a full-page North American advertisement in the Saturday Evening Post showed old "99" busting a bridge in Burma. The accompanying caption read: *"The waist gunner yelled over the intercom 'Take her up a bit Captain, we're shipping water back here.' That is really low-level bombing!"*

On November 29th, just two days after arriving at Warazup, and for the first time in its history, the 490th was bombed by the enemy.

Otsie and many of the others were impatiently waiting for a balky movie projector to be fixed. "The Sea Wolf" might have been showing that night, maybe "Guadalcanal Diary" or "Tall in the Saddle"—it made no difference. The men were starved for stateside entertainment and the nightly movies were the biggest thing going. As the projector was being worked on, a lone Mitsubishi G4M1 "Betty" bomber appeared overhead. It was already dark, and the plane could barely be seen.

"Who's flying tonight?" Somebody asked.

"Hell, that ain't one of ours," someone else answered. All eyes looked up toward the drone of the two MK4A Kasei radials.

"Shit—that's a goddamned Jap!"

Ever since arriving at Warazup, the men had been badgered to dig foxholes. Some were faithful in doing it, some weren't. In the entire history of the squadron, there was no record of it ever being attacked.

But tonight it happened. The enemy dropped incendiaries and frags, putting a number of small potholes in the runway. The bombs struck near the control tower and trailed over to the Ledo Road. One or two tore open a gas pipeline at the south end of the runway. Howard Bell remembers that when the bombs started to explode, men jumped into holes they hadn't dug—while some of those who'd spent an afternoon digging in the hot, Burmese sun couldn't find an empty one.

A few of the guys received minor injuries. The gas pipe and the field were quickly repaired, but they were in Burma now, and nobody knew if these night bombings would be a regular routine or not. The next day, without much urging, everybody was out digging foxholes, and those who'd already dug theirs were digging them a little deeper.

On the day that night attack occurred, Otsie had flown on the first assigned mission from the squadron's new base.

Early that morning, twelve Mitchells led by Bob Lundin took off from the dirt field. Takeoff at Warazup was to the north because of winds. The flights climbed out north and then turned south, passing back over the field on their way to the targets. Today they were after the Tonbo railroad and road bridges.

It would prove an unsatisfying mission and cost the Bridge Busters the first fatality since Otsie joined them. Just half of the railroad bridge was destroyed, while the road bridge escaped the raid untouched. At two and three hundred feet, the Mitchells had come in low, dropping both five hundred and thousand pound bombs, tearing up buildings and hidden gun positions with their .50s and 75mm cannon.

But they soon learned that the Japanese were serious about hanging on to Burma. From Tonbo and nearby Sedaw, heavy anti-aircraft fire arched up as each plane made its run. On one pass, engineer Walt Edwards was hit in the legs—and on another, turret-gunner Frank Zinga was badly wounded.

Squadron area—Warazup, Burma. Showing staff vehicles and orderly room in foreground. At Warazup, they lived in the famous British desert tents that were developed over the years in the tropics and in desert operations. Their construction consisted of a tent inside a tent, with four to six inches of air space between the two layers, so that in summer the air could circulate to keep the tent cool, and in the winter it would act as insulation for warmth. The tents were a lend-lease item from the British to the Americans.

As the flights returned from Tenbe, the crew chiefs surveyed the damage: Three of their aircraft would need patching up, and Zinga's Mitchell had been particularly hard hit—coming home with the tail turret out, the left vertical stabilizer damaged, and the aileron central cable partly severed.

Led by Dick Johnson, Ed Kitta, Bob Bennett, Herb Schwarz, and Elden Cross, the battered Mitchells all returned safely to Warazup, but Sergeant Zinga's wounds were fatal. He died late that same night at the 48th Evacuation Hospital at Myitkyina.

Frank Zinga had been an engineer-gunner, not a radioman. But like Otsie, he'd been a Chicago boy and soldiers from the same hometown tended to seek each other out when stationed far from home. When word came back to the squadron that Zinga had died, it brought the war home to Ots.

There weren't many differences between them. Both from the same town, the same part of the country. The mission that killed Zinga, the mission that ended his young life forever, was no different than the ones they'd been flying almost every day. A routine mission took Frank Zinga away—away from everything he'd ever known and loved, while the same mission brought Ots home safe and sound, hungry for lunch and looking forward to the customary drink of whiskey given to all the crews on a safe return.

But they forced themselves not to dwell on losses. Zinga was dead. His name would be scrubbed from the roster and once that happened, nobody talked much about him anymore. It was pretty much the same with anyone who was lost.

"Man, those are the breaks," those who returned would say with a fatalistic shrug. "The old fickle finger pointed at somebody else's sorry ass today."

They understood that it could be them tomorrow, or the next day, or two weeks from then. One day soon, each man came to realize, he'd either be shipping back to the states, gloriously drunk on decent whiskey and no longer giving a rat's ass about the war, or else he'd just as easily be in small pieces and scattered across a scorched, black smear of Burma jungle.

But even in the face of danger and death, there was humor—although it was often somewhat black.

As a pilot, Bob Bennett was assigned to fly a planeload of PX supplies from Assam down to Warazup. Earlier, another pilot had flat refused to fly the aircraft and warned Bennett to pull down on the tail guns before taking off.

Bob remembered weighing about one hundred thirty pounds in those days and when he grabbed the guns and brought his weight down, the nose wheel lifted easily off the ground!

Bennett had the load rearranged and talked four East Indians into flying back with them to add balance in the front. "I often wonder what would have happened if we'd been forced to bail out," Bob remembered. "They were four Indians with no chutes."

After unloading at Warazup, the supply plane took off to the south, did a one-eighty and came back low over the mess hall. They were just finishing the roof when Bennett and his crew blew most of it off.

And George Chapman remembers that at Warazup, someone found a British Bren gun carrier in the jungle where it had been abandoned after becoming mired down in the mud as Allied troops were pushing the Japs back south. Some of the guys dug it out and got it running, figured out how to operate it, and had a great time running it up and down the squadron street—until the CO told them to turn it over to an army unit.

With Warazup being located on the Ledo Road, the dust-raising convoys of trucks that passed through often stopped overnight. Black drivers would swap a case of beer from their cargo for a bottle of Carew's gin, and it was often said that the Chinese drivers would steal the goddamn socks off your feet while you still had your shoes on. Any loose stuff was child's play for them.

Theft was endemic with the Chinese, and line chief Clyde Dyar remembers an incident that happened after the squadron left Warazup for their new base in Hanchung, China:

"The 490th was stationed at Warazup, Burma, in the spring of 1945," Clyde recalls. "Having run out of worthwhile targets, we were ordered to move our operations to China. An advance party flew to Hanchung to check out the new base, and word came back that it was very primitive. There was only a single grass runway running east and west with no buildings on the flight line, and an old monastery in town for troop housing.

"The GIs were at their best and most resourceful when our orders came to move to Hanchung. Many of the lend-lease British desert tents that we'd been living in became the subjects of 'reverse lend-lease,' also known as 'midnight requisition.' We took more than a few of these fine tents to China and set them up along the flight line as homes away from home. We kept all our posessions in these tents.

"At Hanchung it was a mile and a half from the flight line to the mess hall. At chow time, we'd pile into a weapons carrier and head over for something to eat, leaving Chinese soldiers to guard the airstrip. Very soon, cartons of smokes began disappearing from our tents.

"One of the guys—I'll call him Mac—decided to stay put one night and find out who was stealing cigarettes. He didn't have very long to wait. Once the rest of us were gone, one of the Chinese guards came into the tent and helped himself to a carton of Camels.

"Mac let the guy get a distance away from the tent before he yelled at him to halt and drop the stolen smokes. When the guard started to run, Mac yelled 'Stop!' once more, then raised his carbine and dropped the cigarette thief in his tracks.

"The proper Chinese authorities were notified, but by this time it was getting dark and no one knew what to do. Somebody suggested putting the body in the ambulance until morning, forgetting that one of the squadron's medics was making his home in the ambulance, using one of the litters for his bed.

"That night this particular medic was in town drinking, and after too much of the local liquor he returned to find the Chinese soldier in his bed. He tried to wake the corpse with poor result and finally realized the man was dead.

"Two or three days later the Chinese came and took the body. Mac was rotated back to the states for his own safety, and the medic swore to lay off the local booze. It wasn't long before somebody else joked that the moral of the story could be 'Don't mess with my Camels.'

"It seemed funny at the time," Clyde remembers. "But it's too bad a human being had to die over a carton of smokes."

15

Ots logged a lot of hours the first two weeks of December. The month would shape up as one of the most successful in the squadron's twenty-nine months of operations against the enemy. December saw them set a new record for bridges destroyed in any one-month period.

They blew apart twenty-five, and inflicted major damage on five more. Out of forty-three spans attacked, only thirteen remained undamaged. For the year just ending, the Bridge Busters destroyed or severely damaged one hundred and twenty-two bridges and damaged forty-nine others enough to put them out of commission for days and weeks at a time. The end of the year would see a record unmatched by any other single unit in the Army Air Corps.

The squadron also switched over to a new schedule of combat operation. Now, they would fly for six consecutive days, including moonlight sweeps against targets of opportunity out of Myitkyina, transition flying on the seventh day, followed by a general day off for everybody on the eighth.

A little more than two weeks before Christmas, Ots got a five-day leave. With little else to do but see as much of the world as he could, he hitched a ride on one of the squadron's B-25s heading to Calcutta for supplies.

Located near the Bay of Bengal, the city of Calcutta had been founded in 1690 by the British trader, Job Charnock, as a post of the British East India Company. When Ots arrived, he thought that he'd never seen such filth and misery in his life. Calcutta smelled like a sewer. Beggars were everywhere, as was the hideous sight of leprosy. On the filthy streets all around him were people missing noses, ears, or portions of their faces.

Cripples were in abundance, too. Men, women and children without arms, missing legs, or stumbling along blind. He'd been told to eat no ice cream, and to drink no water, cold drinks, or milk.

Radio reports had told of mass starvation in Calcutta and Ots soon realized the reports were true. Thousands of poor, starving people shuffled around the streets like zombies, homeless and slowly dying, they could only wrap whatever rags they wore around their wasted bodies and lie down to sleep at night in gutters, doorways, or on sidewalks.

Each morning, just before dawn, thieves would kick each body to see if it was still alive. The corpses were quickly stripped of anything of value, and later in the morning the city trucks would load the thin, stiffened bodies of the dead and take them to the constantly burning mass funeral pyres.

In Calcutta, field grade officers put up at the Great Eastern Hotel. Lower ranking officers and enlisted men used the Grand Hotel. Both were located on Chowringee Street. Down the street was Firpo's restaurant.

Ots had more than enough of Calcutta after two days, but as bad as the city was, the Japanese weren't shooting at him there, and he stuck out his leave until he could catch another ride back.

He returned to Warazup in mid-December, and a few days later wrote a letter to his sister, Erma: *"I just got back from rest camp today. Had a five-day leave in Calcutta. Didn't do much but look around and get disgusted as hell with India. I've never seen anything so miserable in all my life. These people just aren't civilized at all."*

The Bridge Busters quickly settled in at Warazup. Work details began laying out a baseball diamond and an open-air movie theater. The communications people rigged up a public address system and began broadcasting popular music, specially transcribed programs, and a daily 15-minute feature of world news by Sgt. Glen Henton and Cpl. John Poister.

Sgt. Lee Kruska started publishing "The Fishwrapper," the squadron's daily newspaper, and on Christmas Eve, they celebrated the formal opening of an Enlisted Man's Club.

For the holidays, both the officer's and enlisted men's mess halls were decorated with Christmas ornaments, and outside stood a fully-lit Christmas tree and nativity scene that had been assembled by Chaplain John Dwiggins, S/Sgt. John Garrison, and chaplain's assistant, Pfc Ralph Hansen.

Aircraft armorer Doug Knokey and several others were relieved of duty around Christmas, and were impatiently waiting for orders to go home. One morning, Knokey remembers, six or eight of them were "volunteered" to dig a cesspool for the mess hall.

They were told to dig a hole, fifteen feet square and fifteen feet deep, at least a hundred feet from the mess. With everybody bitching and moaning—all of them anxious to get the hell out of Burma and go home—the "volunteers" worked a few hours and then realized that they just might have to reenlist for at least one more hitch if they were going to dig a hole of those dimensions in that Burmese gumbo.

A few of them, being ex-ordnance types, hunted up T/Sgt. Fred Bakker in ordnance, and "borrowed" a hundred-pound bomb. Using a posthole digger, they went down ten or twelve feet, cut down a block of dynamite to fit in the tail fuse end, lowered the bomb into the hole, and then touched it off.

Knokey is still convinced that most of the mud blew a hundred feet straight up in the air and fell right back down into the hole.

This stunt put the whole squadron into the finest unrehearsed alert ever—all the tents were emptied and the slit trenches were filled in record time. The mess hall itself, was a grass-roofed, burlap-walled building that didn't fare too well. The blast didn't knock it down but it rearranged some of the shelves.

One of the squadron's senior officers, blessed with a sense of humor and wise to what had happened, told Knokey and the others that they should "pray for a plane to arrive on its way back from China and start them on their way home before somebody else started thinking 'Courts Martial.'"

Christmas came, and although everybody tried to put a game face on it, Christmas was always hell for soldiers overseas. Like most everyone else, Ots and his tent buddies tried to drink their loneliness away, and paid for it the next day. He later wrote to Mildred:... *we got good and 'stinkin' on Christmas. All on Indian liquor and that's no good, but what else? The tent was such a mess the next morning that our bearer wanted to know if the Japs had come at night.*

In spite of the loneliness of Christmas far from home, the base saw a few prominent visitors that month, including Major Leaguers Paul Waner, Luke Sewell, and Dixie Walker. The ballplayers may not have been quite as popular as Paulette Goddard was back in India, but they were nevertheless heartily welcomed as symbols of the USA and home.

The squadron got drunk again on New Year's Eve—at least many of them did.

Don Harkins welcomed 1945 in a slightly different manner. On New Year's Eve, as navigator in a single Mitchell, flying out of Myitkyina late at night with pilot George Chapman, Don's moonlight mission took them over Heho Airfield where they dropped their bombs exactly at midnight. The lone Mitchell took some fireworks from the ground but made it back safely, with a relieved and happy crew singing Auld Lang Syne.

The calendar pages turned and the war rolled over into another miserable year.

Overseas mail to and from a remote spot such as Warazup was slow. What was written in a letter might be totally out of date by the time the reader got it. Such was the case in January when Otsie wrote to Mildred and told her that after a hundred combat hours, he'd recently received an air medal for missions flown.

Warazup, Burma
January 3, 1945

Dear Sis…

Let's see now, I'll read your letter again (only the fourth time) and see if there are any questions I can answer for you.

Speaking of weight, I'm normal again and always was. You see, I blame that on the poor photography. I sent some pictures to Zoe taken a couple of weeks ago. No doubt you'll get to see them and draw your own conclusions.

Your mentioning my six missions makes me feel like a new man. It may surprise you to learn that at this writing I have twenty-two to my credit. Not bad, eh? Never thought I'd be able to survive the excitement. As far as Zoe knowing, I already told her. Perhaps it was a little pride that made me spill the beans. But on second thought, I felt it was better for her to know.

By the way, I've got one medal and am within reach of another. Proud of your kid brother? But I can't understand my still being a corporal. Guess

I'm the original T.S. Kid. Would you like to punch my card? Kidding aside, I may make sergeant any day now.

Assam is in eastern India, but that's old stuff now as I'm not there any longer. Guess I move faster than the mail does. However, keep looking and watch the newspapers. Our squadron has been getting a lot of stateside publicity. Anything that has to do with the war in Burma, read over once or twice—malum? (Indian lingo for 'understand').

Brazil and Trinidad is nothing like the travel folders state. In my estimation, every country out of the U.S. is nothing but filth and poverty.

More than once I wanted to ask you to send me some stationery but didn't want to impose on you. Now that you mention it, I'll say yes. Please do. It doesn't have to be fancy. Tissue second sheets are about as good as any. Now to make it official: "Can you please send me some writing paper and envelopes?" Thanks.

I guess by now you know that I received the bracelet. I'll bet you picked it out. Very nice and I consider it one of my good luck charms.

Don't worry about hearing from Pep. I was able to write only because we made frequent stops but in Pep's case he can't do that while in the middle of the ocean somewhere.

I'm sending you a small clipping out of a GI newspaper. Perhaps it will give you some idea of what we are doing.

On the Central Burma Front, planes of the 490th Bombardment Group were up to their favorite bridge-busting activities. They got three railroad bridges at Mongmit, a bypass at Tangon and Tantabin, a bridge northeast of Tabin, and another at Mandaunghla and Sissongy. They knocked down four additional bridges near Mandalay.

Write soon, hello to Jimmer and to the Vesely's. And above all, tell Mom I'm OK and lots of love for her.

Otsie's twenty-second mission was flown on the same day he wrote this letter. They went against the Aungban airfield southeast of

Mandalay. This was a high altitude mission in which he wasn't doing any shooting. Instead, he was busy on the radio and watching out his port and starboard bay windows for any Japanese fighters that might try to jump them.

But this time out, even over an air base like Aungban, they weren't sweating enemy fighter opposition all that much. Escorting them to the target was the luxury of twelve P-47 Thunderbolts from the 80th Fighter Group.

Capt. Ed Tengler was mission leader. Tengler was a fine pilot and well liked by everyone. In less than four months, he'd be made commanding officer of the 490th.

On this mission, each of three flights was assigned seventeen hundred feet of Aungban's main NW-SE runway. They unloaded forty thousand-pounders on Aungban, but heavy clouds at the point of release affected bombing accuracy. Even with the clouds, from over twelve thousand feet, they scored two direct hits on the runway and blew apart a hangar at the south end of it. The rest of the bombs were ineffectual and scattered along the west side of the runway.

Two days later, the squadron put up sixteen B-25s, the largest number ever in a 490th combat mission. This was to be a low-level mission over three separate Japanese airfields, and would result in the loss of one airplane and an incredible story of survival.

Ots wasn't flying that day, but like all those who stayed on the ground, he had his fingers crossed for those who were.

Taking off from Warazup that morning, mission leader Sterling Reynolds climbed out and waited for everyone else to group before banking south towards the targets. One of those was Aungban again, and that made everyone edgy. Visiting the same target so soon after the last strike usually put them under heavy fire from beefed up defenses on the ground. They weren't sure about Lai-Hka and Kunlon airfields, but they had a hunch that Aungban might be a son-of-a-bitch.

They were right. Even though the Mitchells managed sixteen direct hits on the runway, they took heavy, accurate fire from the ground, and three out of the four planes on this flight were hit by at least twelve gun positions.

Lai-Hka was flattened by a total of twenty-nine bombs, and the runways at Kunlon were heavily cratered. Here again, three gulls took heavy fire from below, and one of them—piloted by 1st Lt. Quentin O. Ball—soon began belching smoke from its right engine.

The other Mitchells in the area soon heard Ball talking to his wingman. He was limping along on a single engine and trying to decide if he could clear the mountains to get home.

A few minutes later, Ball's crew decided to pull the plug on it and bail out. The navigator, Lt. Benjamin Brill remembered it years later: "When we got hit I was sitting in the right seat and looked at the engine on the right side to see a hell of a hole on top of the housing, where a shell had exited. We couldn't feather the engine and had no chance with the windmilling. I looked over at Quentin and we both thought 'Oh shit'—then he made one of the lowest altitude bailouts out of the top hatch of a B25 in a complete nose down attitude. It's unbelievable he didn't get cut to pieces when he jumped."

The other crews heard them decide to bail out, and as soon as Ball's crew cleared the ship, it turned gently to the right, then broke violently to the left and smashed into the side of a hill.

Gathering up and hiding their chutes, the crew of the crashed B-25 stumbled into each other on top of a small hill. There were only three of them—Sergeants Al Nichols, Junior Miller, and Chris Weber.

"Where's Ball and Brill?" They asked each other. "Did they make it out OK?"

Nobody knew. No one had seen them come down.

Making sure nobody was badly hurt, the three enlisted men took stock of their situation. They were flat in the middle of enemy territory, with only their sidearms and limited rations, having lost most of them in the jump.

They each glanced over at the greasy, black plume of smoke that was hovering over the trees. It would be a dead giveaway of their position.

"We need to get the hell out of here," they all agreed.

But after walking for two and a half days through thick jungle, they discovered they'd been traveling in circles. They finally hit a trail and met several natives who spoke broken English, and were directed to a village just outside Kalegwe. On their way to it they spotted a B-25 rescue plane circling the area.

"They're looking for us."

In the village, they were fed, given blankets, and told there was another American in a village to the east.

"That's either gotta be Ball or Brill."

The next morning they climbed into an oxcart and traveled to a village three miles away, where they were fed again.

"Where's the American?" They all asked.

"Not here now," the village headman told them. "He hide from Japs in jungle. I get now."

The headman left them eating and went on alone, returning a few hours later with Lieutenant Ball. Counting noses, the pilot saw they were still only four.

"Where's Lieutenant Brill?" He asked. "He make it OK?"

"We dunno, sir. None of us saw either of you come down."

Again, they heard the familiar sound of two Wright Cyclone engines above. It was another B-25, flying low, looking for them. They shouted and waved but couldn't attract its attention.

At the urging of the headman they rested and then went on to another village nearer the mountains. Here they were given more food and slept until that night, when all four were shaken awake by another native. His name was Shuben-Yal, he told them, and he was the headman in this village.

"Japanese men look for you at Kalegwe," Shuben-Yal said. "I take you to hide in the hills."

They followed him and stayed hidden for several days. Another native, by the name of Piyna, brought them food and water. Although happy to be safe, the crew was still worried about Lieutenant Brill.

"He's either lost, captured, or dead," someone suggested. "But hell, nothing we can do for him now."

They'd been in the bush a week when they again heard the sound of a single B-25 in the area. "They got to be looking for us," Lieutenant Ball suspected. Quickly the four men spread out a parachute in a nearby rice paddy. The white silk finally caught the eye of the searching B-25.

The plane came over low and slow, dropping a handwritten note that said: *try to clear a 300 ft landing strip—long enough for an L-1 to land.*

With Piyna's help, they recruited some machete-carrying Burmese and hurriedly cleared trees and brush to lay out a rough, improvised strip. A little over two hours later, two L-1s and several P-47s returned, escorted to the site by the B-25.

One of the L-1s broke and tried to land, but came in too hot and smashed into a tree, almost tearing off a wing and twisting the plane around. The pilot, Sergeant Lindgren, stepped out of the little airplane angry but unhurt. Now there were five Americans in need of rescuing.

The B25 dropped another note, telling them to improve the strip. It also dropped a 4-man kit but the parachute failed to open and the kit was smashed to pieces on the ground.

Whoever was coordinating the search, Quentin Ball thought, was damned serious about getting them back. The next morning, while they were again clearing jungle to improve and lengthen the strip, a C-47 flew over and the men stared upward as a small, dark figure left the airplane and came floating down toward them.

The jumper was a Burmese regular officer named Captain Santone. He knew the territory, Santone explained, and had been sent to help get them out.

The C-47 made a second, lower pass, dropping food, picks and shovels. In the afternoon, two more L-1s were back. Piloted by Sergeant Phillips, one of the little Stinsons came in and put down on the improvised runway.

"You guys about ready to go home?" Phillips called out as he taxied back to them. Straws were drawn and the winners were Chris Weber and the other L-1 pilot, Sergeant Lindgren. Phillips went bouncing down the runway but found too late that he needed more room to take off than to land, especially with the weight of two extra men aboard. With the pilot giving it full throttle and hauling back on the stick, the Stinson still ran off the end of the strip and smashed into a tree, ripping off its entire undercarriage.

"Shit," Phillips growled as the three pulled themselves out of the wrecked airplane. Now there were six on the ground, along with Captain Santone.

In the second L-1, the pilot, Sergeant Gooders, saw what happened, and began his approach into the little jungle airstrip. Gooders put it down too hard and tore off a wheel. He too, climbed out unhurt, but disgusted and angry at himself.

With three wrecked planes, they decided to start out on foot. Santone told the Burmese to burn the wrecked L-1s that night and he quickly recruited a Gurkha guide named Kalahda from a nearby village.

All the while that Lieutenant Ball and his crew were hiding from the Japanese and attempting to make their way slowly back to safety, the squadron was pressing ahead with missions, and Otsie was flying a lot of them.

On January 11th, the Bridge Busters went after Lashio again. A dozen Mitchells strafed and dropped bombs on storage buildings at New Lashio. Many of them were blown apart by direct hits, while others were badly damaged by near hits. The attacking airmen saw one huge fire burning as they strafed the area at low level with both .50s and 75mm cannon.

Machine gun fire was encountered from the vicinity of the Lashio bridges, as well as from a boxcar at the railroad station. Otsie and the other gunners tore into it on every pass and the position soon fell silent.

Two Mitchells were hit by small arms fire from New Lashio. One received only superficial damage, while the other, piloted by Lt. Gerald Hannaford, had its left tire shot out. Hannaford, who usually flew with a small dog named "Bombsight"—who'd now become an unofficial squadron mascot—got back safely and successfully landed at Warazup.

16

On January 14th, Ots climbed up the rear ladder and got himself settled at the radio and waistguns. The mission that day was to be another low-level attack against a Japanese rest camp, along with three bridges, personnel areas and storage sheds at Nampawng. With a large part of the target consisting of enemy personnel, para-frags had been loaded and would be used against the rest camp ten miles south of Lashio. These were fragmentation bombs attached to small parachutes so that they'd float instead of fall—allowing the crews to release them at extremely low levels. They were after more than wood or steel spans that morning. Today's targets were Japanese soldiers.

Mission leader Capt. Rollin White took his twelve airplanes in and virtually obliterated the rest area. More than six buildings were totally destroyed and a number of others were badly damaged—with the entire area left in flames. Caught by surprise, how many Japanese died in the raid would never be known for certain.

The flights went on to blow apart two road bridges at Hayti and the Bypass Bridge at Nampawng. Following a bombing and strafing attack on Nampawng village, three warehouses and fourteen basha-type buildings were set ablaze and destroyed.

Otsie was scheduled to fly again the next two days. The 16th and 17th of January saw a high altitude raid against Namtoc on one day, and a twelve-plane attack against the Hohko bypass bridges the next. The evening after the Namtoc raid, Ots ate supper and went back to his tent to write some letters. One was to his sister, Millie:

Warazup, Burma
January 16, 1945

Dear Sis…

Your newsy letter came today and believe me it was appreciated. I'm glad you're going to write whenever you have news instead of waiting to hear from me.

I'm glad you sent that quotation from the Times. I've often wondered about things like that. Nobody seems to go into detail as much as you. Most everything was true about that story, except for the number of planes involved. If you divide that by five, you might get the right answer. We aren't a large outfit.

I've been flying like mad last week, logging plenty of time, but feeling pretty tired. Went up today and will go up again tomorrow. Day before yesterday I flew twice. You can see I'm pretty busy. Besides this, I've got to clean my guns, load bombs, and what's left?

By the way, I wasn't on the mission transcribed on Christmas, but I was at the target about three or four times previously. Sure was a hot spot, but I've seen worse. It won't be long before we start operating around "where the flying fishes play." That's going to be something.

In the Burma jungle that same day, Lieutenant Ball and his crew reached and crossed the Nampac River, but their meager rations were beginning to run short. Two days later, on the morning of the 18th, the tough little group walked out of the hills into fairly open country. Although they had no way of knowing it, this same day was to prove especially bad for their comrades back at Warazup.

That afternoon, Otsie and the rest of those who hadn't been scheduled to fly were on hand to witness the return of what had turned into a hard-luck mission against the Japanese airfield at Nawnghkio. They would soon learn that one of the squadron's hottest pilots, Capt. Andy Squire, who was also assistant operations officer, had lost his life.

Val Verrutii remembered it this way: "Andy was mission leader and flying number 111, the first strafer model we received."

This was the same airplane that Otsie and his stateside crew had ferried over a little over two months earlier.

"It had eight .50 cal. guns in the nose, plus the four package guns for the pilot to fire," Val Verrutii went on. "A real low-level attack weapon. The day it went down, we were after the airfield at Nawnghkio, near Mandalay, which was very heavily defended. The mission, six flights of twos, were spaced ten minutes apart, each of us loaded with four time-fused thousand pound bombs to be dropped at low-level. Andy was lead plane on the mission, and I was in the lead plane of the fourth flight. When we came around a hill there was so much smoke and dust that we could barely see the runway, but we flew down and dropped our load. We could see many huge craters and that the field had already been destroyed.

"Just off to the left we saw the black smoke of a burning B-25 that was later confirmed to be 111."

Each flight had pounded the airfield from low altitude, dotting the runway with bomb craters and strafing anti-aircraft positions on both sides of the field. But on turning for home, the Mitchells had begun to take heavy machine gun fire from the nearby railroad station.

Along with four others, Squire's gull was hit and drifted off with its left engine streaming smoke. Five minutes later, much too low to parachute, he and his crew went in, crashing and burning ten miles northwest of the target.

Andy Squire would race no more cars.

Bill Shivar still remembers that day. He was a 1st lieutenant, flying navigator for Gerry Hannaford—on the second flight to the same target. They had taken off about a half hour after Squire and were about twenty miles out, approaching Nawnghkio, when they saw thick, oily smoke billowing up from the jungle below and ahead of them.

Not knowing what it was, Bill noted it on his map as they continued on toward the target and made their runs, dropping their bombs and hightailing it back to Warazup.

When they landed, everybody seemed to be asking everybody else if they'd seen Andy Squire. Bill said no, but that he'd noted an oil fire in the target area. He was immediately put on a plane to Myitkyina where he flew three flights with Air Rescue, leading them back to the area of whatever it was that was burning. By that time, the smoke had cleared but the Air Rescue crew thought they could see what looked like the shine of metal down below.

"The jungle was so thick," Shivar remembers. "There was no way we could land."

On the way back to Myitkyina, assuming that what they saw was probably Squire's plane, Bill couldn't help but ponder the vagaries of fate. At the morning briefing, he'd noted that Andy Squire's navigator that day was to be 1st Lt. Walt Bogart.

Bogart had trained with Gerry Hannaford—Shivar's pilot—back in Columbia, South Carolina, and Bill briefly thought about switching right seats with Walt and going up with Andy Squire, so that Bogart and Hannaford could fly together again. For whatever reason, he changed his mind at the last minute and decided to fly the mission as scheduled.

That small decision saved his life.

As the battered flights returned to Warazup that afternoon, the squadron almost lost another crew.

Flying his 37th and last mission, 1st Lt. George Chapman, from the small town of River Falls, Wisconsin, and another of the 490th's fine, veteran pilots was hard hit as well. His hydraulics and bomb bay had been destroyed by 37mm antiaircraft fire and heavy bursts from a Japanese machine gun had torn apart his left tire.

This is how Chapman remembered it. "It was January 18th, 1945. I believe there were six two-ship elements that flew the mission. I was pilot of the last two-ship unit. By the time we came over the target, the Japs had us in a crossfire. We saw the smoke from the B-25 they'd shot down. I believe it was Captain Squire.

"We dropped our bombs at low altitude, all guns blazing. On the way back to Warazup, the crew tried to check the damage. I turned the controls over to my copilot, 1st Lt. Harold Ludeman, and climbed over the bomb bay to inspect rear damage. The radioman hadn't been at his station, but was firing a waist gun. Lucky for him, as a shell had come up through the open bomb bay and right through his seat. Back at Warazup, we were the last plane on the mission to return. I dropped the landing gear and then made a pass or two at the tower. They could see no problem. The crew trusted me more than they did their chutes, so they didn't bail out. There was an air-evac aircraft at the end of the runway with props turning, waiting to take off.

"At the time, I had more than a thousand hours as a pilot. I touched down on the runway, but the left tire had been shot out and the plane immediately veered to the left. I remember seeing a refueling truck near the runway. I saw the driver jump out and run for his life. He made it, but I hit the fuel truck. It knocked out our landing gear and we skidded to a stop on our belly. There was spilled fuel burning on the left front and left rear of the B-25. The top hatch in the pilot's compartment was popped open. The copilot exited. The engineer got out. The copilot landed on his head. I don't know if I was thrown into the instrument panel or if I landed outside on my knees. A blank space in my memory.

"The two crewmen in the rear escaped through a side hatch. The radioman, Jim Bryant, came around the wing tip and dragged me to a spot at the end of a pile of pipe—part of a pipeline project. The .50s were popping off and the slugs were coming through the pipes at our end.

"They took me to the first aid tent. My biggest concern was for our crew. I could account for five, but not my copilot. Someone said he was safe in his tent. My navigator and I were airlifted to the 234th General Hospital in Assam. It took me almost a year to get back to flying."

Pfc Bernie Capelli remembered the same incident this way: "I still wonder how they all got out of that burning plane. Van Burleigh and I had just completed our fifty missions and were assigned fire truck duty while waiting to rotate home. It was a beautiful day at Warazup and we'd removed our fatigue jackets to enjoy a lazy, sunny day. Our truck was parked at the far end of the runway. An army ambulance and a gasoline tanker were parked beside us. Van was unhappy with our position so we moved up runway to a spot directly across from the bamboo radio tower, which was about mid-runway.

"We'd barely settled into our new parking spot when a red flashing signal came from the tower letting us know that Chapman's approaching B-25 was in trouble. Chapman was bringing the plane in hot and he roared past us going much too fast to stop before the end of the runway. Right after the plane passed, Burleigh drove out on the runway and chased it. We'd driven about fifty yards when we saw the plane's left wing hit the gasoline tanker. The plane ground looped and burst into flames that shot two hundred feet in the air. I jumped from the truck and ran toward the fire, figuring no one could be alive in that inferno. I hesitated for a moment then ran around the wall of flame and got a shock.

"Only one wing was burning. The rest of the plane was intact. The fire was roaring and .50s were starting to explode. Sergeant Bryant was yelling at me that the crew was safe and to get away from the airplane before it exploded."

Both being radiomen, Otsie knew Jim Bryant well. After risking his life to pull Chapman from the burning wreckage, Bryant was considered a genuine hero in the squadron. Among the veterans of the 490th, that status would stick with him his entire life—until he died of cancer in 1988.

The same day these events occurred, Lieutenant Ball and his party of survivors had reached the Irrawaddy River. The far shore was Allied territory and they decided on an attempt to cross it on improvised rafts made of hammocks and filled with leaves.

The first raft was barely twenty-five feet from shore when it began to sink. Junior Miller and Al Nichols began to swim back to shore.

Without calling to the others for help, Sergeant Weber, who couldn't swim, sunk beneath the brown, muddy water and was never seen again. The other two rafts also returned to the east bank with Lieutenant Ball and Captain Santone finally deciding that a boat was the only safe way to cross.

They waited for night and then made their way downriver. There was no hint of danger until they stumbled into a Japanese patrol. They heard a sentry shout *"Tomare*—Halt!"

The Americans froze. When the sentry shouted again and worked the bolt of his rifle, the group scrambled for cover in the surrounding bushes. The quiet jungle night was shattered by gunfire and a Japanese grenade actually hit Sergeant Nichols in the head, bounced off and exploded just six feet away, but no one was hurt.

The Japanese patrol hurriedly set up a machinegun and sprayed the entire area. Captain Santone and Sergeant Lindgren were hit almost immediately. Santone was killed when a flashlight in his pocket went on as he was raising his carbine to fire. The light gave away his position.

Wounded, Lindgren raised himself up on an elbow and asked Sergeant Gooders for his Thompson gun. As he did, he was hit again and killed.

With bullets like hornets around them, Sergeants Miller and Nichols picked up their fallen comrade's weapons and crept away into the underbrush. In the confusion, they became separated from Lieutenant Ball and the others.

Before crawling off, Nichols took a compass from the pocket of Captain Santone. The captain's body already felt cold.

A few minutes later, hunkered down in a nearby gully, Miller and Nichols found themselves under heavy fire again. But the Japanese were just firing blindly in the dark. When it stopped they again began to creep forward, and after roughly half a mile, they crawled under some bushes and tried to rest until dawn.

The next day they spotted three small native fishing boats a hundred feet upriver.

"Maybe we ought to wait for night," Nichols suggested.

"I don't want to wait for anything," Miller said, impatient to be across. "We're too damned close, and those Japs might still be looking for us."

Taking their chances, the two men made their way to the boats in daylight. Using the butts of their weapons as paddles they managed to cross the river into allied territory. They walked north less than a mile and in the first village they approached, they met a British patrol that escorted them to British headquarters three miles upriver.

The squadron was aware of the stubborn efforts being carried out to find Ball and the others, but they had precious little time to think about them.

On the 21st, Ots was part of a ten-plane high-level mission against Heho Airdrome. It gave him and all the others aboard the Mitchells a good feeling to see twelve Thunderbolts alongside, escorting them to the target.

Powered by 2100hp Pratt & Whitney radials, the P-47s were formidable machines. Nicknamed "Jugs" by the airmen, they had a maximum speed of almost five hundred miles per hour and carried six or eight fixed, forward-firing .50s along the leading edges of each wing.

At this stage of the war, Japanese pilots were thinking long and hard about taking their dwindling supply of Zeroes up against American Thunderbolts, and aside from expected flak, everybody could feel a little looser on these high-altitude, escorted missions.

But the next day they were back on the deck again, with mission leader Dick Johnson taking them against the stores and personnel areas at Panglong and Tawhsang. At Panglong, the 75mm cannon was used, demolishing a machine gun position with a direct hit.

The cannon was a brutal weapon, and a tricky one to use. Don Harkins remembers that "In the H Model Mitchell, if we were to use the cannon, the navigator moved into the well behind the pilot to load it. Loading was one shell at a time, and a good team could get off four or five rounds on an attack run. The navigator would load, tap the pilot on the shoulder, and the pilot would fire. He was supposed to wait for the shoulder tap before hitting the fire button. Otherwise, if he had his finger on the trigger, the cannon would fire as soon as the navigator shoved a shell into it—and the navigator would lose a hand."

After having been successfully tested with the standard Army 75mm field gun, the older G model Mitchells had been fitted out with these big guns. The cannon was mounted forward in the crawlspace. The gun was nine and a half feet long and weighed close to 900 pounds. Mounted in a cradle to absorb the shock, it extended under the pilot's seat to allow for a twenty one-inch recoil. Aside from the hazards that Don Harkins remembers, feeding the brute wasn't an enviable job for navigators. Slamming those fifteen-pound shells into the breech in the crowded space available took both strength and skill.

In the H models, the newer, lighter cannon was coded as the T13E1. But it was just as hard to load and even with some weight shaved off, the newer 75 was still a beast. It was the heaviest air weapon ever to fly into combat and when it was fired, many crews swore, the recoil seemed to stop the aircraft's forward motion for just a split-second—at least that's the way it felt.

Ots finished out the month with three more missions. On the 23rd of January, a heavy front moved in and lousy weather prevented another attack on Heho. The alternate targets were Hsumhsai and

Aungban airfield. Twelve planes took off from Warazup, but three turned back due to weather and one due to a shortage of fuel. Ed Tengler led the mission, and once again, twelve Thunderbolts escorted them to the dance and brought them home again.

The next day took the flights over Hsumshai airfield at an altitude of six thousand feet, and on the 25th they went back to Heho, attacking and heavily cratering the main runway. They dropped their loads from twelve thousand feet and flew between at least sixty bursts of flak. Antiaircraft fire was heavy but relatively inaccurate, with only two planes returning with minor damage.

Don Harkins still remembers January 25th. His was one of the two gulls that were hit: "I was flying with Maurice Graves, my tent mate and one of my favorite pilots. We were in an "H" model and carrying four thousand-pounders.

Don Harkins' original stateside crew. (l to r) 1st Lt. John Petree (pilot), S/Sgt. Gary Eeelman (armorer/gunner), S/Sgt. Jim Spence (engineer/gunner), S/Sgt. Walter Howie (radio/gunner), 1st Lt. Don Harkins (navigator), and T/Sgt. Walter Block (crew chief).

"On the initial run, flak hit our bomb bay. We thought we'd bombed on the lead ship, but when the rest of the squadron started making a diving turn to the left to avoid any more exposure, Graves couldn't make the maneuver.

"The bombs were still stuck in the bay and the weight of them made us too heavy to stay in formation. Finally we managed to pull out and the lead ship's bombardier took us to Aungban airstrip to try again.

"Over Aungban we still couldn't drop and Graves had to bring us back to Warazup—landing with four thousand pounds of high explosives under our sorry butts.

"I'm still convinced that was the best landing Maurice ever made. Fun and games in Burma."

And that same day, two of the prodigals finally came home.

A few days earlier, now safely in British hands, Sergeants Nichols and Miller went on to Thabeikkyin where they were fed, clothed and treated. That evening they rode a jeep to Onbauk and two days later they were taken to Inainggale where they were interrogated by Intelligence, and an officer of the 14th Army. From there they were sent to Myitkyina and returned to the squadron on January 25th.

Lieutenant Ball, Sergeant Gooders, and Sergeant Phillips, along with the Indian Gurkha, managed to get across the Irrawaddy and made contact with the same British patrol a day after their comrades did. They reached Myitkyina on January 23rd. Ball was admitted to the 48th Evacuation hospital for observation and returned to the squadron on February 2nd.

It was back at Warazup, that Quentin Ball finally learned that his missing navigator, Ben Brill, had also been reported safe in Bhamo.

"I remember Colonel Pichney's 201 outfit," Brill later said. "An OSS Group, mostly Burmese. I ate monkey stew prepared in my honor in a Shan village a few miles south of Mogok. I remember an airdrop of hundred pound sacks that contained salt, K-rations, a slab of opium about a foot long and two inches thick, and a case of toilet paper.

"In debriefing, I told them that if they gave me enough opium why hell, it wouldn't be too hard to walk from Rangoon all the way to Ledo."

At the Aviation Dispensary in Bhamo, Brill had an infection on his chin and was treated with penicillin. The flight surgeon in charge admitted that he'd never used the stuff on anyone before, and when the antibiotic didn't seem to work in the conventional way, the doctor dripped it directly into the open wound, where it seemed to work just fine.

Miller and Nichols told their interrogators that they never harbored any doubts of being rescued or reaching safety, and that Captain Santone had kept them going with his confidence and knowledge of the country. "He took charge of our group," the two men related. "He acted as doctor, guide and our advisor on the ways of staying alive in the jungle."

The natives took care of them too, treating them in a friendly manner and keeping them supplied with food. The Burmese told them over and over that they didn't like the Japanese, and the two headmen insisted: "Japanese no good. British good. American very good."

That same day, the squadron hit the village of Loilem from almost twelve thousand feet. Looking out his small windows, Ots saw lots of smoke below. Direct hits had destroyed twenty buildings in the personnel and stores area. A few secondary explosions resulted in two oil fires. Twelve planes left Warazup that morning and twelve came back for lunch.

No sweat today. The fickle finger was pointing somewhere else, but Ots was still on edge. He was getting close to going home, but the fear was building, too. He was a little surprised. He thought that after this many missions he'd be able to handle fear. But it was just the opposite and getting worse each day. It was a fear that woke you up at night and dogged your ass all day long. The only time it went away, he realized, was during the missions themselves—when everyone was just too busy to be scared.

But after awhile, even flying failed to dull the fear, and having Andy Squire and his crew go down in #111—the same plane he'd come over on—didn't help much, either. On an afternoon at the end of January, Bob Hyde and Harold Peppeard noticed that Ots seemed unusually distant and preoccupied.

"What's wrong, Al?" Bob asked. No one but his family and friends back in the old neighborhood called him Otsie, and for obvious reasons he refused to be called Adolph during his time in the Air Corps. In India and Burma, it was always Al.

Ots just shook his head and tried to stay quiet about whatever was eating at him, but Bob finally got him to open up.

"I don't think I'm going home," Ots told both his buddies that afternoon. "I'm afraid I'm not gonna make it back."

"Hell, man," Bob and Harold agreed. "Most of us are afraid of that. You talked to the flight surgeon?"

"No, he'd probably think I was nuts."

"Well, you ain't nuts," Bob said. "We're all scared. Why the hell should you be any different?"

Otsie said no more about it, but Bob remembers that soon afterward, Ots made his way to a small, nearby Catholic chapel located along the Ledo Road. He talked to the priest, made his confession, and took Holy Communion there.

After that, Bob recalled, it was business as usual. If Ots had a premonition, he wasn't going to let his fear show, but he still hinted at it in a letter to his sister, Millie.

Warazup, Burma
February 4, 1945

Dear Sis...

Received two of your letters and truthfully have never heard so much news before. Yes, the last letter I sent to you was the build-up to a citation.

I'm in for an award, but I don't like to mention it yet because it isn't official yet. Just don't say anything to anybody.

I made my 35th mission yesterday, and honestly, I'm getting nervous as hell. If you can fly every day, it's okay. But if I lay off a day or two I hate to start over again. Guess you know how it is. Things happen now and then which don't help the situation at all.

You don't have to worry about me sticking my neck out, though, for I shrink to half my size.

Had a day off today so I went hunting. Didn't do any good but as tomorrow is a general day off, we are going out in strength and should have a little luck. We've been getting quite a few chickens and doves lately and they really were good.

Some of the boys went out last night and got two deer and a two thousand pound Asiatic bison. This afternoon, two of the ack-ack boys went out and got a tiger that was six feet long. Plenty to do around here.

Days are getting longer so I guess summer is just around the corner. I hope I can get away from here before the monsoons start. I understand that's really rough. Well, Mil, guess I'll close. I've got so many letters to write. I've got to write Mom for her birthday. I got her a $15 money order and I hope she puts it to good use. What I mean by that is taking a couple of days off work. Say hello to her and the rest of the family. Thanks for the buck. I'm saving it to buy a good drink when I hit the states again.

Love,
Otsie

The next day was a general day off, and on the shore of the Mogaung River, a squadron picnic had been organized. While some of the ground crews were pressed into service repairing a few of the damaged Mitchells, the rest of the Bridge Busters had a fine time with a big picnic lunch and plenty of beer. Some of the guys stripped and went swimming, while others played poker, craps, or baseball.

With a number of pickup games going, Lt. Bill Hilgefort would later write in his diary: *Squadron holiday—played a red hot ballgame and got beat 5 to 4 in nine innings. Lost a case of beer.*

It was the best time they'd had since coming to Warazup, yet in less than two weeks twenty of the men at that picnic would be dead.

Part Five—Kehsi Man Sam

17

1st Lt. William Benjamin Plunkett III was awake at 5:00 a.m. on the morning of February 15th, 1945. He awoke with a heightened sense of awareness to everything around him. He'd been chosen as group mission leader today.

Bill Plunkett was 22 years old, a handsome young man from Little Rock, Arkansas. He'd proven himself a good, steady pilot, serious about the job that his outfit had to do. From all accounts, he was well liked by the crews who flew with him.

Like every other young pilot at Warazup, the United States government had seen fit to give Plunkett sole responsibility for an aircraft worth almost $150,000 in 1945 dollars. Although the vagaries of chance were beyond his control—he undoubtedly also felt responsible for the lives of the four other men flying with him.

The Plunketts were Arkansans going back for generations. In addition to tillable land, Bill's father and grandfather owned the Plunkett-Jarrell Grocer Company—a wholesale grocery business with statewide branches. Although Bill came of age during the Depression, he and his two older sisters had few wants or worries. They enjoyed a summer home in Michigan and spent every summer there.

He often thought about family and friends back home. He and his girl had been a steady couple all through school. They'd been engaged shortly before he enlisted, and he was thinking of her today, just as he had been the day before—on Valentine's Day.

Bill loved tennis, but Warazup was remote—surrounded by jungle and having only a baseball diamond. There were no British clubs nearby where a court might be found.

Before the war, he'd enrolled at the University of Arizona where the winters were warm, and tennis courts were played on all year round. Two years later, he'd decided to become an engineer and transferred to Vanderbilt in Nashville, Tennessee.

He had only one semester to finish before graduating, but the war was grinding on and Bill's urge to fly was even stronger than his love of tennis and his talent for engineering.

Lt. Bill Plunkett. His flight school graduation picture.

Against his family's wishes—they were urging him to finish school and wait to be drafted—he enlisted in the Air Corps early in January 1943, taking his Basic at Sheppard Field and leaving Savannah, Georgia, September 8th, 1944—to pilot a brand new Mitchell across the sea to India.

Shortly before Ots arrived in the CBI, Bill Plunkett had joined the squadron in Dergaon, India, in eastern Assam, where it had been operating since the end of August.

All during the 1944 Allied summer offensive against the entrenched Japanese in Burma, the 490th had been assisting ground troops by providing low level air support—strafing and bombing enemy troop concentrations and striking at the bridges leading into Myitkyina which was under siege by the Allies

On today's mission, Operations had assigned 2nd Lt. Donald Thorn as Plunkett's navigator. Like radio/gunner Otsie Malovich, Don Thorn was from Chicago. Thorn's mother, Agnes, was a widow, with two sons in the service—both in the Air Corps. She lived on south Loomis Avenue with her daughter, Eileen.

Agnes Thorn had sent her youngest son off to war with gifts of a fine camera and a black and gold Parker pen and pencil set with his name engraved on it. Don Thorn was not as experienced as Plunkett would have liked, but he'd heard nothing negative about the lieutenant's abilities.

Sgt. JD Cobb would be their engineer/gunner. Cobb was a short, stocky airman who'd joined the 490th as a corporal in September, part of a six-man crew that brought over a new J model from the States. JD's pilot had been Ed Mackay, and the copilot was Ernie Evenson.

Evenson and a crew of six were killed less than a week earlier, in a low-level attack against the same target they were going after today.

For some reason, JD Cobb had always gone by his first initials, and even the army wasn't certain of his given name. Aside from Otsie, he was the only other married man on the crew. His wife Edna lived on south Flower Street, in Santa Ana, California.

Engineer/gunner Cobb worked out of the dorsal turret and was thankful that these Mitchells carried no ball turret slung beneath the belly, as did the bigger B-17s. They were all familiar with the grim story of a crippled 8th Air Force flying fortress that was returning over the channel from a raid on Germany. The B-17's hydraulics had been damaged—rendering the landing gear inoperable. To the horror of the crew, the track that allowed the ball turret gunner to rotate his bubble and open the small exit door had been torn to pieces, too.

Making it back to the English coast with tears in his eyes, the pilot had had no choice but to make a wheels-up belly landing with his ball turret gunner trapped helplessly below.

Sgt. Adolph "Otsie" Malovich in Warazup, Burma.
This picture was taken by his tentmate, Sgt. Bob Hyde,
sometime during the winter of 1945.

Aboard #977, Sgt. Otsie Malovich was on the radio and waist guns, and at the tail they had armorer/gunner Sgt. Stephen Collins who'd volunteered for this particular mission, taking the place of a buddy who was sick.

The planes were to leave Warazup at 6:00 am that Thursday morning, staggered at fifteen-minute intervals. There were nine Mitchells on this day's mission—number 442. Their primary target was to bomb what remained of the heavily battered warehouse district at Kehsi Man Sam, then go on to sweep the surrounding roads with cannon and machine gun fire.

From November to February, the Japanese were being pushed back from their bases in the north. Kehsi Man Sam had become an important supply and staging area for them as they struggled to hang on in Burma. Because of this situation, it also became more and more of a priority target for the 490th.

Everyone in the squadron knew that Kehsi Man Sam was a longer distance away than many of their other targets. If they got into trouble there, the odds were high against making it back to Warazup.

Twelve planes had hit Kehsi Man Sam the day before, destroying about half the buildings there. They'd gone in at an altitude of two hundred and fifty feet, strafing and dropping more than a hundred and sixty-eight hundred pounders on the complex. Two trucks and nine oxcarts were also shot up on the nearby roads. The Mitchells received heavy machine gun fire, but mission leader, 1st Lt. Warren Mancke had brought the entire group home with no casualties or losses.

But Kehsi Man Sam was proving to be a spooky, bad luck target. The morning that Otsie and Steve Collins scrambled up through the rear hatch of number 977—Kehsi Man Sam had already cost the 490th eleven men and two aircraft.

Two weeks earlier, 2nd Lt. Elvin Bishop and his crew, 2nd Lt. Clyde Bauer, and Corporals Ed Farrell, Willis Rule, and Jim Hoenig, were killed when they crashed at Kehsi Man Sam while attacking it. The aircraft burned and exploded, but no ground fire was reported during its bomb run.

Sgt. Tom Harvey was flying his third mission that day. Operations had scheduled him to be on the lead ship with Lieutenant Bishop and Corporal Rule, but Jim Hoenig came by and asked him to swap planes because Hoenig had gone through school with Rule. The pilot said it would be OK, so the two of them traded places.

Hoenig and the rest of the crew died instantly in the exploding Mitchell, while Tom Harvey survived the war.

Once again, the fickle finger.

Nine days later, another small road bridge at Kehsi Man Sam was destroyed, but attacks on the main bridge were unsatisfactory. Mission leader, Capt. Rollin White, took eight Mitchells in against the bridges. The last plane to attack dropped its bombs and then hit a tree three hundred feet east of the target. The impact sheared off five feet of its right wing. The aircraft rolled belly-up and plunged to earth, exploding and instantly killing its six-man crew, 1st Lt. Ernie Evenson, 2nd Lieutenants Roswell Reno and John Kenner, S/Sgt. Ken McJury, Sgt. Jerry Hohner, and Cpl. Jim Martin.

*Steven Collins before the war.
Probably his class picture
from the University of Georgia.*

In the tail section this Thursday morning, Stephen Collins was settling in behind his guns. This was his 41st mission—the same amount as Otsie had.

Stephen's middle name was Mercer, after his mother's family, and back home in Cobbtown, that's what everyone called him—Mercer. But Warazup was a long way from Georgia, and in the CBI, it was just Steve.

His great-great grandfather Joseph Collins had brought a team and covered wagon out of Bertie County, North Carolina, settled in Tattnall

County, Georgia in the early 1800s and had five sons, one of whom was John—Stephen's great grandfather.

Ben L. Collins, Steve's father, had seven sisters and one brother, and was a rural mail carrier in Cobbtown. Stephen himself was a graduate of South Georgia Teacher's College and the University of Georgia. Before the war, he'd been a schoolteacher—bright and kind, according to the memories of his niece, Pat Moyle, who still keeps his medals—guiding children, giving tests, and grading homework.

Now he spent his days flying low-level bombing missions over heavily defended targets, arming and firing twin .50 caliber machineguns—the stinger in the hornet's tail. Collins had come over on the same operations order with JD Cobb, their engineer today, but Collins crossed the ocean in a different airplane—another new J model, piloted by 2nd Lt. Leslie Berry.

Otsie sat on the small drop-down bench near his starboard gun. As he felt the vibrations of the Mitchell's engines and waited for Bill Plunkett to take off, he was thinking about his own fears and the crews of Elvin Bishop and Ernie Evenson. Ots had known the enlisted men aboard both those planes, and he was feeling on edge and jumpy—he'd been that way for two weeks now.

"*I made my 35th mission yesterday,*" he wrote in a letter to Mildred ten days earlier. "*And honestly, I'm getting nervous as hell. If you can fly every day, it's okay. But if I lay off a day or two I hate to start over again. Guess you know how it is. Things happen now and then which don't help the situation at all. You don't have to worry about me sticking my neck out though, for I shrink to half my size.*"

If he was outwardly calm, it was a false front. He would do his job, but although each time a man went up it brought him closer to being rotated stateside, Otsie knew by now, as all of them did, that every flight you flew narrowed your odds against survival.

Well, most of them thought, with an easily acquired streak of fatalism, *you buy the ticket, you take the ride.*

18

The mission schedules had been posted the night before. The crews attended briefing that morning, receiving target information, intelligence, weather reports, and takeoff times. Like the others, Plunkett's crew did a careful walk around on aircraft number 977, while Sergeant Collins double-checked the bomb bay to make sure all ordnance was secure.

They had a little time to have a smoke and wrestle with their nerves while Plunkett went over last minute procedures, making sure everyone knew what was expected of them. Finally, he checked his watch.

"Okay guys, time to crank it up."

Plunkett, Thorn, and Cobb climbed up the front crew ladder, while Otsie and Steve Collins scrambled up through the aft hatch. The Mitchell they were flying today was an H—built two years before. The H carried a five-man aircrew consisting of what the army called multi-MOS (Military Occupational Skill) personnel. Only the pilot and tailgunner had single roles. The three other positions were navigator/cannoneer, engineer/dorsal gunner, and radioman/waist gunner.

It soon became an irreverent joke among the crews that this configuration enabled fewer people to fuck up more areas than ever before.

The H was a strafer, equipped with four fixed .50s in its solid nose, four more in individual blisters on each side of the fuselage, two flexible .50s in the top turret, and four more flexibles in the two waist gun positions and in the tail. In addition, it carried a 75mm cannon and a maximum bomb payload of four thousand pounds—making number

977 and other models like it, the deadliest twin-engined medium bombers of the war.

The B-25 strafer came in two configurations, the H and the later J— and each was a lethal piece of work. But the older model H, carrying four .50s and a 75mm cannon in the nose, was a two-sided coin. For the five man crews that flew them, their deadly potential could work both ways—against the crew as well as against the Japanese. The H model strafers made the crews edgy. They liked the massive firepower you could bring to bear with the devastating 75, but no one thought much of the aircraft's lack of dual controls. The strafers were often the lead ships—the first ones in—blazing away and tearing up enemy defenses with their concentrated fire. But at the altitudes they were flying, they were exposed to heavy ground fire—usually a lot of it. The Japanese gun crews were firing 20mm machine cannons up at them, along with heavier 75mm antiaircraft ordnance.

Heavy fire from the ground could easily hit the pilot and if that happened, most H crews figured they'd bought the farm. At the altitudes they were flying, there would be little chance of anyone else aboard being able to wrestle a dead or badly wounded pilot out of the left seat and taking control.

Don Harkins says that on a low level mission, most of the navigators felt that there would be no way the navigator could reach over, pull the pilot out, climb into the pilot's seat, and gain control in time to avoid a crash. Although everybody agreed that they'd damn well give it one hell of a try.

At medium altitude and with help from the engineer/gunner, they thought it might have been possible, but the H crews didn't think much of going up with only a single pilot, and the pilots knew it. Some of them, the smarter ones, made it a point to encourage their navigators to fly the aircraft. Don remembers that he got a lot of stick time, including instrument flying. This made for a happier crew, knowing there was a navigator who could bring the plane back if the pilot was killed.

Buy the ticket, take the ride.

Behind the armored-floor of the nose, #977 was divided. Topside was the flight deck and the dorsal turret position, while the lower level consisted of a narrow tunnel about four feet high leading to the front entry hatch.

Plunkett and Thorn sat side-by-side, amid a maze of dials and switches, knobs and indicators, lights, various buttons, and gauges whose functions controlled the airplane. The main instrument panel was forward, while the rheostats, power-plant controls, and emergency hydraulic selector valve were to Plunkett's right.

Above and to the rear of the flight deck was engineer-turret gunner, Sgt. JD Cobb, manning twin fifties with four hundred rounds each.

Malovich and Collins were separated by only fifteen or twenty feet, but they were isolated from the flight deck and from Cobb in the top turret, by the bulkhead of the bomb bay. Communication was by intercom.

Bill Plunkett settled in his seat and checked his watch as he went through preflight check. Seeing they were on schedule with their preassigned takeoff time, Plunkett pushed his mixture to full rich, set the props, clicked the booster pumps to on, snapped the energizer switch to the right, primed the starboard engine, waited twenty seconds, then flicked the toggle to start position.

The engine whined, coughed, and then caught—running roughly for a moment before smoothing out. Going through the same procedure, he fired the port engine and the medium bomber shook with the vibration of three thousand horsepower.

Lowering the flaps to fifteen degrees, he kept an eye on his oil gauges as the two Wrights warmed up at twelve hundred RPM. Plunkett had to make certain that the oil temperature showed an increase, and that their oil pressure held steady at forty pounds per square inch.

As they taxied into position, the morning sun glared through the pitted and scratched windshield, making both the pilot and navigator grateful for their army-issue Ray-Bans.

Out of Warazup, the gulls always took off and landed to the north. As mission leader, Plunkett's was the lead plane. When he was ready, he put flaps full down and set his stabilizer at three-quarters. The Mitchell was tail-heavy with full power against the brakes. When they were suddenly released, the shuddering plane lurched ahead, trundling slowly forward at first, then gathering more and more speed as Plunkett eased back on the yoke and lifted the bomber up and over the trees, closely followed by their wingman in the second plane.

The pilots brought up their landing gear and raised flaps. Both aircraft climbed to the north for about four minutes, reaching for altitude and giving the others a little time to get off the deck and into position before turning south again and passing over the field toward the warehouses at Kehsi Man Sam.

At seven thousand feet, they leveled out, backing off the flaps and throttling back to save fuel, adjusting power settings and checking their position.

Once in the air, Otsie, Collins, and Cobb put a few short bursts through their guns to check them. Looking out the small bay windows on either side of the fuselage, Otsie could see the rugged terrain of northern Burma as it fell away below. He saw the land blanketed by rectangular fields in which farmers plowed, plodding slowly behind huge carabao, occasionally stopping to wave as the climbing bombers passed overhead.

Their primary target was what was left of the Japanese warehouse district—those buildings that hadn't been hit the day before. They hated to revisit the same target the next day. The enemy was always ready and ground fire was usually heavy.

They continued on a southeast course at seven thousand feet, flying over the Namyin and Shweli Rivers and past previous targets—Bhamo,

Namhkam, Hsenwi, and the railhead at Lashio, which was where they crossed the Yao River, heading for the target.

Twenty minutes later, Thorn called out over the roar of the engines. "Kehsi Man Sam dead on at thirty miles out."

They were closing.

"Roger that," Plunkett said, pointing the nose down and beginning a descent to fifteen hundred feet.

As they neared the ground, warm air updrafts began to slam into the aircraft. Otsie hated rough air and felt his stomach knot as they began to bounce around. Descending down through it, the aircraft smoothed out, and he now saw only a green blur of jungle hurtling past beneath the starboard wing.

Plunkett had just checked the oil temp and pressure gauges for the last time. Satisfied with these, he was now flying by feel, his eyes glued straight ahead, searching for the targets still quite a distance off.

More than three miles out from the bridge, scattered and hidden in the trees, light small-arms fire began coming up at them, along with a few Japanese batteries firing 20mm machine cannons. The enemy anti-aircraft gunners tracked the Mitchells that were boring down on the warehouses, trying to lead the bombers just as Otsie had once learned to lead fast-flying mallards with his 12-gauge pump gun.

Now the intercom began to crackle.

"Right side waist! Get those fifties going. Tail, cover our ass."

They could already feel the shudder of the six fixed .50s hammering out bursts from the nose. From up above in the dorsal turret, Sergeant Cobb pounded away with his two guns, raining hot, empty shell casings down onto the flight deck's floor.

Suddenly they were bouncing around in rough air again—coming in so low over the trees that Otsie felt his stomach turn and sicken.

As they closed on Kehsi Man Sam, the ground-fire intensified. Plunkett wasn't even messing with the 75mm cannon. The target wasn't right for it and he was too busy lining things up.

Seated next to him, Don Thorn was frantically trying to spot the tracers arching up from ground fire positions so that either Plunkett or Cobb could nail them with the .50s. At the same time, Thorn was trying to keep his eyes on the other Mitchells that were approaching—so that there'd be no collisions—and figuring out an emergency escape route out of the target area in case they lost an engine or had one taken out by ground fire.

At the waist and tail guns, Otsie and Steve Collins each hung on to their bucking .50s as they squeezed off heavy bursts at the Japanese ground positions flashing by just below them.

They rocketed above the green canopy of jungle so fast it seemed as if they might easily overshoot their target.

The hammering of the nose guns kept on, and both waist and tail guns were pounding away as well. As they closed on the warehouses, Plunkett could see that a few of the buildings were still smoking from fires set the day before.

He quit the fixed .50s and turned his attention to his bombsight. Once he activated the bomb bay, the doors were opened into the slipstream and the crew felt a tremendous drag and heard the labored howl of the Wrights as they struggled to overcome the inward rush of air.

Plunkett lined up the target in his sight and fought to keep the Mitchell steady as his eyes darted quickly from direction indicator to air speed indicator to altimeter and then back to his indicator again. Now the bomb release lit up—*blink, blink, blink*—and the crew felt each bomb snap free of its shackles.

What happened then will always remain a mystery.

19

Ken Shugart wrote about the mission in his diary that day: *Plane #977 went over the target and continued south...must be the controls or pilot were hit by ground fire. It never turned back.*

The words written in Bill Hilgefort's diary hit even closer to home: *Bad luck still with us. Today it was Plunkett, my tent mate...went out at six this morning to bomb Kehsi Man Sam and sweep the roads. Was last seen at the target...no radio contact.*

The official 490th Bomb Squadron mission report for February 15, 1945 stated: *15 Feb. 1945—What remained of the warehouse district at Kehsi Man Sam was wiped out by nine B-25s which dropped 216 100 lb bombs from low level of 300 feet. Buildings to the south were also attacked, several being destroyed by direct hits and fires. The entire area was strafed on the bomb run. Two other planes sprinkled 48 100lb bombs on the personnel area at Loilem. A few direct hits on buildings were noted but extent of damage is unknown. The area was also strafed. Meager, inaccurate machine gun fire was encountered. One plane was hit in the propeller by a .25 caliber bullet. Source of fire was not known.*

One plane failed to return from the mission.

It was last seen near Kehsi Man Sam at 0930 hrs, under control and not in distress. Reason for failing to return is unknown. Crew as follows: 1st Lt. W.B. Plunkett, pilot; 2nd Lt. D.E. Thorn, navigator; Sgt. J.D. Cobb, engineer-gunner; Sgt. A. Malovich, radio-gunner; Sgt. S.M. Collins, armorer-gunner.

This was the fourth plane and crew lost during the month, an anytime high for the squadron. Previous top had been three crews in any one month.

The missing Lt. Plunkett was mission leader. Flight leaders were 1st Lts. L.V. Berry, C.A. Farrand, G.K. Hannaford, 2nd Lt. J.C.Petree and F/O Fjeldheim. Mission No. was 442.

The official mission report states that ground fire was meager and ineffective, but it often didn't take much. Clyde Dyar remembers the time in China, when a B-24 made an emergency landing. The pilot, a young major, was dead in the left seat with a single bullet wound that had entered under his chin and smashed into his brain. The round had ripped up through the aircraft's floor—directly between the pilot's feet. Later, on looking the Liberator over, ground crews found that this was the only bullet hole on the entire airplane.

An additional report said: *"This aircraft departed Warazup, Burma, enroute to Kehsi Man Sam, on a bombing run and strafing mission. No word has been received from Search and Rescue in regard to this missing plane and crew.*

And the following is a somewhat contradictory statement from Lt. William H. Dugan on 15 February 1945: *"I was in aircraft #781 and approaching our intended target from the east. About two miles from the target I met #977 flying east. He had evidently already dropped his bombs. His altitude was approximately 800 feet and I could see visible signs of trouble. I tried to call the pilot, Lt. Plunkett, to tell him that the weather was extremely bad on the route he was taking. I received no answer. That was the last time I saw the plane. There were numerous thunderstorms in the area toward which he was heading and quite a bit of turbulence. Visibility was also very poor. The approximate time I saw this plane was at 0930 hours."*

*1st Lt. William Dugan.
He was the last man to see
Mitchell # 977 still in the air.*

Why wouldn't Bill Plunkett have answered Dugan's call? Was the radio knocked out? Was Plunkett already dead, or too badly wounded to operate his radio? Maybe Thorn was hit, too—unable to navigate, unable to get a dead pilot out of the left seat.

Whatever was happening inside that aircraft, #977 stayed in the air and traveled east as far from the target as Tang Yan, where the airplane finally plunged to earth.

Adolph Malovich and Stephen Collins—both isolated behind the bomb bay bulkhead in the Mitchell's fuselage—rode it down together.

Ten days later, another bulletin dated Feb. 25, 1945, stated that: *"word was received by Air Jungle Rescue that this plane crashed as a result of engine failure. On reaching the scene of the accident, two bodies were found hanging in a tree from parachutes. Further investigation has failed to reveal any additional information, and MARC# 12381 lists all the crew as dead."*

In regard to #977, this report was erroneous.

Five days before Plunkett went down, on an attack against the Laihka Bridge, 2nd Lt. Al Dugas lost an engine on his bomb run. Dugas salvoed his ordnance and the mission's lead ship attempted to give him navigational assistance as he struggled with the crippled Mitchell. Dugas disappeared into bad weather and was thought to have attempted a crash landing. His plane was eventually located on the ground, nosed in and broken in two. It hadn't burned on impact and nearby were two parachutes, partly opened, with the bodies still in harness. Along with Lieutenant Dugas, the crew consisted of 2nd Lt. Bob Nelson, Sgt. R.E. Barnes, Cpl. H.W. Gorham, and Cpl. Don Mathews.

I'm convinced that this was the aircraft described in the bulletin of Feb. 25th.

Otsie's last mission is filled with unknowns.

Line chief Clyde Dyar wrote: *"I can't remember your uncle after all these years although I sure remember the loss of the B-25, February 15, 1945. I remember that there were conflicting reports of what happened. This was a low-level mission with the bombs equipped with delayed action fuses. Also, the bombs were a new type that had been known to explode by just dropping them on the ground without a fuse being installed. Some thought the bomb dropped by the lead plane may have exploded early, or the bomb on your uncle's plane exploded on contact with the ground. No one really knows for sure..."*

In three official letters to Zoe over a twenty two-month period in 1946 and 47, the army stumbled over its own feet trying to explain the reasons that caused the crash. On January 27, 1946, Brig. Gen. Leon W. Johnson wrote: *"...during this mission, Sgt. Malovich's bomber was returning from the target after the bombs had been released and was last seen at 8:30 a.m., about two miles east of Kehsi Man Sam flying in an easterly direction at an altitude of eight hundred feet. The pilot of another aircraft attempted to contact Sgt. Malovich's plane by radio to warn the pilot of unfavorable weather conditions, but the message was not acknowledged. Inasmuch as Sgt. Malovich's plane was not seen or contacted by radio after this time the circumstances surrounding its disappearance are not known. However, the plane may have been lost as a result of inclement weather as there were numerous thunderstorms and excessive turbulence in the area towards which it was heading. It is regretted that no further information is available in this headquarters relative to Sgt. Malovich's disappearance."*

This letter seems to correspond with Bill Dugan's original report on the day of the crash. However, nineteen months later, Zoe received a second letter from Maj. Gen. Edward F. Witsell, Adjutant General of the Army: *"The aircraft was last seen in the vicinity of Kehsi Man Sam, apparently in no difficulty. A Search and Recovery team later recovered human remains from the wreckage of a plane in the vicinity of Kehsi Man Sam but no individual identification could be established. According to information submitted by a native local official, while the plane was making bomb runs on bridges in the above-mentioned area, it was caught in its own blast during a low run, at which time it crashed and burned. He further stated that no other plane crash was reported in his state..."*

If number 977 was caught in its own bomb blast as this second letter states, and as Clyde Dyar has speculated, why did the official squadron report state that: *"...it was last seen near Kehsi Man Sam at 0930 hrs, under control and not in distress. Reason for failing to return is unknown..."*

Don Harkins takes a different view. In speculating on it, he writes: *"What I don't understand is why Plunkett would have been so close to the target area after he'd bombed. Under normal conditions, he would have vacated the area and been miles away looking for other targets. Did he violate the rule of clearing the area for other incoming planes? Plunkett was far more experienced than that. Thorn was rather inexperienced as a navigator. Did he get lost? Why was Plunkett going east from the primary target when the better targets (of opportunity) were elsewhere, and when Warazup was to the north?*

Engine failure would have to be from enemy fire. I never heard of two engines failing (at the same time) and the B-25 could have certainly made it far out of the target area on one engine, again unless Thorn was confused about his location..."

In a later e-mail, after reading the correspondence from Generals Johnson and Witsell, Don goes on to say: *"If the plane was at 900 feet or 500 feet, it really doesn't matter. What does matter is why Plunkett didn't respond to the radio call. Why would he have dropped low-level when he was carrying instant-fused bombs that would have brought the plane down? It makes me wonder if Plunkett himself had been hit by ground fire, and the plane was out of control. If it was a B-25H there was no dual control and there was no way the navigator could have pulled Plunkett out of the left seat and taken control when they were so low..."*

In June 1999, Ed Tengler—once the 490th's CO—answered my letter to him concerning the crash and loss of crew. *"It is quite possible that I could have flown some missions, of which I had almost a hundred, with your uncle as the radio gunner aboard. If my memory is correct, the B-25 crashed on the return from a mission. Another crew saw the crash and after getting a report from them, we sent another B-25 to the scene but they couldn't find any signs of survivors.*

In the CBI at that time we had some Air-Sea Rescue operations that immediately took over... they had light planes and even a chopper or two that could land in the area... Burma is a rugged country. Lots of jungle and the countryside was described as being like a washboard. Finding a level place for a forced landing was always a real challenge..."

An unofficial flight, the plane and crew that Tengler sent out to search consisted of his tentmates, Sgt. Bob Hyde and Sgt. Harold Peppeard, along with pilot, 1st. Lt. Ken Schaible, and navigator Orville Christensen—four of Otsie's original stateside crew. They were never able to locate the wreckage and whatever happened that long ago day, no one would ever know.

20

By early spring of 1945, tactically and strategically, the Japanese in Burma were defeated. The squadron hadn't left a single supply line into Northern Burma intact. The Japanese had been cut off and now it was they, with no air power and no supplies, who were on the retreat. By late March, the Bridge Busters had just about run out of decent targets and it was determined that the squadron had completed its mission in Burma.

Capt. Ed Tengler. Commanding Officer of the squadron in China. Back from a mission.

In April 1945, Lt. Colonel Erdin was transferred to HQ, 10th Air Force. Now it was Capt. Ed Tengler who would assume command, and it would be his job to move the Bridge Busters from Burma into China.

On April 12th, as the squadron was busying itself to relocate from the Warazup base to a new one in Hanchung, word was received that at Warm Springs, Georgia, earlier in the day, Franklin Delano Roosevelt had died from a massive cerebral hemorrhage.

The news raced through Warazup like a wildfire. Most of the men were stunned. Roosevelt had been president of the United States since most of them were young boys still in school. They knew no other political leader.

That evening was subdued, quiet, as most of them pondered the future of the war with FDR gone.

The last mission from Warazup was an uneventful leaflet drop.

They'd be transferred into Chennault's 14th Air Force and rejoin their old group, the 341st, which had been sent to China many months before.

A few days before the 490th was scheduled to go over the "Hump," General Davidson paid them a visit. He thanked all those who were gathered around him for their heroic efforts in Burma, and with tears in his eyes, bid a sad farewell to his favorite squadron.

In Mid-April, the squadron left Warazup for Hanchung, China. The air echelon made the move in their B-25s and a few C-47s, while the ground echelon arrived thirty eight days later, having traveled over the Ledo and Burma Roads and over mountain passes almost fourteen thousand feet high. The convoy commander, Ordnance Officer, 1st Lt. Gabe Szabo brought thirty-two of his original thirty-nine trucks through. With him were two other officers and almost eighty enlisted men.

John Poister still remembers his abortive flight from Warazup to China and back to Warazup again, when they were brought back in their crippled airplane by flight surgeon Doc Wadsworth who calmed the nervous pilot and convinced him that bailing out wasn't necessary.

As the crew was jettisoning all their gear out the back door in an effort to cut weight and gain altitude, Poister recalls being handed a medium-sized wooden box marked "Blood Plasma."

Figuring they'd need all of their medical supplies in the likely event of a crash landing in the jungle, he didn't heave it out the door but rather pulled it aside in the nick of time.

When they finally brought the aircraft back to Warazup, Poister learned that box he thought was plasma had magically turned into beefsteak. They had a real beef and bourbon party that night in their tent—hosted by their grinning flight surgeon.

When they arrived in China, the 490th joined Brig. Gen. Russell Randall's 312th—the West China Raiders, a well-known 14th Air Force fighter wing.

As they settled in at Hanchung, another news bulletin came over their radios. Adolf Hitler was dead—a suicide in his Berlin bunker. A week later, German General Alfred Jodl signed an unconditional surrender of all German armed forces at General Eisenhower's headquarters in Reims. The next day, May 8th, was declared V-E Day—the European war was over.

To the men who'd been fighting in the Pacific, the news was welcome, but curiously far removed. The war in Europe hadn't been their war, and most felt that the news of its end would have little impact on their lives.

They still had the Japanese to deal with. They'd all heard of the butchery at places like Tarawa and Iwo Jima, and of the fighting still raging on Okinawa. Throughout Asia and the Pacific, the Japanese were dying hard. Whatever else was said of them, the Japanese had always managed to die hard. The 490th still had their war to fight.

There wasn't much to the Hanchung Base at first, but it slowly grew and improved. In June, the Special Services section put up a recreation building that had a game room and ping pong tables, a small library and reading room, and a supply room for baseball, touch football and volleyball equipment.

When it wasn't serving meals, the mess hall stayed open to serve coffee and donuts on nights when no movies were available. Overworked mess personnel did the best they could to serve decent food with what little they had. Any variety of fresh fruits or vegetables was virtually nonexistent.

Most of the food was being requisitioned from local farmers. A mess team paid the squadron a visit in order to improve the chow. Soup began to be served at every noon meal, and a single toaster was installed in the center of the hall.

An administration building was put up and quickly occupied by Headquarters, Quartermaster Supply, and the Medical Section. When the injections were made available, the squadron medics were kept busy giving shots for typhus and plague to all air and ground personnel.

Along with movies three or four nights a week, the sports program was becoming better organized, too. The Bridge Busters had two baseball teams—one made up of officers and the other of enlisted men. That spring and summer in China, the enlisted men led the league with three wins and no losses.

On July 27th, the Bridge Busters held a banquet, using the squadron fund to buy everything they needed. It was to be a welcome break to the fear and tedium of a long war.

Along with sliced corned beef, a baked duck dinner with all the trimmings was served. They rustled up juice, and soup, turkey salad, baked dressing, and cranberry sauce, sweet pickles, creamed corn and mashed potatoes. Along with coffee, they had canned peaches for desert. Somebody produced Chinese champagne, which proved popular and was soon in short supply. Even menus were designed, printed, and numbered.

At the end of the meal, a short program was given by the officers and enlisted men. It included a few ribald stories and a lot of jokes. Finally, a one-act skit was put on, written and directed by Sgt. Charles Thomas, with organ accompaniment by Pfc George Myfelt. At the end of the evening, door prizes were given to those who held lucky numbered menus.

While they'd been in Burma, ordnance would issue shells and the few shotguns the squadron had. Because fresh meat was scarce, pilot Harry DePew and a few of the others would go hunting for "Burma Chickens." These were black jungle birds that looked like chickens and were pretty good eating.

One of the officer's tents had a gasoline cook stove and a large, heavy frying pan. They'd cook the plucked and cleaned birds in grease from the mess hall and eat them with their fingers.

They did the same thing in China, but here the game was the colorful and familiar ringneck pheasant. Having no shotguns, the Chinese were never able to hunt them so they ran around like tame birds.

Hoping for at least a little sport, Harry and the others would have little Chinese kids run through the fields like bird dogs and flush the ringnecks so that the GIs could shoot them on the fly.

Along with pilot Bill Dugan and bombardier Bill Short, Harry would often get a jeep from the motor pool and take it up into the mountains that ringed the Hanchung base. It was a rare outing when they didn't come home with a jeep full of fat birds.

"Practically all of us had dysentery," DePew recalls. "And everybody welcomed fresh, uncontaminated meat. Some of us suffered severe weight loss. Ed MacKay normally weighed around a hundred and eighty pounds, but he was now down to one forty-five. Our Flight Surgeon, Dr. Wadsworth, told us that sulfa drugs wouldn't do any good because we'd just get sick over and over again."

Line Chief Clyde Dyar (r) with their tent boy in Hanchung, China.

Even though the squadron was settling in, Commanding Officer Tengler was soon faced with many problems. Many of the unit's key personnel, both in the air and on the ground, had been rotated back to the States. The squadron was full of new men who had to be broken in on their jobs. The aircrews were flying over terrain that was unfamiliar, but just as dangerous as that of Burma.

To Tengler's annoyance, people kept telling him that the 490th had seen their time in the sun: "Your boys may have pasted a lot of bridges in Burma," some were saying. "But things are a lot different here—the bridges in China are flak traps."

"Hell, you guys have lost all your old men," was another common opinion. "From now on, you'll be running on your reputation. Things are a lot different here in China."

It was true, Tengler worried, that the targets were much more heavily defended in China, and the bridges were bigger, longer, and better built. But to the CO's satisfaction, on their first mission out of

Hanchung the Mitchells that were still wearing the Skull and Wings blew apart twelve spans of the Chungou Railroad Bridge, a vital link on the Tung Pu railway and one of the most important Japanese supply routes into China.

The crews hadn't lost their touch.

Or their sense of humor. The runway at Hanchung ran directly east and west. The jury-rigged tower was made of empty 55-gallon avgas drums stacked in a pyramid five or six high. Regulations stated that before crossing the runway, one had to get permission from the tower.

Line chief Clyde Dyar remembers that one afternoon, a good 'ol boy from Mississippi called the tower. "Hello towah," the voice drawled. "Ah'm on the north end 'o the east-west runway. If you'all heah me, give me the green light."

Barely able to keep from laughing, the tower operator answered: "You'all ain't where you think you is, but go ahead anyway."

And yet, fate still reached out its bony finger to claim more lives. Even during the squadron's short stint in China, two more planes and crews were lost.

On May 10th, in an attack on the Ping Han Bridge with fighter escorts, 1st Lt. John Pennington's Mitchell was hit by ground fire and crashed. 2nd Lieutenant Wichmann was in the right seat, while engineer and top turret gunner Sgt. John Lees and Corporals Jess Smith and Gene Falkowski were also lost.

Harry DePew still remembers the mission. Pennington was his buddy and their mission leader that day. "John was first plane in," Harry recalls. "I was second. We followed each other in about twenty seconds apart. Our thousand pounders were fused with an eight to ten second delay and we had to be careful not to get sucked into each other's bomb blast and flying debris.

"The bridge and railyard was heavily defended that day. To minimize our exposure to ground fire after we released our bombs the technique was to break to the right, hug the ground, and go like a bat out of hell.

"But John continued straight in because it was customary for the lead ship to strafe and knock out as much opposition as possible. From both sides of the rail yard, we could see hundreds of tracer rounds lined up on him. His right engine started to smoke, but by then, I was concentrating on the target. When we finally pulled out, I couldn't see John, so I tried to radio him.

"The voice that came back was one of the fighter boys. 'It's all over for him,' the voice said. 'That black smoke about five miles away is him. His gas tank exploded and blew the right wing off.'

"That night," DePew says. "I drank way too much."

And twenty days later, on a strafing mission against Sincheng Bridge, 1st Lt. Bob Hanson, along with his entire crew was lost to enemy fire.

Another mission Harry DePew remembers was out of Sian, China. It was a high altitude raid against the large railroad yard and repair depot at Kaifeng. There were four gulls on this mission, each of them carrying twenty four hundred-pound bombs. Fifteen or twenty minutes out from the target, flying on strict radio silence and deep into Japanese-held territory, the flight received a radio message.

It was an English-speaking voice, Harry remembers, and the man was asking to speak to mission leader Ed MacKay.

"I know your commanding officer, Major Tengler," the voice insisted. "I had dinner with him last week."

"That a fact?" Captain MacKay said. He and the others were suspicious. A great many Japanese spoke excellent English, and it wasn't impossible that somehow the enemy had learned the name of the 490th's CO.

Finally, after a great deal of pleading by the voice on the radio, MacKay decided to take a chance.

"OK, go ahead."

"I'm with the OSS," the man said. "I'm here at the Kaifeng yards. The Japs have moved most of their locomotives, ammunition, and boxcars into large sheds a mile or so from Kaifeng. If you bomb the yards it will be a waste of ordnance."

"That so?" MacKay said, talking to the man further, drawing him out and trying to make sure that whoever it was, the voice was on the up and up. Finally, the captain was convinced the man was who he said he was and the flight changed course, with the voice directing them from somewhere on the ground with the use of high-powered binoculars.

When MacKay's raiders dropped their bombs, the voice on the ground became excited. "I see your bombs falling," the man said. "They look good. But I've got to get the hell out of here."

Capt. Ed MacKay
At Warazup, 1945

That was the end of his radio transmission, and when their bombs slammed home, Harry DePew remembers, there were large explosions, fires, and great, greasy columns of coal-black smoke that billowed up to nine or ten-thousand feet. They later learned from Intelligence that their mission had destroyed seven locomotives, along with ammunition and oil tanker cars that had been hidden away in large sheds—just as the mysterious OSS man had told them.

One particular Hanchung mission still stands out in Clyde Dyar's mind: "Lt. Bert Snow, the best pilot I ever flew with, was on a search and destroy mission in an H model—with the big 75mm and all its bristling .50s. This was strictly a strafing mission with no bombs aboard. Their targets were railroad tracks, rolling stock, rail yards, and flak towers. Their record for the day was a hundred and fifty miles of track destroyed, six flak towers blown to bits, three rail yards and four locomotives hit.

"When Bert brought his plane back to Hanchung," Clyde remembers. "He was out of ammunition, his windshield and side windows had been shattered by flying debris, and there was telephone wire wrapped around the right engine. They came home a tired, but happy crew!"

But everybody was pretty certain there was more to come. There was a lot of talk and anxiety about rumored future missions against the Yellow River Bridge—one of the most important, and heavily defended, in Japanese-occupied China. And true to rumor, crews and airplanes were sent to Hsian to go after it. Most of the squadron had the willies about this target, and a lot of them thought the mission to be suicidal. The bridge was very heavily defended and in the past, flights of B-29s hadn't been able to take it out.

The squadron was flying against an increasingly desperate enemy. By this late in the war, the Japanese were stubbornly hanging on by their fingernails. From the first of June through early August, the 315th Bomb Wing of the 501st Bomb Group had hit nine different Japanese oil refineries on Honshu a total of fifteen times.

Rumor had it that there wasn't enough gasoline left in the home islands to run a motorbike through Tokyo.

The 490th was hurting too, and the first priorities at Hanchung were gasoline and ammo, medical supplies, spare parts, and clothing.

A total of twenty-one raids would be flown against the Japanese from the 490th's new base in China, and although no one was aware of it at the time, on August 4th, 1945, the squadron flew its last mission—resulting in the destruction of the Sinyang Bridge.

As he began the Potsdam Conference with Winston Churchill and Josef Stalin on July 17th, President Harry Truman learned of the successful test of an atomic bomb in the New Mexico desert the day before. He immediately called a meeting of his staff to discuss the import of this terrible new weapon.

One of the president's first questions was to his Chief of Staff, Gen. George C. Marshall. What would it cost us, Truman asked, to invade the Japanese mainland?

A minimum quarter of a million casualties, Marshall answered without hesitation. Perhaps as much as a million on the American side alone, with as many casualties among the Japanese.

Truman then turned to Secretary of War Stimson and asked which sites in Japan were presently devoted to war production.

Hiroshima, among others, Stimson replied. And Nagasaki.

In the small hours of the morning on August 6th, almost three thousand nautical miles east of the 490th's base at Hanchung, three bomber crews took their last sips of coffee and swung up into the aluminum bellies of their silver B-29s. The lead ship, overly heavy with its top secret cargo had been christened the *Enola Gay,* in honor of the pilot's mother.

Capt. Richard H. Johnson. The squadron's last CO. From September to November of 1945. He was to bring them home.

In the darkness, and followed by two observation planes loaded down with heavy cameras and scientific instruments, the Enola Gay lumbered heavily down runway Able on North Field and slowly lifted off from the tiny island of Tinian, in the northern Marianas.

With Col. Paul W. Tibbets, Jr., commander of the 509th Bomb Group, in the left seat, navigator Capt. Ted Van Kirk put the heavy bomber on a steady northwest course over the Philippine Sea and toward the Japanese city of Hiroshima.

At 8:15 a.m., a single atomic bomb, nicknamed *Little Boy*, was dropped over the center of the city. It's initial blast immediately killed eighty thousand people, injured another seventy thousand, and leveled half the city's structures.

The atomic bombing of Nagasaki occurred three days later, when, at 3:37 in the morning, three more American B-29s took off from Tinian. One of them, piloted by Maj. Charles Sweeney, was named *Bock's Car* and carried a ten thousand-pound plutonium bomb named *Fat Man*.

Sweeney's bomb killed almost forty thousand and injured a similar number. As at Hiroshima, half of Nagasaki was obliterated.

Shortly after the second bomb destroyed Nagasaki, Captain Tengler received orders to cease all offensive action. There would be no more combat missions for the tired crews of the Burma Bridge Busters.

On August 14th, the *Domei* News Agency announced that the Japanese government, with Tokyo in flames and two of its major cities flattened beyond belief, had reluctantly decided to accept President Truman's Potsdam Ultimatum and it's unconditional terms of surrender.

Back in the States and throughout the Pacific, people went wild with joy and relief. Radio/gunner Francis Posey was home on a 45-day leave. He got married on August 1st and with the announcement of Japan's surrender, he and his wife drove into town and Francis suddenly found himself leading a parade.

Until the ammo ran out, the news caused a lot of gunfire at the Hanchung base, and armorer George Townsend spent thirty minutes under his bunk praying that he wouldn't be hit by friendly fire on the day the war ended.

It was true. The war was over.

From their inception in February 1943, the Burma Bridge Busters had flown a total of six hundred and fifteen missions, and dropped over eleven million pounds of bombs.

In two and a half years of combat operations, the 490th hit every type of target under every conceivable condition. They flew in monsoons, over high, jagged mountains, thick, steaming jungles, against skilled Japanese fighters and through heavy curtains of enemy fire—and they did it over some of the most dangerous, least hospitable terrain on earth.

In two years, the Burma Bridge Busters emerged as one of the most distinguished bombardment units of the war. In its history, the squadron accounted for a hundred eighty-seven bridges destroyed and fifty-three more badly damaged. On the entrenched Japanese in Burma, the squadron cost the enemy thousands of casualties, while blasting to pieces his supply lines, his communications, fortifications, and his hopes for conquest in southeast Asia.

The 490th also suffered one hundred and fifty-four men killed or missing in action. This was in a small unit that fought a largely unheralded war and that rarely had more than fifteen operational aircraft at any one time.

But these statistics, however impressive, fall far short of describing the men who made them a reality. This was a small group of young Americans who came together in a far-off corner of the world—with the task of waging war against a fanatical and well-trained enemy determined to overrun and plunder the resources of China, Burma, and India.

In spite of their youth, and despite the isolation of being half way around the world from everything they knew, and everyone they loved, every member of the squadron accepted the risks, and many sacrificed their lives.

In a horror of fire, impact, and twisted steel, they died for places named Nawnghkio, Laihka, Kadu, and Kehsi Man Sam—nondescript places that don't appear on most maps, and probably never will.

"Back then, we were all just kids," 1st Lt. Don Harkins recalls from a time now more than half a century distant from his service in Burma.

And as Capt. Howard Bell has written with unsettling candor: "The men of the 490th, thrust into a forgotten theater by chance, fought and died without rancor—as was normal in those days."

What greater tribute could be paid?

Epilogue—Grand Rapids

III

"Harold Ludeman," Boogie intones. "Ludeman...Ludeman."

"Robert Kapika. Kapika...Kapika."

In a voice that has begun to crack, he completes the silent roll and turns to Clyde Dyar at the podium. "We have twelve men missing, sir," Boogie says in his deep, West Texas drawl. "I fear they are lost."

As I look around me at this banquet that is taking place more than half a century after the events in this book occurred, I realize with great regret that the closest I'll ever be able to get to my uncle is now—in this Holiday Inn ballroom in Grand Rapids, Michigan—among these men still living, some of whom undoubtedly flew with him, hit the same targets, fought the same enemy, and harbored the same fears.

These are the lucky ones I'm spending the evening with tonight. Fate reached out and gave them a pass to come back home and live long, full lives. To them and to those who never returned, the rest of us owe something beyond imagining.

Don Harkins once put his feelings into words in an e-mail to me: *You can hardly imagine the weight lifted off my shoulders when the Flight Surgeon came to my tent one afternoon in February of '45. He sat down and talked awhile, about nothing much, then smiled and told me 'Harkins, you're grounded from combat. You'll be going home in a few days—start packing.'*

Amen to that, I thought. But you know—my heart still breaks whenever I think about those who weren't as lucky. Bless their souls, they were the real heros.

This generation of aged warriors, these unassuming old men who were barely out of high school when they fought their war, are now leaving us at the rate of eleven hundred a day.

In awe and sadness, I look around the room, at each of their faces, and I think how incredibly well they did the terrible job that was given them.

This nation will be fortunate to ever see their like again.

So, among all the squadron's losses, the nation's losses, then and since, my uncle and four other good men died that February Burma morning in 1945. Five young lives were casually spent in the winning of a war. In the big picture, the grand scheme of things, their loss meant little except to those back home who loved and cared for them.

In the aftermath of the war, and for a good number of years thereafter, people throughout America and throughout the world, mourned lost sons, fathers, and brothers.

Bill Plunkett died owing $200 to a buddy, 1st Lt. Julius Williams, who was in the 81st Squadron, 12th Bomb Group. Bill borrowed the money the day before he went down—the debt was later settled by his estate.

Otsie's personal effects were sent to the wrong address. The Effects Quartermaster wrote 'Hamilton' instead of 'Hamlin' Avenue. At the time, no such street existed in Chicago.

Don Thorn's mother was a widow, poor, uneducated, and extremely saddened when she received what remained of her son's belongings:

Oct. 7th, 1946
Colonel Glenn Ross:

Dear Sir,

I read your article in the Southtown Economist about sending men to search for missing men in Burma-India. Dear sir, you will be looking for my son. Lt. Donald E. Thorn was a navigator/bombardier on a B-25 Mitchell bomber, was with the 490th Bombing Squadron, lost over in that territory. He was lost February 15th, 1945 (and was listed as missing since) although officially reported dead.

I am so heartbroken over losing him. I am a widow nine years. All alone now. My oldest son is a regular Army aviation man in Quito, Ecuador. He is in the service nine years.

So you see, I do feel badly over the loss of my son, especially not knowing anything about him. I know his soul is saved, and that his body is only a cloak for his soul, but it is his dear body that I took such great care of, and now it lies somewhere (where) no one knows.

I never received any medal nor any citation, and I know he wrote and said he did receive some. But I never received nothing. All I got (was) a sad telegram that he is dead, and a box of his dirty shoes and rolled up uniforms. He had an expensive fountain pen and pencil set, and two empty wallets, and he had a wristwatch of his own and two the government issued. Nothing of this sort came back.

I know he didn't have it on his person, so you see, I guess as soon as they hear a plane didn't come back, well, their boxes are ransacked.

I wonder if these boys didn't die in vain.

Please look for my son and let me know. The whole crew of five men are missing. My son from Chicago. Lt. Plunkett from Little Rock, Arkansas, and three others. Thank you kindly.

Mrs. Agnes Thorn

Now a young widow, Zoe Malovich overcame her illness. A combination of a stubborn will to live and the breakthrough antibiotic streptomycin brought her home again. Soon after the war ended, she met Roy Novak. Three years after Otsie's death, in the middle of the postwar boom, they married and moved from the old neighborhood to the suburbs of Brookfield, Illinois.

Zoe kept in touch with my grandmother and Otsie's sisters for awhile, but she was still a young woman with a new family and another life to get on with now. Eventually the Christmas cards stopped coming—which is how it should have been.

By now, the country was experiencing the explosive growth of the postwar years. Mildred and Erma's husbands had returned home unhurt and eager to begin building a life for themselves and their young families.

America was standing tall on the world stage. The industries that had beaten Germany and Japan were now turned inward again, building the products and providing the goods that Americans wanted. Automobiles, washing machines, and refrigerators were being manufactured once more, food was abundant in the stores.

The nation was awakening from its long nightmare of war.

Near the end of March 1949, almost six years since he'd first gone away, Josephine Malovich received an official letter from the War Department:

28 March 1949
Sgt. Adolph Malovich, 36 743 591
Group Burial
American Military Cemetery
Barrackpore, India

Dear Mrs. Malovich:

The Department of the Army desires that you be given the most recent information concerning your son, the late Sergeant Adolph Malovich, A.S.N. 36 743 591.

His remains were initially buried with others of his comrades who met their death in the same incident. Since that time the American Graves Registration Service has, without success, explored every clue that might lead to individual identification of the remains, and has at last been forced to conclude that only a group identification of the remains is possible. They are now casketed and, pending return to the United States, are being held at the United States Army Mausoleum #2, Schofield Barracks, Territory of Hawaii.

All remains in this group will be brought back simultaneously for interment in Fort Sam Houston National Cemetery, located at Fort Sam Houston, Texas...this particular National Cemetery was selected in order that no undue burden of travel might be placed on any one family wishing to attend the services.

You and the next of kin of the other men will be informed of the date and time of the final interment sufficiently in advance to permit you and any interested persons to attend the ceremonies...

Sincerely yours,

E.V. FREEMAN
Colonel, QMC
Memorial Division

So, they booked a room at San Antonio's Gunter Hotel and boarded the westbound train out of Chicago's Union Station that August. My mother and my grandmother traveled across the country to watch a brother and son buried—to put some closure to it after all the long and painful years.

But the mystery refuses to quit. In researching this book, the author learned that a Burmese native, a chief of the Ngente Region, may have witnessed the crash. He certainly located it almost immediately. A lengthy report filed with the Department of the Army in April 1977 states: "*WWII wreckage of a twin engine US aircraft and remains of its crew are reported near Tang Yan (2224N—9824E) Burma. Source of information (an area resident) has not seen the wreckage personally, but claims that his 80 year-old uncle, a former chief of Ngente Region (also called Musmu) of Wa State, knows the exact location and has had in his possession for years a ring taken from a body at the site. The ring is a class ring from the University of Georgia, Class of 1940, and is inscribed with the name Stephen XXllins. (The first two or three letters of the family name are obliterated). The source believes that the wreckage and remains of the crew are still located at the site.*

When asked why the wreck is only now being reported he stated that his uncle is in need of money after having been forced out of Tang Yan by the BCP. He asks 50,000 kyat for the ring. Coincidentally, another attaché informed me that an individual (possibly the same man) was trying to sell a University of Georgia class ring for 200,000 kyat about three months ago, apparently believing that the red stone setting was a ruby. The source intends to return to the Shan State in four or five days and wants some indication of US interest in the ring and the wreckage.

I have addressed the matter informally with a representative of Burmese Defense Services Intelligence who said that if the claim has validity, I.E. the ring belonged to a US airman who was lost in Burma during WWII that Burma Defense Services would cooperate in locating the site and assist in removing the remains..."

So, what are we to make of it? This last memo is dated April 1977, and states that the wreckage and remains of the crew were still located at the site. If this is indeed true, who are the remains located beneath the stone marker at the Fort Sam Houston National Cemetery? The In Memoriam printed in the neighborhood paper on the third anniversary of the crash may carry much more meaning than the news writer was aware of:

> In loving memory of beloved and dear husband and son.
>
> SGT. ADOLPH MALOVICH
>
> Three long years have passed since he has sacrificed his life in the Pacific Islands on February 15th, 1945.
> Three years have passed since you no longer are with us—
> resting in strange faraway lands where there is no returning road. No one visits your resting grave, only mild winds

> quietly carry the sadness of our hearts to you. Rest in peace, dear, beloved husband, son, and brother: your memory will be with us as long as we shall live.

Adolph "Otsie" Malovich and the crew of Mitchell 977 died far from home. They perished much too young and much too easily in a war that many people thought would bring an end to war. His death and the long wait to bring him home was probably not all that unusual in the postwar years, and the heartache of those distant days is now barely remembered. It was so long ago.

But as I stood over that grave at Fort Sam Houston almost thirty years ago, with the five names engraved upon it, I still remember thinking how very fine it would have been to have known him.

To have known all of them.

Appendix

Wartime Letters from Adolph Malovich
1943–1945

1943

Clearwater, Florida
April 25th, 1943
(To Mildred Vesely, his sister)

Dear Millie:

Sorry I couldn't write you any sooner, but I'm sure you understand how things are when you first get in. No time and always on the go, from morning to night.

Well, I'm going to start from the beginning and tell you what I've been doing.

I was at Camp Grant for two days for shots, uniforms, and aptitude tests. The Tuesday of the 13th we were put aboard a train and our destination was unknown.

We found out we were going to the Air Force at St. Petersburg, Florida, and during the trip we ate in dining cars and were served by waiters—very good meals but we did not have any sleepers so we had to sleep the best we could. Saw many beautiful sights on the way, but when we reached camp we were the most disappointed group in the whole army. The town of St. Pete is beautiful and we were nine miles away. A part which they call The Jungle.

Plenty of snakes, crocodiles, lizards, and other reptiles. The camp was not so hot but we were only there for processing and stayed there for only seven days. While there we had lectures and tests. I went out for radio and made it, so I was pretty lucky.

Friday, the 23rd we were shipped out and sent here to Clearwater, Florida, where we will receive our basic training for approximately twenty-eight days. From here we will be shipped to a technical school. New York, Chicago, or Scott Field. I'll bet you don't know which one I'm hoping for.

Now let me describe the place we are staying at. It is the former Belleview Biltmore Hotel on a high bluff overlooking the Gulf of Mexico which is only one block away. Civilians had to pay as high as $25 per day to stay here! Shower, bath, toilet and sink in every room.

We have an 18-hole golf course, tile swimming pool, tennis courts, badminton courts, and the most beautiful winding roads lined with palm trees. Grass all over the place and it is very clean. There are two theaters in the hotel, we eat four to a table in the dining room and every flight has their own day room which includes pool tables, ping-pong tables, record players, and games. We also have golf clubs, fishing tackle, bats, balls, and all sports equipment.

However, all these things can never take the place of Zoe, for I certainly miss her an awful lot. Have you seen her lately? How is Jimmer, Pep, and everybody? Is Mom OK? Will you send me Pep's address so I can write him? Well, Mil, I have about twelve letters to write now so I guess I'll quit for now. So until later, so long.

Love,
Otsie

My address is:

Pvt. Adolph Malovich
Squadron 515, Flight C
601st Training Group, 63rd Training Wing
Clearwater, Florida

P.S. Mom has a picture of the hotel—ask her to show it to you. Write soon, hello to everybody.

Clearwater, Florida
April 25th, 1943
(To Erma Peknik, his sister)

Hello:

How are you people? Sorry I couldn't write sooner. So, today being Sunday, I thought I'd write to everybody. That means I have about twelve more to write.

This life isn't so bad but it is pretty tough. The trouble is that its too far from home. We're living in a big and beautiful hotel right on the Gulf of Mexico. I described it in Millie's letter so she'll probably show it to you and you can get an idea of what its like here. I haven't had any KP or guard duty yet but I think my time is coming pretty soon. I'm going to be here for about twenty eight days and from here I will go to a radio school. New York, Chicago, or Scott Field. Hope its Chicago, for I am pretty lonesome here.

The weather here is pretty hot and has been up to 100 degrees already.

Doesn't take long for a guy to get burnt here. It hardly ever rains here but when it does you have to tie everything down. I understand they had a hurricane here last month. Well, I'm going to close now and will be able to write more the next time as I won't have so many letters to write then.

Love,
Otsie

P.S. How's Tommy?

Clearwater, Florida
April 29th, 1943
(To Mildred Vesely)

Dear Sister:

First of all, I want to thank you for your letter. Yours was the first that I received since I entered the service. And you can't imagine how nice it is to hear from home. I really appreciated it and never will forget your thoughtfulness. The reason I didn't receive mail from anyone else was because I told them not to write as I was expected to be shipped out at a moment's notice from St. Pete. I gather from your letter that you didn't receive the one I sent you.

When you do receive it you will find a different address on the bottom of the page. The letter you sent me at St. Pete was delayed for a couple of days and then forwarded to me here. Thanks again.

Well Mil, I will truthfully tell you that I was depressed while at St. Petes. The place was like a jungle. Hot as hell during the day, and cold at night. We were there for seven days and removed our clothing only when we showered. There were snakes there, crocodiles, and lizards. Some of the most deadliest snakes in North America shared the camp with us. However, that was good experience for us as they say that anyone who could live in "The Jungle" for a week will make a good soldier.

Now that this experience is in the past we have something to look forward to here, and our spirits are bolstered to a very high point. We live in such a clean place now that it makes us mad because we are always cleaning. We have to scrub the floor, tub, sink, and toilet every morning, and wash woodwork every week.

The neighborhood is clustered with millionaires and you should see some of the houses here. As yet, we have not received any passes to town but that is secondary here as we have everything here in the form of entertainment to occupy our spare moments. You'd be surprised how few boys leave the post every night. They had a big show here last night, but I could not go as I stood a 24-hour guard.

I wish you could see the ceremonies we have here every Wednesday and Saturday. We stand Retreat on Wednesday and have Review on Saturday. The color and formalities send chills up and down my spine, and I can truthfully say that we are beginning to look like soldiers—not the rookies we were a few weeks ago.

Its pretty hot here, too, and am getting a wonderful coat of tan. I go to bed about 8:30 when I don't go to the show and am up at 5:30. And one thing that is surprising is the two breakfasts I eat every morning, with a quart of milk.

Well Sis, I'm going to stop now as I want to write Mom yet and it's about 9:30. So, until next time. God Bless you and Jimmer.

Love,
Otsie

P.S. I'll write Pep in a couple of days. Write soon. Regards to the Veselys. I got two letters from Zoe tonight. Boy, am I happy.

Clearwater, Florida
May 13th, 1943
(To Erma Peknik)

Dear Erm and Milt:

Got your letter and was surprised to get it after such a long silence.

Things are becoming easier now and they are really pushing us through. Basic training used to be 13 weeks but the Air Corps gets only 18 days so you can imagine how hard we are working. Tomorrow we will go to the rifle range and that will complete our training. I can't say what will come next as I don't know myself. We are always kept in the dark.

I went fishing Sunday but did not have much luck as the tide was out and we could not get far enough out as the coast is constantly patrolled here. Right around here is where they caught those eight Nazi saboteurs.

I went to town Sunday and walked and walked. I drank plenty of orange juice, about a half gallon. Oranges here are cheap. So is the juice but I wanted to ship some home and it would have cost me $6 per crate, that is including shipping and packing.

I'm sorry to hear that Tommy is in danger of getting the measles, but if he takes after me I'm sure he'll be alright.

There is a measles epidemic here I think, for about 30 of our boys are in quarantine for that reason.

I'm going to have to cut this short again as the show starts in about 8 minutes and they have the picture about Africa which you spoke about and I would like to see.

I'm getting very tan and my hair is turning white. The sun here is awfully hot but the air is clean and healthy. The ocean sure is beautiful. From our drill field (the fairway of the 9th hole on the golf course) we could walk over a cliff and fall right to the ocean. That is just a picture of how close we are to it. Very often we see sharks in the bay and they sure are plentiful. The boys here go alligator hunting on Sundays at a small island about a mile offshore. Very often they catch them and we have two of them as pets with sergeant stripes painted on them. Well, I must say goodbye now, so write soon, won't you?

Love,
Otsie

P.S. Say hello to Mom and give her my love.

Clearwater, Florida
May 23rd, 1943
(To Mildred Vesely)

Dear Millie & Nefew Jim,

Well, a month is already past and I have had a lot of experiences to tell my future children. The Army isn't so bad but its being away from something dear that is so hard to stand. I do my damndest to be a good soldier and am succeeding, but I'm sure I could do a lot better if I wouldn't get those lonesome spells at times.

I'm feeling fine and getting along swell. Never gigged yet and no extra duty so I shouldn't have anything to complain about. Although I am pretty crippled up today due to a soccer game. I did not want to go on sick call today as I may miss something if I am quartered. At Tent City I was so sick one day that I thought I'd die, but I lived through that so I guess I can make out tomorrow.

You may not believe this but I haven't done any gambling since I'm here. Its just that I have no interest in it. Whenever I get a little spare time, when my mind is not occupied, I start thinking about My Love, so I just sit down and write her a letter. I wrote to her four times in one day already, and very often twice.

So Tommy might have the measles? Well, there seems to be a measle epidemic here, as quite a few of the boys in our squadron have them. They are the German measles so it is not so bad. Just a rest for them. You're looking forward to seeing Pep. Well, I'm looking forward to seeing Zoe, too, and can't hardly wait for that day. I had KP last week, but it wasn't so bad as I was in the chow line dishing out the food and not in the kitchen. I saw the boys chopping onions and were they crying.

I'm standing guard tonight from 12 till 2, so I must cut this letter short and get a little sleep if I can. I intended to stay up till midnight but I think it won't be possible as I'm getting terribly sleepy now. Give the little nefew a big kiss for me, will you? Does he ever ask for his uncle Otsis? Say hello to Mom and tell her that she owes me a letter. So until next time. Write soon and long, won't you?

Sincerely,
Otsie

Hello to the Vesely's.

Clearwater, Florida
May 26th, 1943
(To Mildred Vesely)

Dear Sis—

    To begin with, let me tell you that your letters are very eagerly read. They are very nice, just like a big sister should write to her little brother. I thank you for all the compliments.

    So my little nefew is a sick boy again. I bet this Florida sunshine would be just the thing for him. Does he still want Uncle Otsis to play with him? I'll send you some pictures as soon as I'm able to. I've tried so hard to buy a camera. But there just doesn't seem to be any. I wrote to Jim Brachtl and he might be able to get one for me.

    I've heard all about the Chicago weather and I know just how it is. Here we see hardly any rain at all. Last night we almost had a hurricane. I understand they come this way at times.

    I do consider myself lucky being at this place but am very unlucky being away from my love. I guess you know how it is.

    I haven't done any deep sea fishing as the boats are not allowed to go out. Submarines are in the vicinity at times, but I did do some fishing but didn't have any luck. I'll send you and Jimmy something as soon as I'm able to. I was plenty broke for awhile but am on my feet again. When I go into town I'll look around.

    I, too, was hurt on the obstacle course (don't tell Zoe). Nothing serious though. I hurt my back but didn't want to lose any time so I didn't go on sick call. I'm OK now and ready to get hurt again. It really is rough, but I guess it's all for the good.

    How is mother? I sure enjoy reading her letters. They are misspelled but readable. Don't tell her anything for she may not write. They really are cute. Well Sis, I've got about six more letters to write, so I must close now. Write again, and give Jimmer a kiss for me.

Love,
Otsie

Clearwater, Florida
May 26th, 1943
(To Erma Peknik)

Dear E & M;

Sorry about the delay but have been pretty busy the last few days.

I'm in the groove now and am able to take it like a veteran. We are finished with Basic and expect to be shipped soon. When, I don't know, but according to rumors we should have moved a week after we got here. This place for gossip is just like 32nd and Hamlin.

No, I haven't gained any weight but lost my fat ass and waist. I'm getting solid now, and tough as nails. I'll send pictures just as soon as I get some.

So, you're planning to go to Merkles(?). Boy, I wish I was going there. I did some fishing here but didn't have any luck. We see plenty of sharks here in the bay and yesterday we saw a lot of porpoise.

We are going to parade on Memorial Day in town. That means that another uniform must go to the laundry. We sweat so much that they can be worn only once and it costs sixty cents to wash and iron. Plenty of dough, but they all rob you out here.

We were on the range the last two days and had plenty of target practice with the carbine, tommy gun, and rifle. And all for free, too.

How is Tom Tom? Growing up I suppose, and talking like nobody's business. He sure is a cute. Takes after me, that's the reason.

I'm exceptionally tired today and it's pretty hard to write in that condition, but I didn't want to delay my mail any longer. So if you find this letter kinda crummy you'll know why.

I'm going to sleep now so I'll say goodbye until next time. Are you still a W.E.?

Regards,
Otsie

Scott Field, Illinois
July 7th, 1943
(To Erma Peknik)

Dear Erm & Milt & Tommy—

Well, here I am, being more prompt. It's hard to find things to write in such a short time, for the days here are always alike. Same routine and it gets awfully boring at times.

You probably know that Zoe was here this week. And boy, was I glad to see her again. The trouble is that time goes so darned fast. We had a nice time and am looking forward to her next visit here or my next trip home.

I got a letter from Mary & Jerry Pekarek and they are going up to Minnesota. It's too bad Milt can't go along with them.

I know what the "Liberators" are, for we have quite a few of them here. They are the U.S.'s largest bomber. Looks quite clumsy though. I hope I'm assigned to a B-26 for they are much smaller and faster.

Where was the carnival you went to? On Cicero Ave.? Was it the Royal American Shows? We saw their headquarters when we were in Florida.

You would like to know what I'd appreciate the most. Well, I'll tell you. Everything, no matter how small, is appreciated. It's the thought of being remembered that counts most, but if you want my frank desire, it's the cash. You see, there are always things to buy. Ties, socks, shirts, stationery, and we always try to look our best with clothing that is not GI. I get along OK on my paltry salary and have no complaints but a little surplus, too, would be OK. Although, please don't neglect yourselves on my account. I know every dollar counts, (I've got a lot of experience) so take it easy.

I'll bet Tommy is pretty cute now. Does he talk a lot now? Is his hair still white? It's time for chow now, and there isn't anything new to write. So, until I hear from you again.

Love,
Otsie

Scott Field, Illinois
July 7th, 1943
(To Mildred Vesely)

Dear Millie…

Now you may get peeved 'cause I'm answering your letters so promptly, 'cause news is scarce I know, and letters are hard to write.

Me? I'm okay physically, but mentally I guess I'm going a little mad. Between radio and Zoe you can imagine how my mind is working. I'm going in circles all the time. Zoe left me only two hours ago and I already miss her like the dickens. I hope to hell I can come home for good soon.

Ha! I can just picture Jimmer beating heck out of Billy. I guess he's going to be a real scrapper.

I too, passed the 64 twice and must go again the 19th of August. So much fuss. It gets me down all the time. On my day off, too.

I'll bet Bally(?) is pretty sorry that he enlisted. He didn't know when he was well off. Did you hear about John Marvin(?) (Fritz's husband). He was sent to the infantry and of all places, to Alabama. Fritz feels pretty bad about it and I don't blame her.

I don't know where you got the idea that I was going to be shipped soon. I've yet to stay here for three months, then gunnery school in Texas, Nevada, or Florida for three months. Then to Salt Lake City for assignment to a bomber, then three more months of flight training. I hope it goes fast because there's a furlough waiting for me. Also those sergeant stripes and a pair of wings. I promised Zoe I'd give them to her and she was so tickled. She's swell, isn't she?

Scott Field is composed of 60 to 75% of washed out cadets. Whoever told them they would be officers when they left here told them a big fib 'cause Scott does not graduate any as officers.

They take your time. I can't be a general till I'm about 60 years old. Besides, there are no promotions while in school.

Well, kid, guess I'll close down now. So until next time. Be good. Say hello to the Vesely's and Jimmer.

Love,
Otsie

Scott Field, Illinois
July 18th, 1943
(To Mildred Vesely)

Dear Sis…

Forgive me for not writing sooner, but you see I didn't write to hardly anybody for about 3 weeks. I didn't have time or else I was too busy.

Before I forget. Do you know Marvin Stone? From J.H. If you do, give him regards from Bob Shubert. He is my buddy. The one who's wife came here with Zoe. This fellow Bob knows Marvin and you might mention that he's from the Northwest Baking Co. Quite a coincidence. Wednesday night we went to the opera in St. Louis and Bob bumped into a friend of his, who is now an Army officer, that he didn't see in five years. There were eleven thousand people there so you never know what's going to happen.

I agree with you that Illinois is nothing to look at compared to other states, but I wouldn't trade it for any money.

Glad to hear that you enjoyed your trip. It's only too bad they can't last longer. Zoe and I both feel that way about it.

We had a very nice time when she was here. I'll let her tell you about it, for if I go into details I'll never finish. I've got to write to Mom today or tomorrow. I'm telling you, I'm ashamed of myself for letting my writing go the way it did.

I don't think I told you but the course here has been extended for twenty weeks and the last two will all be in the air. From there I go to gunnery school for another twelve weeks, and then, I too, will wear a pin of silver wings. By the time I get out of school, the war will probably be over, but don't think I'm hoping it isn't, for I have no desire to be a hero of any sort. I just want to be plain Mr. A.M.

Thursday next week I will go to school from 7pm till 1am. I guess it will be OK for I'll be able to get some sleep.

I'm afraid I won't be able to come home anymore on my 36-hour passes, as they are really tightening down. The reason is that too many of the boys have gone AWOL and in the Army we all suffer for a few boy's mistakes. Ah, but such is life. Grin and bear it.

Well Sis, I guess I'll have to be on my way again. So thanks very much for your letter. I apologize once more and won't let it happen again. So until next time. God Bless you and Jimmer.

Love,
Otsie

Tell Jimmer Uncle Otsis says hello. Send Mom my love. I'll write her tomorrow.

Scott Field, Illinois
July 24th, 1943
(To Erma Peknik)

Dear Milt & Erm:

No excuses for not writing sooner. I guess I was a little lazy and a little tired.

It seems like a long time since I was home and it seems as though it was months since Zoe was here.

I am now going on my 7th week of school. It is getting more interesting as we are building our own transmitters and broadcasting with them. Although it is interesting, it is a lot harder and I must be on the ball all the time. My new shift is from 7pm till 1:30am. Get to sleep about 2am and up at 9:00. It's a lot better though, for we don't have to get up when it is dark. That's one thing I hated before.

We had a USO show here last week which was pretty good, although I think our boys have it all over the professionals. It seems we enjoy their shows much more.

My day off last week was spent at the swimming pool in Belleville. It's hard finding things to do. I also spent a lot of time at the USO club. They have a nice place there. I might mention that the Servicemen's Center in Chicago is well known wherever I go. Everybody has nice words for it and also the city.

How is Tommy? Does he talk any more? And how does Milt like his job at Burish's(?)? What does he do there? Good to hear that he is working at such a nice place.

Well, I guess that's about all for now as things to write about are hard to find. You see, one day is no different from the rest. The routine gets quite boring at times. Did Milt do any fishing yet? If he'd like to go why don't he get in touch with Zoe's brother Jerry. He goes almost every Sunday. Well, so long for now.

Love,
Otsie

Scott Field, Illinois
July 26th, 1943
(To Mildred Vesely)

Dear Sis:

Well, I must say you are very prompt in answering letters.

You are right about us studying. God, we eat radio, sleep radio, talk radio. In fact some of us are getting "code happy." It's OK though, but you can imagine how we feel after getting code for three hours steady. Yipe! I'm getting goofy.

You know Mil, 60% of the students here are washed out flying cadets and some of them think that this course here is a lot tougher.

I see that Pep is doing a lot of travelling. After Scott, I'll go to Tyndall Field, Florida, Las Vegas, Nevada, Texas or Arizona. I'll be in the Tech Training Command for about eight or nine more months.

Our barracks are like Pep's, without the air-conditioning. Perhaps he's spoofing you on that. The food here is wonderful. They say nothing but the best for the Air Force.

We have all types of planes here and get to see many experimental planes. Every day they are testing an XP55—a new plane that looks awfully funny and looks like it flys backwards. It is supposed to fly 700 miles per hour. Looks something like this (sketch). Crazy, isn't it? We all call it the 'wing' 'cause that's just what it looks like when it flies.

Well Sis, I guess that's all for now, so until next time, God Bless you both. Give my hello to Jimmer.

Otsie

My squadron is putting on a show tomorrow. Heard it will be pretty good. I'll tell you all about it.

Scott Field, Illinois
August 15th, 1943
(To Erma Peknik)

Dear Milt & Erma:

This letter will be short for there isn't much to write at present but I did want to write and thank you for the money. It sure did come in handy, for when I got it I had eighteen cents in my pocket. I sure was glad to get it and appreciate it very much, but you shouldn't have sent so much. Thanks a million. I'll close now but will write in a few days and forward any news if any. Thanks again.

Otsie

Scott Field, Illinois
August 19th, 1943
(To Mildred Vesely)

Dear Sis:

Received your letter and frankly speaking I think you should get a job in the morale division of the O.W.I. I'm not being sarcastic but I'm only trying to point out that you put your feelings so well into words that you should do it professionally.

True, Mil. There are many more like me. I've had just about everything before I left. Nice home, swell wife, good job and a bright future. All set to raise another Tommy or Jimmer, and what happens? I'm trying to make the best of it and I think I'm doing a good job of it, too.

You ought to see our guardhouse. There are about fifteen hundred prisoners in it and almost all are AWOL's. I could be in there, too, if I really didn't try.

Another thing. A guy picks up a newspaper and what does he read about? Arguments in Washington, waste of money, etc. Stuff like this shouldn't be going on in times like these and I get very disgusted about it. Enough of that. Let's get back to the brighter side of life.

Now something about Scott. The days are cool now and the nights are cold. The result: a cod' in de nos. Lot better than all the heat we've been having. Last Friday it was 92 degrees at midnight. So you can imagine what it was like during the day.

We have two heavy bombardment squadrons now stationed here. Consists of thirty flying forts. Looks nice when they are all massed together. Maybe someday I'll be in one of them, although if I had my choice, I'd choose a B-26. But who gets his choice in the army?

I go to school an extra hour each day and will do so for 24 days. Learning aircraft identification. In a few weeks I'll have radio compass, and some navigation. I am going to start taking 20 words per minute in code in about one week. And believe me, this stuff is enough to drive one mad. In fact, one of our boys went off his bean last week. I don't know what from.

As though I don't have enough to do, I'm going to join the glee club. Nuts, don't you think? But I always did like to sing and it's a lot better than shooting craps or playing cards like some of the boys always do. It's funny how some of these boys are. So irresponsible and "I don't care" attitude. Some even try to wash out intentionally. I don't know how they can be that way.

Another pleasant weekend has gone by. When Zoe was here, I mean. Seeing her really does a guy a lot of good. She's coming here in a couple of weeks again. And then I'll change shifts so I'll be able to come home once in a while.

I was issued another uniform yesterday, so I have five of them now. I tried on my OD's yesterday and I lost so much weight since I got them that I'll have to have them completely altered. Then I'll get a garrison hat, one of sloppy ones and I'll be a sharpie. You know garrison hats are not allowed to be worn by enlisted men, that is while on duty, but our C.O. General Hays encourages it. Nice guy.

Well, I guess this is about all for now so till next time, so long.

Love,
Sad Sack Otsie

How is Jimmer? Tell him I got some nice new cuss words I'll teach him when I come home—army style. Due to the paper shortage you may use the reverse side of this sheet to make out your grocery list. Say hello to everybody.

Scott Field, Illinois
August 19th, 1943
(To Erma Peknik)

Dear M & E & Tom,

Well, I promised I'd write in a couple of days so here I am. Nothing new has happened as usual but will try to write something that may be interesting.

I think summer is all over here. Last week we were practically roasted and now this week the days are cool and the nights are cold. We sleep with comforters already.

I was issued another uniform a few days ago so I have 5 of them now. I lost weight, you know, so I'll have to have my OD's altered completely. Tried them on and I look like a sad sack. Can't wait to wear them for it's hard to stay neat in khakis.

I went to St. Louis Tuesday and saw "This is the Army." A very good show. Don't miss it.

A few nights ago, a fellow in my squadron went off the beam. Took eight guys to hold him down when they caught him. He bit the O.D. and was screaming and hollering. He also tried to choke a sergeant. It's too bad he didn't succeed.

I go to school an extra hour each day to learn aircraft identification. It's a good thing but the whole afternoon is shot to hell. For everything goes on in about three weeks. I'll start to learn the radio compass and study navigation. Many new things are being added to the course. The boys are starting to fly already and so will I in a couple of months. We have two new heavy bombardment squadrons here now, consisting of 30 flying fortresses and it is quite a sight to see when they are side by side. You can't imagine how big they are until you get next to one of them. The tail is about as high as our house. Plenty of noise too, when they all start up at one time.

Zoe is coming here in a couple of weeks again, and when I go on the second shift I'll be able to come home again. Am anxious to, for I miss the old neighborhood, too. Like to see the kids. I'll bet Tommy is pretty darn cute and smart. Do you think he'll be afraid of me when he sees me? I guess I'll have to bawl Mom out for not answering my letters. She bawled me out once so now it's my turn.

Well, I guess this is about all for now. Can't think of anything else to write that would be of interest. I almost think this letter will be pretty boring but I guess you understand. So until the next time, so long.

Love,
Otsie

Thanks again for the fin. Came in mighty handy.

Scott Field, Illinois
August 28th, 1943
(To Mildred Vesely)

Dear Sis:

Your letter was long and interesting, but you shouldn't have felt that I was going to be mad at you. True you know. We get bitter at times when we are pushed around, but it wears off.

Things are much the same here. Nothing ever changes. Although there has been a change in code. It seems that they have plenty of radio men now, so they really are making things tough. The code speed was stepped up somewhat and it will be a few days before we can become accustomed to the new speed. We receive under all conditions, lots of static, music mixed in, noise interrupting, and all. At times, it is terrible but we've got to make the best of it. Yesterday, I finished my receiver so I can say I built a radio all by myself. It plays pretty good, too. I probably told you I built a transmitter a few weeks ago, so I had my own broadcasting station for awhile. One thing we all will get out of this is the fact that we won't have anymore radio repair bills when I get home. When you really get into it like we do, a person finds out what a racket these radio men have.

I heard from Mom and Erma yesterday. Mom must be pretty busy. The next time you write, please don't tell me about Junior Raven. I heard it three times in one day.

Only two more weeks until Zoe will be here. Can hardly wait for the day.

Believe it or not, but I have ten letters to answer today and I'm going to try to get them all finished.

By the way, why don't you ask Zoe if she would like to work at your place. It would be very convenient for her and I'm sure the work would be much easier for her.

The cool weather is here again and I hope it stays this time. The weather a few days ago was 102 degrees officially.

Say, why don't you ask me a lot of questions the next time you write? You see, I have so many letters to write that it's pretty hard trying to make them sound a little different. This one will have to be short for I must get on to my other letters. I promise to write more the next time. Hello to Jimmer.

Love,
Otsie

Scott Field, Illinois
(To Erma Peknik)
September 4th, 1943

Dear Milt & Erma:

Sorry I didn't write sooner but these last couple of days have been very busy ones. I'm in the upper class now, so that means more studying now than before.

Did I know about Junior Raven falling? Well, the day I got your letter I got one from Ma and Zoe, and they all told me the same.

So Tommy is playing with the girls now? Well, he's got the right idea. Perhaps he's dating them up in advance.

Things are about the same here. We've had some rain day before yesterday. The first in about a month. The days are hot once more.

In school now, I am operating a radio that is used on the Fortress. Very big and complicated. We had a check on it last night and we had to tune it in 1 1/2 minutes. Well, I did even better and tuned it in one minute and twenty seconds. This radio has about 40 dials on it and we have to use math to find the frequency we are to transmit on. This math was included in the 1:20 so you see we've got to work fast. We also use a frequency meter to zero but (?) our oscillator and transmitter. Every frequency must have a certain length antenna so that includes more math.

Here is the formula we use: (formula)

You may think I'm silly for writing you this stuff. I'm just trying to give you an idea of what I am doing. We are also assigned certain frequencies to work on every night and if our calculations are wrong and work on another we are liable for court martial, so you see everything must be perfect otherwise we would be jamming the regular broadcasting bands.

Carol Bruce and Bernice Cummins were on the field last week. Wonder who's coming next.

My shift will change tomorrow. I'm going on the second shift. Just think, I am here three months already. Only five more months of tech school ahead of me, and then three months of processing. The last three months should be interesting for then I will fly all over the states.

Only about one more week until Zoe comes here again. I guess this will be her last trip until graduation. For I'll be able to come home once in awhile now. It will be for a short while but I'm anxious to see what home is like once more.

Ma told me all about her work and I bet the house looks pretty good. What I wouldn't give to come home for good. Well, how is Milt's job? Getting to like it a little better? They are testing a plane here every day that travels straightaway at 750 miles per hour. Guess I told you about it already.

Well, I guess I'll move along for now so until I hear from you again, so long.

Sincerely
Otsie

Scott Field, Illinois
October 6th, 1943
(To Mildred Vesely)

Dear Sis:

Just wanted to drop you a line telling you how much I enjoyed my visit home. It really was perfect. I was extremely happy then, the first time in a long time, but leaving was pretty hard. Those last few moments are really tough and I mean it. I'm going to get home every possible chance I get.

You shouldn't feel so badly over Jimmer's actions. After all, he's still a baby and in time he'll get out of it. Don't do any worrying about it for it won't get you anywhere.

The ride home wasn't so bad. I had two seats, I rented a pillow, made myself comfortable (took my shoes off) and woke up in St. Louis. That bus ride to the field sure is a lonely one for that is where I do all of my reminiscing. Don't like to, but I can't help it and it only makes me feel bad. I wish this was all over with already. But a guy can wish and wish and it only makes him feel that much worse. I don't think I'll ever get used to the Army life. I guess I'm just a home boy.

I'm writing this in class so I've got to cut this short. If you don't think it worth answering, don't and I'll send you another in a week or so. My instructor just told me to copy code instead of writing, so I'll say goodbye. God Bless you and Jimmy. Thanks again for helping to make my visit home a pleasant one.

Love, Otsie

Excuse the paper and pencil. It's GI.
Hello to Pep.

Take it easy. Don't be too eager—beaver.

Scott Field, Illinois
October 8th, 1943
(To Erma Peknik)

Dear Milt & Erma:

Just want to let you know how much I appreciated everything you've done for my sake yesterday. And especially for those 39 points. Very good, too, and what I wouldn't give for a meal like that right now. Also, many thanks for the two bucks. It comes in mighty handy. Really, I had a very nice time and I hope that it can be repeated in the near future.

From now on, everytime I have the train fare I'll be in so you can look forward to another visit soon. Tommy is such a cute kid and so good that a guy could squeeze him to death. I'm glad he's on my side again. We got along pretty good, didn't we?

I don't know what happened to Mom last night, as we stopped there about 7:30 and she wasn't there, so I had no idea where she could have been. However, Zoe will forward my goodbyes for me. I'll make up for it the next time. Already I am trying to figure a way out next week. The ride wasn't so bad this time as the train was pretty good and not a bit crowded. Slept all the way back and got to the field at 8:30 without any trouble.

Well, I intended to make this a short note for I'm writing this in class and I don't want to get caught. So, hoping to see you soon.

Sincerely,
Otsie

Excuse the pencil and paper. It's GI.

Belleville, Illinois, USO Club
October 26th, 1943
(To Mildred Vesely)

Dear Sis:

It's about time I thanked you for those swell cookies you sent. Thanks very much. You know they didn't last quite two days. But everybody enjoyed them so that gave me just as much pleasure as if I would have eaten them myself.

The reason I didn't write sooner was that I was preparing myself for my final check in mechanics. I should get it tomorrow, and it will last for two days. Boy, am I in for something. I'm pretty confident in myself but when I get into the check room I get so darn nervous that I forget. Those instructors are rats and they try to catch you on everything. Oh well!

Being so close to payday, I am spending my day off at the USO. How thrilling—

It's been raining here for three days now, and it really is cold. But it makes no difference to me for most of my time is spent in the barracks anyway. Things are about the same with me. Still lonesome and waiting for my next chance to come home again. I hope I get a chance to see you then. If not, it probably won't be till Christmas when it can be arranged. I hope to get three days then and if I do I wonder if I'll be able to get a train. Such troubles I got. Perhaps I'd be better off if I didn't worry so much.

Refreshments are going to be served soon and I've got to get in line 'cause I'm hungry. It's 9:30 and I really should be in bed already, for reveille is at 3:30. Nice time to get up, isn't it?

Well, kid, I hope everything is OK with you and going great. Keep your chin up and we'll all be home soon. For good, I mean, and start off where we ended.

So take care of yourself and God Bless you and Jimmer.

Sincerely with love,
Otsie

Scott Field, Illinois
November 9th, 1943
(To Mildred Vesely)

Dear Sis:

Have a little time today, being my day off I'm staying in. Just taking it easy.

You probably heard that I was coming home this week. Well, I was. Had my pass and all, but they restricted the whole field Monday night. And at 2:00 am we had to fall out for a physical check. Isn't that the limit? Well, I'm coming home for sure next week if nothing else comes up.

It's pretty cold here now. Snowed a little yesterday. I developed a cough and it's driving me nuts.

Last Monday I graduated mechanics so I've got it pretty easy now. Go to school only three hours per day. Good deal, I say. At present, I find no difficulty at school. It's a good thing, for they are starting to clean house again and are washing them out left and right.

Here I am with a lot of time but I can't get in the letter-writing mood. Maybe it's because I just got up. 8:00—nice, huh? I'm going to breakfast at 10:00 with the late shift. Understand they have pancakes. I understand you civilians are still putting up with those old-fashioned eggs that you have to break. You ought to try these powdered eggs sometime (joke) Phooey!

You mentioned the condition of my morale the last time I was in. Maybe it's because we were all together again. Made me pretty happy. A guy never realizes what his family means to him until he's away.

Just looking out the window now I see the prisoners cleaning the ashes out of the furnace. What a dull life they lead.

Things are about the same out here. Chicken....—is just as thick as ever. But regardless, I get along very nicely.

How is everything with you, and does Jimmer rule the West Side yet? I mean his mob. He sure is a toughie, but it's good for him. Make a man out of him yet.

Well Mil, try as I may, I can't get things down on this paper. I tried hard but I find it impossible. I guess I've got to quit writing and do some sewing. So here's hoping I'll get to see you next week.

Love,
Otsie

Scott Field, Illinois
November 21st, 1943
(To Joseph B. Vesely, his brother-in-law,
stationed at Thunderbird Field, Arizona)

Dear Pep...

Got your letter yesterday and it really was a surprise. Glad to hear that you are doing so well and wish you all the luck in the world that you make it. I know it's tough. Ninety percent of the guys here are washouts and the stories they tell are pitiful, especially those raw deals.

I know how you feel about your 40-hour check. That's one thing that worries me all of the time. I get checks every day, sometimes two. My final check in theory took six hours. I really sweated that one out, but made a 93.

I'm no genius because I can take 22 wpm in code. In fact, at present I'm taking 25, but I think I've reached my peak. It just gets so dits and dahs aren't counted and letters are taken down by sound. It's easy to distinguish characters in time but it's hard to print that fast.

I'll be here about four or five more weeks. Scott isn't so bad, but there is an excess of chickenshit. I guess it's that's the way all over in the Air Corps. It's a nice place. Modern conveniences and the Special Department is always on the ball. So, as a whole, it's bearable but for the chickenshit and the chow. Things like this can be put up with knowing I can get home once in awhile. One thing good about being a student is no KP or guard duty. School, calesthenics, and barracks detail once in a while. I'll live through it, I'm sure.

We have about two hundred (unreadable) here that are used by students. Many are flown by our boys for there seems to be a shortage of laison pilots and many of the boys here (ex-cadets) have over a hundred hours time, so they fly these.

Last Tuesday, a P-40 came in with his wheels up, hit the runway and burned. The pilot got out okay, but was he pissed off! I've seen about ten crack-ups here already. The Twentieth Processing Group have their headquarters here and there are always about two hundred B-17's on the field. We have two of them to practice procedures in, but they never leave the ground.

Perhaps you'll stop here on a cross-country sometime. Many BT's and AT's do come in for stopovers. I'm a qualified gunner and will likely wind up in New Mexico, Florida, Texas, or Nevada. But at present, most of the graduates are going to Salt Lake City and will get gunnery overseas.

Well Pep, I guess I took up enough of your time, so until next time, lots of luck.

Sincerely,
Otsie

Scott Field, Illinois
November 26th, 1943
(To Mildred Vesely)

Happy day after Thanksgiving—Hope you had just as much turkey as I did. Really, we ate like kings yesterday and can't gripe about anything. No kidding, it was swell. Poor civilians, I'll bet they were eating chicken and ducks.

Well, things are about the same with me. Still trying to get along and being a good soldier as usual. How are you and Jimmer? Fine, I hope.

I'm sorry I didn't write sooner. Can't make any excuses for you know me too well.

I got a letter from Pep the other day and answered it right away. He told me all about Thunderbird, so in turn, I had to write about Scott. See, when there are things to write about it isn't so hard.

Tried calling Zoe up Thanksgiving eve. She wasn't home but I was glad to get Mom at home. I guess you can understand the situation.

I may be home on furlough right after the new year. Can't say for sure but that's what all the boys are getting now. Then from home to Salt Lake, squadron assignment, and then overseas for gunnery. Then the ratings start coming and that can't be too soon for me.

I suppose you're still working hard as usual. I know I am. I mean in school. I've only three more weeks and I'd sure hate to wash out now. Well, Mil, I'm trying to write this in parts for I wrote Mom and I'll write Erma and I know all three letters will sound alike, but what can I do? So, till later—lots of love.

Otsie

Hello to the Vesely's.

Scott Field, Illinois
November 26th, 1943
(To Erma Peknik)

Dear Erm & Milt:

It's about time I thanked you for the cookies and nuts. Those cookies were delicious and if you made them you ought to be proud.

Well, as usual, I'm looking forward to another trip home. I may be able to make it once more, and I'll do my darndest, too.

Did Milt go hunting lately, and if so, what did he get besides sore feet? For a while I was waiting for that duck to come but I've given up hope already.

How is Tommy? Talkative as usual I suppose.

How was your Thanksgiving dinner? Ours was swell and couldn't have been better. We had everything from turkey to ham to candy. It was really swell and we got all we could eat. But already we are paying the price. For supper last night we had rice—nothing else, and this afternoon we had the usual stew. Oh well, it's filling anyway, and I'm getting used to it.

Everything is coming along fine. I'm in my last three weeks so I'm keeping on the ball. I'd sure hate to wash out now. In the last three weeks, 500 students were washed out so you see we're in the Battle of Scott Field right now. Our wits against the damned Army regulations.

By the way, what do you think of the Patton case? Pretty raw, wasn't it? But then too, he probably was under strain. We can't judge until we know all the facts and those we'll never get to know. Personally, I think politics have a lot to do with it.

Well, chow call—so I guess I've got to say so long for now.

Love,
Otsie

Scott Field, Illinois
December 18th, 1943
(To Erma Peknik)

Dear Milt, Erma & Tommy:

Got your Christmas present this afternoon. Thank you so much for it. Personally, I think it was a little too much. But I know you'd be insulted if I sent some back and you know I wouldn't want to hurt anybody's feelings. All kidding aside, I appreciate it very much. Thanks again. Got Mom's gift today, too. So I'm going to write a thank you to her right after I finish this.

Santa Claus must think I've been a pretty good boy this year for he is being very good to me. Since yesterday, I got $24 plus a great, big box from Jerry and Mary (Zoe's brother). People certainly are nice to me and I wish so much that I could show my appreciation to them.

Well, I suppose you wondered too, if I made out all right when I got back. I did, and everthing turned out swell. They missed me at school for Bob left a little earlier than he should have, for they had a double roll call. I can't blame him though, for it was his day off and his wife was waiting for him in Belleville. The instructor happened to be a pretty good Joe so he didn't turn me in. In fact, it made us pretty good friends and he lets me out of school about a half hour every day. Crazy army, isn't it?

Well, Christmas is only a few days off and trees are springing up all over camp. I don't know yet what sort of deal we'll get for the holidays, but I can assure you it won't be in our favor. Jerry and I are going to town tonight. Tomorrow morning we are going to St. John's, Missouri—about five miles from St. Louis. He's got some business there and I think he chiseled a dinner for us.

Well, I had a very good time when I was home last time. Of course it was short as usual, but my furlough isn't so far off. If Milt would have talked about hunting a little more I guess I'd be in the guardhouse now. Boy, I was all primed up. I've got to get back to work now (I'm writing this in school) so I'll close. I hope you all have a Merry Christmas and give Tommy a big hug and kiss for me.

Love,

Otsie

1944

Flexible Gunnery School
Fort Myers, Florida
February 4th, 1944
(To Mildred Vesely)

Dear Sis,

OK, so I'm pretty negligent in answering my mail. Well, let me explain and perhaps I'll be forgiven this time. I knew I would leave Scott soon and I didn't want to write for fear of a mixup in my mail. So, I thought I'd let it go and do it when I got here. So don't feel left out 'cause I didn't write to anybody but Zoe.

I left Scott Monday morning and got down here Wednesday afternoon. A very tiresome trip in day coach. Was very disappointed when I got here for it can in no way compare with Scott. This too, is the real Army and it's pretty rough.

The barracks and field look like they were put up overnight. Very desolate spot. Right in the Everglades.

I had another physical yesterday and was processed. I've yet to go to the pressure chamber. I may start my basic week in school Monday and I certainly hope so. After basic, we go on duty for a week (KP) and then we start the regular school. This will be for six weeks. Four weeks of ground school and two weeks of flying. Everything involves shooting and more shooting, and this place sounds as though the war is going on right here. Training is given in B-17's and B-26's.

I shouldn't be here for no longer than nine weeks so if everything turns out OK I should be home in April for I already signed for my delay enroute. I guess you know enough to know what that means.

The weather here is beautiful. Right now, I'm lying on my blanket in the sand with only my gym trunks on. I should get a pretty good tan out here. On the radio this morning, I heard that it's 28 degrees in Chicago. You poor people. This life makes me feel like a millionaire.

It's not going to be all fun, though. When I start school I'll begin at 5:30 am and quit at 10:00 pm. I've got to keep up with my radio so I'll get this two hours every night.

I met a lot of my old friends here already. It's hard to find them 'cause the place is so big and spread apart.

Well, I suppose you and Pep really took advantage of his furlough. Boy, I'm going to pack about a year in mine. Zoe wrote about the whole gang going out and I was sorry we couldn't have been there. Well, I've still got something to look forward to and if I didn't, I don't know how I could get along here.

Does Pep have any idea where he will go? Perhaps he'll get a good deal out of it anyway. I've got to go now, so I'll close till next time. Say hello to Jimmy and the Vesely's.

Love,
Otsie

Flexible Gunnery School
Fort Myers, Florida
February 4th, 1944
(To Erma Peknik)

Dear Milt & Erma,

Forgive me for not writing sooner. It could have been helped, I know, but I had other plans. That's the reason for the delay.

Here I am in the sunny south again. Lying out in the sun trying to get a tan. Nice weather. Just a little breeze to keep it cool.

I left Scott Monday morning and got here Wednesday after spending 52 hours in a day coach. What a ride.

This place cannot compare with Scott in any way. This is the Army without a doubt. I will start school in about two weeks and will go for six. I shouldn't be here for more than nine weeks so if everything turns out OK I should be home in April. This is almost positive 'cause yesterday I signed for my delay enroute.

This school involves nothing else but shooting. Starting with the .22, then 12 gauge skeet, .30 cal. and .50 cal. It sounds like the war is going on right here, there is so much noise. I'll get between 30 or 40 hours of flying time here, all of it in B-17's.

I've got to keep up work with my radio so I'll get two hours of this every night besides my gunnery. In all, I will start at 5:30 am and quit at 10:00 pm so you see I've got a busy six weeks ahead of me. But this doesn't worry me any for I know that everyday that goes by brings me closer to my furlough and that is the only thing I want right now.

I guess George is in the Army by now. What branch did he manage to get into? He wanted the Air Corps, didn't he? Zoe told me about the whole bunch of you going out. I was sorry I wasn't able to go but my day is coming.

The food is much better here than at Scott. Chicken every Sunday and all we want, too. Christ, I've written about twelve letters already and I'm all petered out.

How is Tommy? Does he ever ask for his Uncle Otsie? That guy sure is a cute one. Well, I'm going to quit now with no excuses. So, let's hear from you soon and I'll try to write normally once more.

Love,
Otsie

Flexible Gunnery School
Buckingham Army Air Field
Fort Myers, Florida
March 1st, 1944
(To Mildred Vesely)

Dear Sis—

Letters must be written now only at minute intervals so you'll have to excuse the delay. Mom and Zoe were the only ones I've written to for some time, but it just can't be helped. Thanks for your interesting and long letter and thanks for asking so many questions. This makes it much easier to answer. Thank Jimmer for his valentine.

First of all let me put you straight. True, I'm in Florida but I'm a long way from vacationing. I'm going to do that in Chicago about April 10th (I hope). I am lucky to be where it is nice and warm. Spent Sunday at the beach getting a suntan. Pretty good, eh?

I don't know where you got your info, but this place is no paradise. I sent Zoe a book on the place with plenty of pictures and the field's history. I'm sure you'll see it. It's quite interesting. Quite authentic, too. Wait till you see the town of Buckingham. You'll die laughing. I guess it's the smallest town in the *world*. I mean that.

Concerning the pressure chamber. Pictures of this are in the book, too. Well, 20 of us went in at a time. Went up to 15,000 feet without oxygen to see what effects it would have. Very surprising, too. I'll get to that later. Came down again and then went up to 30,000 feet. At 27,000 feet, two "volunteers" took off their masks to see the results. Lack of oxygen (anoxia) crept up on them. Unnoticeably, and they were normal in every way but they could not control their minds. When they were on the verge of passing out (death results 3 minutes later) the instructor told them to put on their masks but they couldn't do it, so they had to be helped. This was just an example of what may happen to us if we aren't careful. The next day we went up to 38,000 feet. A few fellows passed out, one got a hemorrhage and the "bends" were numerous. I was OK though. Tough guy, that's me. Well, this was it. After the test those who made it were issued cards permitting us to fly in all high-altitude aircraft.

I'll put in 20 hours of B-17 time here. Then when I go to an OTG I'll fly about 500 hours in whatever type of plane I'm assigned to. B-26 I hope. If I'm lucky I'll get my OTG training here for three months. If not, then its overseas shortly after my furlough.

My day is as follows (this week). Up at 5:00. School at 6:00—radio, skeet range, sighting, weapons and turrets. Tomorrow and Friday and Saturday I'll be in school till 10:00 pm. Otherwise, my day ends at about 7:30 or 8:00. It's plenty rough here and I'm not kidding, but it's a lot of fun when a guy can go on the range and blaze away to his heart's content.

Had a check Friday, got 99% on it. Today I had a (unreadable) check. Tomorrow another. Oh, my!

Scott Field and Buckingham are no comparison. Scott is like a good, clean little girl and Buck is like a dirty little boy. I hope I make myself clear. Look at both those books I sent Zoe (Scott & Buck) and you'll see the difference. At Scott, we were treated like a bunch of school kids, and here we're treated like the killers they are trying to make out of us. In other words, here we are like the Dead End Kids. Understand?

Fort Myers itself is a much prettier town than Clearwater. It's supposed to be the most tropical town in Florida. But these southern people are not very congenial and hate the sight of all "Yankees." It's the truth. If a guy doesn't have a southern accent he's S.O.L.

T.S. that George Peknik got into the infantry. That's rough all the time but it's a good outfit, too. I guess every guy thinks his outfit is the best but I can't seem to fall in love with the Air Corps. In my estimation, I think there is too much discrimination in it.

April 5th should be graduation day for me if I make it. When I get out of here I'll ship with $700 worth of flying equipment. And yesterday an order came out stating that all radio operators will be issued navigation watches upon graduating. These are to be worth around $110, so you see I'll have quite a responsibility looking after my things.

I'm in fine health. Never felt better in my life. I eat like a pig and am getting quite a tan. I don't think I'm putting on any weight but I really should.

In my class there are 121 enlisted men, 50 officers including majors, and 100 navigation and bombardier cadets. The beauty of this is that rank doesn't mean a thing while they are students and it's a lot of fun to treat them on an equal basis.

Well Mil, I tried to explain things the way they are. If there is anything else you'd like to know just ask and I'll try to do my best to oblige.

Say hello to Jimmer and the Vesely's, Mom, Erma, Milt and everybody else. Send me Pep's new address so I can write to him.

Love,
Your little brother,
Otsie

PS—See you soon, I hope! How do you like the B.T.O. Stationery?

Flexible Gunnery School
Buckingham Army Air Field
Fort Myers, Florida
March 5th, 1944
(To Erma Peknik)

Dear Erm, Milt, and Handy Spanky:

Sunday, and a day of rest so I made up my mind to answer all of my mail. First chance I got, too. So don't blame me for the delay.

I suppose you'd like to know what I am doing now so I'll try to explain briefly.

First week we had .22 rifle, weapons and sighting. Second week skeet range (12 gauge shotgun), turrets, sighting, aircraft recognition, weapons and radio. The third week is going to be a little different. What it will be like I don't know yet.

Our schedule is a long and tougher one every day but I don't seem to mind it for there is some fun involved in it too. I don't seem to mind for the time goes by fast and already am starting on my third week. Just think, four more weeks and then I'll be home. I'm getting pretty impatient, too.

Washout worries are back with me again. I wish I could get a little confidence in myself. I'm sure I'd find it much easier. I don't have trouble with my work or exams but still can't get any confidence.

How does George P. like the Army? It's too bad that he got the infantry and the only thing he can do now is to make the best of it.

I understand that Pep is coming home again. Pretty lucky guy I say. Too bad he couldn't hold it off a couple of weeks then we all could have gone out boozin'. Oh well, my day will come soon.

This place seems to be getting better and better everyday so I guess it's just a matter of getting used to it. It still isn't a paradise but it's bearable. Although it's nice and warm here, I can't wait to get up north with the real people. These rebels down here drive a guy crazy. And you'd be surprised how much they dislike the damned "Yankees." It's a fact. That just goes to show how dumb they are out here.

Went to the beach last Sunday. Had a nice swim. Water was warm and the sun was hot. Had a chance to go on a picnic at the beach today but figured I'd be better off to stay here and do some things that had to be done.

Well folks, again I'm going to say so long. Write soon, and I hope to see you all soon. Say hello to Handy Spanky.

Love,
Otsie

Flexible Gunnery School
Buckingham Army Air Field
Fort Myers, Florida
March 21st, 1944
(To Erma Peknik)

Dear Milt, Erma & Handy Spanky,

Got your card yesterday but I was in school till 10:00 pm last night and I didn't have a chance to write you then.

Thanks for the two bucks—it came in mighty handy. Please don't do it again, though, for you're going to need it yourself. Instead of doing it, get something for Handy, OK? Don't think I don't appreciate it 'cause I do. If nothing else, one thing I learned in the Army was responsibility. So do this for me.

I'm sorry to hear that Milt is ready to go. Guess nothing can be done about it. I can't say that my washout worries are over yet, 'cause the washout list doesn't come out till one day after graduation. Nice thing to sweat out, isn't it?

This afternoon we went out on a gunnery mission. Went up in a B-17 and stayed up for five hours. Shot the fifty and camera gun at attacking planes. Lots of fun, but awfully tiresome. I was the radio operator for about two hours and enjoyed it very much. The ride was very smooth in spots but some of the boys got awfully sick.

Zoe finally sent me the pictures we took in your yard some time ago. Jeez, that kid of yours is a cute one. Gave me a lot of pleasure looking at them.

These last two weeks here are hell. Almost 16 hours of school everyday. What gets me is washing out after all this work. Boy, I hope it doesn't happen to me.

I should get home on or about the first anniversary of the day I left. This is an awfully long six months. That's the baloney they gave us. After six months we all get a furlough. Some fun.

Erm, I'm not in a letter-writing mood tonight. I'm kind of tired. I just wanted you to know I got your card. I hope to see you in a couple of weeks. Till then.

Love,
Otsie

Hello to Mom and Mil.

Myrtle Beach
South Carolina
June 21st, 1944
(To Mildred Vesely)

Hello Mil,

I suppose by now you are in doubt whether I'm still in existence. Well, I sort of got over my laziness and due to a little more time on my hands I thought I'd let you know that your kid bro is still kickin'.

My life has been a pretty fast one since I came back from my furlough. Don't get me wrong now. What I meant is that buzzin' arround in these 25's sure is a lot of fun.

I'm a first operator now. Flew solo after only four hours of dual instruction. My crew is satisfied with my progress. I'm satisfied with theirs, so we're all happy. I don't know if you know that my pilot, copilot, and 'bombagator' are all from Chi. We get along like a happy family. No formalities whatever. It's really swell. All of us coming from Chi will enable us to get home some weekend. You just wait and see.

Since being down at Greenville, which by the way is a very nice place—trees and mountains, I've gone to bombardier's school, navigation, and my pilot is going to teach me how to fly. It certainly is a lot of fun and I do enjoy what I'm doing. The work isn't hard but the time we put in is the only drawback. Some boys are flying as much as 12 hours per day.

I'm writing this from Myrtle Beach, SC. We came down here Sunday for a week's gunnery and bombing practice. It's really a farce, for in three days we made only one mission. We are only a block from the ocean and get to go swimming every evening. Even with this form of pleasure I'd just as soon dispense with it and go back to Greenville. I like everything about the place. Food, location, and personnel.

I'll be at Greenville Army Air Base till Aug 23rd and then we'll go to Savannah, Georgia. Pick up a brand new plane and head for the other side. Between you and me I'm kind of anxious to get started on this adventure. There has been some rumor that we may go to the China-Burma-India Theater and if this is true, I consider myself the luckiest guy in the world.

Since being at Greenville I made quite a few trips. Have gone to Miami, Tallahasee, Savannah, and a few more places. I'm just waiting for something going to the grand old place called Chi.

Is Pep still at Scott? How is he getting along and how does he like it? I understand you went down there. Quite a nice place, isn't it? How's Jimmer? Bet he's pretty big by now. Christ, I wish I could get home to see everybody pretty soon. I'm almost positive I won't get another furlough. Kind of makes me sad.

Well, I've got to get ready to go on another mission in a few minutes so I'll have to close. Write when you have time. I wouldn't take as long as I did for people won't like it. Till next time. Say hello to Pep and the Vesely's.

Love,

Otsie

Myrtle Beach
South Carolina
June 21st, 1944
(To Erma Peknik)

Dear Erm—

Well, it's been a long time but do or die I decided that I've just got to write to my family today. Just finished writing to Mom & Mil, so here goes the last one.

How is Milt doing in the Navy? Is he through with his boot training yet? What does he expect to do and where does he expect to go? As yet I haven't heard from him. How's Tom? Growing up I guess. Have you moved yet? I understand you had the whole place redecorated. Did Mom do it all by herself? I'll bet it was quite a job. Well, it's all finished now I guess, so that's that for awhile.

As for me, I'm still on the ball. Flying a lot and doing a lot of operating. I like it a lot so am very much satisfied with my job. Ratings were frozen so I guess I'll have to sweat out a raise. If things would have stayed the way they were I should have been a sergeant last week. But it seems that I am too late for everything.

Greenville is a wonderful place. Lots of mountains, trees, and farms. Much nicer than Florida in every respect. The people in town are very nice to GI's and that's very unusual for Rebels. I've been to quite a few places since coming here. We take off for a different place almost every day. I sure hope it's to Chicago one of these weekends. This will be my only chance to come home before going overseas. And the way time is flying it's almost unbelievable. Since Zoe can't come out here I don't care how much shorter the time is getting. I'd just as soon be over there getting a chance to see something than sweating it out in the states. Besides, I think I'd look good with a couple of medals on my chest.

I'm writing this from Myrtle Beach. Sounds good, eh? We came here Sunday for a week's gunnery and bombing practice. We're kept busy every day but go swimming every evening. It sure is a lot of fun swimming in the ocean.

Well kid, I guess I'll close now. I've got so much more writing to do that it makes me sick to think of it. Write when you have time. Tell Milt to drop me a line.

Love,
Otsie

Greenville Army Air Base
Greenville, South Carolina
July 17th, 1944
(To Mildred Vesely)

Hi Sis:

Wow! What a letter you wrote. The fellows couldn't understand that it was from my Sis. They thought only girl friends wrote letters like that.

Well, maybe I will drop in on you people one of these days. If everything turns out OK it may be this Saturday. I certainly get hepped up about it but usually the bottom drops out of it and we stay in the Rebel section of the U.S.

So Pep hates to go to school. I can understand it for it's awfully dry. But now that I can put what I learned (into practice) I find it very interesting and it gives a guy a sense of responsibility when I am the sole means of getting in touch with anybody or anyplace. B.T.O., that's me.

I've got a hell of a nice crew and we get along like a couple of newlyweds. My pilot is from Chicago, copilot, and 'bombagator' is too. A gunner and engineer are from Texas and are good boys, too.

I've got some time actually flying our plane and it's lots of fun. Of course I can't do anything fancy with it but I'll leave that up to the pilot and he sure is a hot rock. He can make it do anything but talk and when we land I get a kick out of picking the treetops out of the belly of the ship. Some fun.

I haven't been to any of the places you mentioned in St. Louis but if you go there again don't fail to go to the Starlight Roof of the Chase Hotel. It's really beautiful. Zoe and I went there one evening. Just like in the movies. You've got to see the base too, for it's a very nice place. The nicest I've seen yet.

The weather is fine here. Never too hot and always perfect for sleeping. I like South Carolina but don't care for Rebels.

Thanks for the buck, but don't throw your dough around like that. I read the last part of your letter to my roomates about having a drink on the buck and they thought it was a good idea so that's what we did with it. Had a few beers, do you mind? You know how things are just before payday.

Well Mil, guess I've got to say so long again. Tell Jimmer that Uncle Otsis says hello. And send my regards to the Vesely's and Pep.

Love,

Otsie

Hunter Field
Combat Crew Center
Savannah, Georgia
September 10th, 1944
(To Mildred Vesely)

Dear Mil and Jimmer:

Better late than never, right? Sorry I didn't come around to say goodbye but I just couldn't make it. I spent what time I had at the hospital so that was the reason.

I suppose by now Pep is on his way to his new station. Let me know how it goes. Has he any idea of what he's going to do now?

I got here Tuesday morning all set to kill a lot of Japs as we were to stay here only long enough to get our equipment and plane, but something snafu'd and here we are. Fighting spirit all gone and we may sweat the war out here for the duration. All kidding aside, we'll be here for perhaps three weeks. But do you think they'd give us a furlough? You guessed it. All we're doing here is nothing and it's a shame. I'd rather spend this time at home.

This part of the country is hot as hell. I'd give anything to go back to Greenville and some of that cool Carolina weather. Boy, there's nothing like it.

Trying to kill this Sunday writing letters. This is my fifth and my fingers are pretty tired already. But the Air Corps never says die. Tonight I'm going to see Dorothy LaMour in something or other. You ought to slip in this show sometime, you get a bigger kick out of the wisecracks the guys pull off than anything else. It's really a scream. The boys sure are cocky around here.

Well Mil, don't be like me when it comes to writing letters. It isn't nice. So when you have a little time, write your lonesome bro.

Love, Otsie

Hello to the Vesely's

Hunter Field
Combat Crew Center
Savannah, Georgia
September 18th, 1944
(To Mildred Vesely)

Dear Sis—

Having a lot of time to myself now, I decided to start a new policy and that is to answer my mail more promptly than before. Although there isn't anything to write about as we aren't doing anything. I must go through with my plan, as you know letters do not come if one does not write.

It's been raining for almost five straight days and I just love it. Just right for the sack. I'm afraid I'll have to get me a bottle of alcohol soon and start using it, otherwise I'll get bed sores. No kidding, this is the life. There isn't a day that I got up before 9:00 am since I've been here. But you know as well as I that this is the lull before the storm.

We are obviously waiting for a CBI shipment as all the boys we came here with have gone out Saturday night. We saw our pilot and he said we can plan to be here till the fifth of next month. But try to get a furlough and they'll beat your head in.

I haven't seen the town of Savannah yet, outside of the ride we had through it on our way from the railroad station. I don't like these Rebel towns at all and have no desire to go in. When we want a little diversion we go right out the gate, have a chicken dinner and a couple of beers and have enough. No travel worries or financial worries. I understand that everything in town is double the price we pay at the (unreadable). Then too, they have a midnight curfew thru out the south, so as soon as a guy gets into town he's got to worry about coming back.

Thanks for the $2.00 you sent. Seeing as how it was a birthday present, I won't moan about it, but don't ever do it otherwise. To tell you the truth, I spent my last fifteen cents yesterday, so you can imagine how much this gift is appreciated. You see, I haven't been paid last month. I missed payday on account of being on furlough, and then I missed the supplementary payroll due to shipping out. God only knows when I'll get paid again. However, between you and me and one more person I've negotiated a $15 loan. I should get it through the mail tomorrow or the next day. You see, I've got to stock up with soap, blades, and a few miscellaneous things before going over, 'cause these things are impossible to get out there. Our pilot tipped us off. He should know 'cause he's been there before. Well Mil, I think I've written more than I thought I could. It probably isn't too interesting but it makes conversation.

Write when you have time. Hello to Jimmer and the Vesely's, and to Mom, of course. Till we meet again.

Love,
Otsie

Hunter Field
Combat Crew Center
Savannah, Georgia
September 28th, 1944
(To Mildred Vesely)

Dear Sis:

Your letter came two days ago and the package came yesterday. Thanks a lot, everything was practical and I'm sure will come to a good use. Should I go to the South Pacific maybe I'll be able to trade a bar of soap for a great big nigger woman—to do my laundry, of course. I'm only kidding, but the boys did make a few suggestions but you know how boys are.

We are still sitting around doing nothing at all and believe me I'm getting pretty tired of it. I'd just as soon go off to war than have this war of nerves. We had a chance to go to Alaska this morning for coastal patrol, but our pilot turned it down as he has his heart definitely set on going to China-Burma-India. This would have been a good deal but then too, it would mean doing nothing again. If he keeps fooling around like this, there's no telling what will happen to us.

Halfway through this letter and already I'm stuck. No, there's nothing that I'm holding back. These letters are not censored and I'm free to write what I please, but the fact that I'm doing nothing makes it hard to find things to write about.

You asked me what I think of Mom working. Well, I don't like it so much, but due to her short hours and the place she works at, it isn't so bad. But you know Mom, I think she'd die if she didn't have anything to do.

Well, I hope Pep gets a good deal out of his new assignment. Perhaps he'll like it a bit better now. Satisfaction is the most important thing, I guess.

I guess this is about all for now. Write again when you have time. Maybe I'll have more interesting things to write about in my next letter. Between you and I, I hope so. You see, I'm an eager beaver. Hello to Pep and the Vesely's, and thanks.

Love,
Otsie

P.S. I had that beer.

Hunter Field
Combat Crew Center
Savannah, Georgia
October 13th, 1944
(To Erma Peknik)

Dear Sis:

Got your letter this morning and thanks very much for the $2.00. You've no idea how handy it came in at the present time. However, please don't do it anymore 'cause I realize how things are and besides, I'm sure Milt could use it first as much as I can, and then too, you could get something extra for Tommy. Understand?

Well, as far as my going back to Greenville was concerned, it turned out just as I thought. Purely rumor. We were called out yesterday for another showdown (?) and we were to leave today, but again something is snafu'd and we are still here. Perhaps tomorrow will tell the tale. We've got our airplane and are all packed up. We will be headed for India, traveling by way of South America. If I know my pilot well enough, I think we'll have another vacation in South America. By the way, we will be paid $7 per day while traveling, with an expense account of a large amount. It won't be so bad.

I'm sorry to hear that Milt was hurt, but the rest will do him good and I'm sure he doesn't mind being in the hospital for awhile. There were many times when I tried to figure out a way to get in myself. Georgia is turning cool now and it's time to pull out if we want to miss winter this year. I understand it gets cold here at times.

Well, we're here five weeks now, and it's been a vacation with nothing to do. Sleep as late as we want to, no formations, roll calls, PT, or anything. The whole day is entirely our own. I've seen every picture that came to this field for that's about all there is to do. We go outside the gate once in awhile for fried chicken and beer, and that consists of our nightlife. I guess the rest is well deserved, for we certainly flew our pants off at Greenville.

Well, I've got other letters to write so I'll close. Keep writing to Georgia until you get my APO. Thanks again for the $2.00. My engineer and gunner thank you too, for we've been sharing all we've got for the last few weeks.

Love,
Otsie

Hello to Mom, Tommy, and Milt.

Hunter Field
Combat Crew Center
Savannah, Georgia
October 13th, 1944
(To Mildred Vesely)

Dear Sis:

Your letter came yesterday and as usual was very interesting and long. Just the way I like them.

Nothing much has happened lately. We've been taken off the New Guinea shipment and have been put on a CBI shipment. We all thought we'd go to China, but lately the 14th Air Force in China have been losing their bases, so evidently we'll go to India. We were to leave today, but as usual things have been snafu'd lately, and we are still sticking around, wearing the seats out of our pants. When we do go, we will hit the POE at West Palm Beach, Florida where we will have our plane modified and from there we will go to South America. The captain figures on taking his sweet time going over so I imagine we'll get to see a lot of South America. While traveling, we will be allowed $7.00 per day for expenses and we also will get a lump sum for same. You can see it's a pretty good deal considering most everybody else goes across by boat.

Sorry to hear Pep has shipped, but it really isn't so bad. Don't you think the both of us did a pretty good job staying here as long as we did? I'm sure everything will turn out OK. Tell Jimmer thanks for the buck, from all of us, but please don't do it again. Don't get me wrong, it's appreciated, but if I knew you had more than you could use it would be different. Understand me?

I'll see if I can pick up some nice souvenirs during my travels, and in that way I'll try to repay you for what you've done—because I want to. Georgia nights are becoming very cool lately, and I can imagine what the weather at home is like. Truthfully, I'd rather have the good ol' Chi weather.

I guess you know that I spoke to Zoe on the phone the other day. It sure was swell, but I certainly hope she can come home for good one of these days. I feel so sorry for her being cooped up the way she is.

Well, time to go, so I'll close again. You can write to this same address unless you get my APO in the meantime. Thanks again for everything and I'll see you soon.

Love,
Otsie

Hello to the Vesely's and Pep.

China-Burma-India Theater
Moran, India—Assam Province
November 21st, 1944
(To Mildred Vesely)

Dear Sis...

Thanks for your letter of the 23rd. Took a long time reaching me and it sure was a welcome sight.

Well, I'll try and tell you all I can.

We left the states on the 21st. Flew our own plane over and had a pretty nice time doing so.

We covered approximately 20,000 miles and stopped at places such as Puerto Rico, Trinidad, Brazil, Ascension Island, Africa, Arabia, and India.

I'm finally settled now, assigned to the hottest bomb squadron in the CBI Theatre, namely the 490th. Naturally, I can't tell you exactly where we are, but I can go as far as saying that we're somewhere in Assam Province.

The location isn't bad at all. We have nice quarters—a big tent made up to suit ourselves and plenty of conveniences. We do a little hunting, I mean for game, too. Cook outdoors once in awhile, so it's just like one big camping trip. The food is good and have plenty of time for myself, which is spent trying to find something to do. Movies every other night, which is a big event here.

I made my sixth mission today. They are quite something which I won't even try to explain. I don't want Zoe to know that I'm actually a part of this war yet, for she'd only worry. So I tell her that I'm still in training. Keep that from her, will you? I'll get around to telling her when I add a few more to my list.

Well, I guess that's all for me right now. I don't like the idea of Mom working so hard, so do what you can to make her quit. I know it's too much for her.

I'm glad to hear that everything is okay at home. I still can't help worrying about Zoe, however. I sure hope she can come home soon.

Well, I'm going to quit now, so tell everybody hello and I'll write as the letters come in.

Love,
Otsie

New Address is:

490th Bomb Squadron
APO 629
c/o Postmaster
New York, NY

16434-CF-12—meant nothing more than shipping number and crew number.

China-Burma-India Theater
Warazup, Burma
December 16th, 1944
(To Erma Peknik)

Dear Sis:

Now I guess I've got more people worried about me. If letters are late in coming, don't think of anything else except a delay someplace. I'll write as often as I can to keep you posted, OK?

I just got back from rest camp today. Had a five day leave in Calcutta. Didn't do much but look around and get disgusted as hell with India. I've never seen anything so miserable in all my life. These people just aren't civilized at all. Things around here are pretty much the same and kinda quiet now. The movie has been set up and got a few records in. Not the latest, but good.

Glad to hear that Milt made good in school. I guess he'll have a pretty good deal aboard ship. Millie wrote me about the two kids playing cowboys all the time. I'll bet they won't even recognize me, or I them, when I get back. Well, we'll have to start all over again.

Erm, I'm not in a writing mood tonight, but I wanted to write a letter to keep you people from worrying. I'll write Mom in a day or two and give you all the dope I can. I sent Zoe some pictures. I guess you'll probably get to see them. I'm closing now. Lots of love to all. And Mom, I know you're reading this over Erma's shoulder, so go easy with that hammer and God Bless you. Merry Christmas!

Nervice in the Service,

Otsie

1945

Warazup, Burma
January 3, 1945
(To Mildred Vesely)

Dear Sis…

Your long letter came today and thanks a lot for it.

Let's see now, I'll read your letter again (only the fourth time) and see if there are any questions I can answer for you.

Speaking of weight, I'm normal again and always was. You see, I blame that on the poor photography. I sent some pictures to Zoe taken a couple of weeks ago. No doubt you'll get to see them and draw your own conclusions.

Your mentioning my six missions makes me feel like a new man. It may surprise you to learn that at this writing I have twenty-two to my credit. Not bad, eh? Never thought I'd be able to survive the excitement. As far as Zoe knowing, I already told her. Perhaps it was a little pride that made me spill the beans. But on second thought, I felt it was better for her to know.

By the way, I've got one medal and am within reach of another. Proud of your kid brother? But I can't understand my still being a corporal. Guess I'm the original T.S. Kid. Would you like to punch my card? Kidding aside, I may make sergeant any day now.

Assam is in eastern India, but that's old stuff now as I'm not there any longer. Guess I move faster than the mail does. However, keep looking and watch the newspapers. Our squadron has been getting a lot of stateside publicity. Anything that has to do with the war in Burma, read over once or twice—malum? (Indian lingo for 'understand').

Brazil and Trinidad is nothing like the travel folders state. In my estimation, every country out of the U.S. is nothing but filth and poverty.

More than once I wanted to ask you to send me some stationery but didn't want to impose on you. Now that you mention it, I'll say yes. Please do. It doesn't have to be fancy. Tissue second sheets are about as good as any. Now to make it official: "Can you please send me some writing paper and envelopes?" Thanks.

I guess by now you know that I received the bracelet. I'll bet you picked it out. Very nice and I consider it one of my good luck charms.

Don't worry about hearing from Pep. I was able to write only because we made frequent stops but in Pep's case he can't do that while in the middle of the ocean somewhere.

I'm sending you a small clipping out of a GI newspaper. Perhaps it will give you some idea of what we are doing.

> **(Clipping)** On the Central Burma Front, planes of the 490th Bombardment Group were up to their favorite bridge-busting activities. They got three railroad bridges at Mongmit, a bypass at Tangon and Tantabin, a bridge northeast of Tabin, and another at Mandaunghla and Sissongy. They knocked down four additional bridges near Mandalay.

Write soon, hello to Jimmer and to the Vesely's. And above all, tell Mom I'm OK and lots of love for her.

Love,

Otsie

PS—Wrap the paper up good. Better put it in one of those Stonewall cartons—good plug???

Warazup, Burma
January 16, 1945
(To Mildred Vesely)

Dear Sis...

Your newsy letter came today and believe me it was appreciated. I'm glad you're going to write whenever you have news instead of waiting to hear from me. Believe me, I write often, the mail just gets tied up somplace.

I'm glad you sent that quotation from the Times. I've often wondered about things like that. Nobody seems to go into detail as much as you. Most everything was true about that story, except for the number of ships. If you divide that by five, you might get the right answer. We aren't a large outfit. That's why our achievements mean so much, for we surpass other squadrons who are much larger than ours. Malum?.

I think I mentioned before that we got good and 'stinkin' on Christmas. All on Indian liquor and that's no good, but what else? The tent was such a mess the next morning that our bearer wanted to know if the Japs had come at night. They didn't, but we certainly did expect them. Glad to hear that Pep finally got a pretty good deal. You won't have to worry about him so much now. That's what kind of a job I'm going to buck for when I get back. "Chairborne Troops of the Paragraph Troops." Good, huh? I read it in a book once.

I've been flying like mad last week, logging plenty of time, but feeling pretty tired. Went up today and will do so again tomorrow. Day before yesterday I flew twice. You can see I'm pretty busy. Besides this, I've got to clean my guns, load bombs, and what's left? I've been reading about the cold waves in Chicago. Brrr! The heat isn't torrid here. Nights are cool and days are just right. Still enjoy outdoor showers and swimming when the chance presents itself.

By the way, I wasn't on the mission transcribed on Christmas, but I was at the target about three or four times previously. Sure was a hot spot, but I've seen worse. It won't be long before we start operating around "where the flying fishes play"-Malum? That's going to be something. Mil, I'd like to write you more, but honestly I haven't got any more stationery and neither has anybody else in the tent. We've been chiseling for awhile now, and I hate to do it again. I ran out of Airmails too, so forgive the *Free* mail until yours arrives. Hope you got my request for I sure am in a bad way. Till I get more stationery—thanks again for the nice letters. Love to Jimmy, Mom, hello to the Vesely's and Pep. Write soon.

Love,

Otsie

Warazup, Burma
January 24th, 1945
(To Mildred Vesely)

Dear Sis:

Thanks for your letter. Glad to hear you say that Mom received three letters from me. Felt pretty bad when she bawled me out. You know I can't control the mail when it leaves me. I try to write as often as there is something to write about. But there is that old saying: "No news is good news." My time isn't too limited, but the thing is what to write. Understand?

No, I'm sorry to say that I haven't received the other box you sent. The bracelet was the only thing I received and that was because it was sent First Class. I'll get the others I'm sure, but can't say when. Just in case I don't get it, how about telling me what was in it. Curious, you know.

Six below zero! Can't imagine it gets cold like that anymore. But here I walk around with only shorts, trying to get a nice suntan. Fish when we have the time, and nicest of all—taking a bath in that nice cool, crystal-clear river. Of course, we have showers but it's more fun that way. But don't think I wouldn't mind enduring that weather at home.

Can't say that I didn't wake up without a hangover on New Year's Day. Never again. In the future I'll take your advice and write to both Mom and you at the same time. You can do the same but don't forget I want your letters and Mom's too. In the same envelope of course. I'm not going to let you get away with things that easy.

Well folks, time to sign off. Got to get some sleep as I'm up again tomorrow. Four out of five this week and I'm tired as hell.

Hello to the kids—how about some pictures? Write soon. Till then, God Bless you all.

Love,

Otsie,

Love and kisses

Warazup, Burma
February 4th, 1945
(To Mildred Vesely)

Dear Sis…

Received two of your letters and truthfully have never heard so much news before.

Let's see now, I'll have to re-read your letter again and see what questions I have to answer.

Yes, the last letter I sent to you was the build-up to a citation. I'm in for an award, but I don't like to mention it yet because it isn't official yet. Just don't say anything to anybody yet, OK?.

"Bocy" went to Aberdare when he went for a rest. Can't say more, for I wouldn't know for sure.

I made my 35th mission yesterday, and honestly, I'm getting nervous as hell. If you can fly every day, it's okay. But if I lay off a day or two I hate to start over again. Guess you know how it is. Things happen now and then which don't help the situation at all. You don't have to worry about me sticking my neck out, though, for I shrink to half my size. It helps too. I'll explain all when I see you people again.

I think I wrote and told you that I received a letter from Pep. I answered it as soon as I got it as it probably won't be long before I hear from him again. He was right about the comic strip, but please exclude the females. That is definitely out.

Had a day off today so I went hunting. Didn't do any good but as tomorrow is a general day off, we are going out in strength and should have a little luck. We've been getting quite a few chickens and doves lately and they really were good. Some of the boys went out last night and got two deer and an Asiatic bison that weighed two-thousand pounds. This afternoon, two of the ack-ack boys went out and got a tiger that was six feet long. Plenty to do around here.

Days are getting longer so I guess summer is just around the corner. I hope I can get away from here before the monsoons start. I understand that's really rough.

Well, Mil, guess I'll close. I've got so many letters to write yet. I've got to write Mom a letter for her birthday. I got her a $15 money order. Hope she puts it to good use. What I mean by that is taking a couple of days off from work. Say hello to her and the rest of the family, to the Vesely's, and Pep and Jimmy.

Love,
Otsie

Thanks for the buck. I'm saving it and intend to buy a good drink when I hit the USA.

This was his last letter. Otsie was killed eleven days later.

Printed in the United States
4966